Fabulous Places

to get married in London

Fabulous Places

to get married in London

crimson

This edition first published in Great Britain in 2007 by
Crimson Publishing
Westminster House, Kew Road
Richmond, Surrey TW9 2ND

A catalogue record for this book is
available from the British Library.

ISBN 978 1 85458 402 1

Design: Andy Prior

Printed and bound in Turkey by
Mega Printing.

Contents

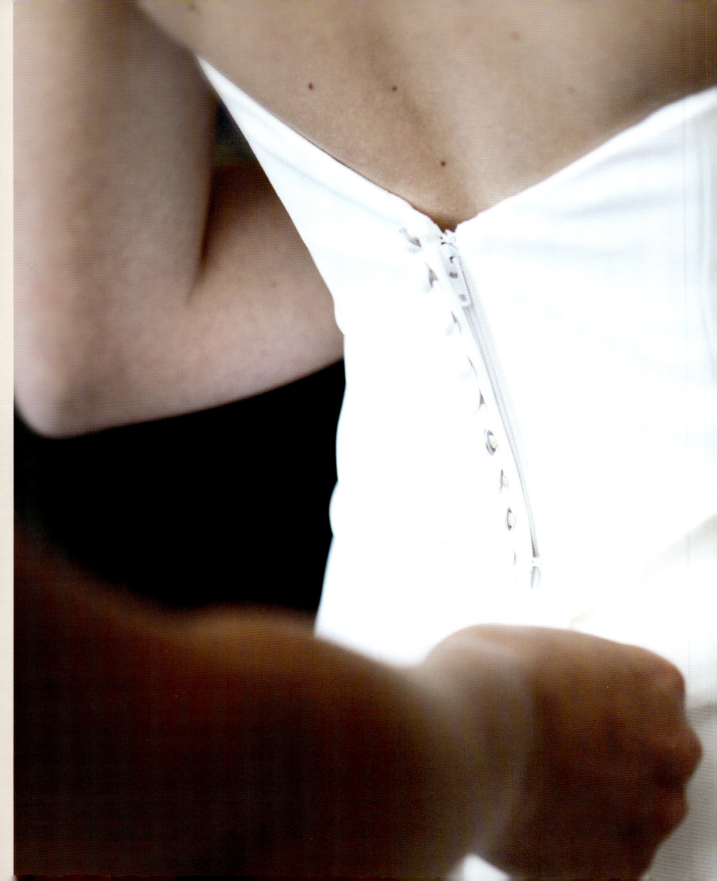

Introduction

London has never been defined by one particular era. It's a city where the Tower of London is dwarfed by the futuristic Gherkin; where the Millennium Bridge links the Tate Modern on the south bank with Sir Christopher Wren's majestic St Paul's on the north. It is a palimpsest of history, the old is juxtaposed with the new and this means a dazzling – almost bewildering – choice of venues for anyone planning a wedding. So how to find somewhere truly fabulous?

Since the Marriage Act of 1994, a host of historic monuments, galleries, hotels and clubs have been licensed for civil ceremonies, as well as being able to hold the reception afterwards. We've selected 48 of the capital's finest locations, from the ornate halls of medieval guilds to minimalist boutique hotels, for a flavour of what's on offer in this vibrant city. If the merits of one of London's museums hadn't occurred to you, perhaps we can inspire you to cast your net a little wider? Does Richmond Theatre offer the sense of drama you seek? Will your guests dine amongst dinosaurs at the Natural History Museum? There's a wonderful diversity in *Fabulous Places to get married in London* and, we hope, plenty of enjoyment in discovering parts of London for the first time.

Each location has its own magic – some can host a ceremony, others a reception, and many cater for both – but what they all share is a certain *Wow* factor that could bring your dream wedding to life. The venue is a key decision and usually one of the first you make – without a where, it's not so easy to decide on when, how or who. This book is designed to help you make that first decision, so that the rest of the plans fall seamlessly into place. And remember, your venue doesn't have to dictate the style of your day. You may be drawn towards a historic venue, but there's nothing to stop you having a contemporary theme; a ceremony at ZSL London Zoo, surrounded by 5,000 animals, can still be bursting with tradition.

However, we know that looking fabulous is not the only criteria, so along with an in-depth description, each venue has been painstakingly researched to give details of function rooms, capacity and wedding services. We also have the answers to any housekeeping question you may have, from accommodation, catering and parking to whether you can light candles, let off fireworks or make a dramatic entrance in a helicopter.

For years, film directors in the capital have set the scene with an old red Routemaster driving past Trafalgar Square. Throw in a black cab and a shot of Big Ben and you've typified England's capital. With *Fabulous Places to get married in London*, we aim to show that London is all of this… and a whole lot more. An iconic city for an unforgettable day.

Notes

While we have tried to ensure that every detail in this book is correct at the time of going to press, we intend this information to be a helpful guideline only and recommend that you always contact and visit your chosen venue before making any decisions.

Civil partnerships

Please note that all ceremony venues in the book welcome civil partnerships, although this is not referred to explicitly throughout for reasons of repetition and flow of profiles.

Capacity and numbers of guests

- The number of guests permitted at each venue is subject to the venue's discretion.
- The number given under 'Capacity' on the first page of each venue's profile is the maximum capacity that each venue has indicated they can accommodate in their largest function room for a seated ceremony, seated dinner and standing reception.
- A number in brackets after a location denotes the maximum capacity for the space specified.
- Other specific figures given are:
  Licensed for ceremony: Seated capacity
  Reception: Seated dinner capacity (wedding breakfast)
  Evening: Standing capacity (evening reception)
  Drinks reception: Capacity for standing drinks reception (usually before dinner).

Prices and rates

- All prices mentioned in the book include VAT. Prices given are often an approximation and are subject to change at the venue's discretion.
- The 'Guide Price' given for each venue refers to the following:
  Per guest (not including venue hire): Food/drinks only
  Per guest (including venue hire): Food/drinks and venue hire divided per person
  Venue hire only: Cost of hiring the venue excluding food/drinks or extra charges.
- Where a corkage charge is given, all amounts are per 75cl bottle unless otherwise stated.

For a Fabulous
Ceremony

Chelsea Register Office

Fabulous because...

Following in the footsteps of the famous, couples can hold their ceremony at this iconic venue set in the Royal Borough of Kensington and Chelsea, the most prestigious register office in London

Location: King's Road, Chelsea

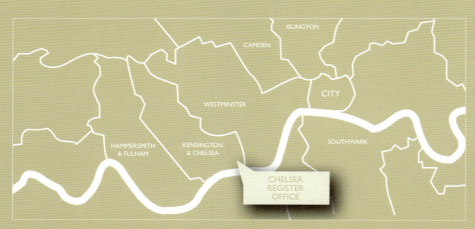

Capacity: Ceremony 40

Minimum number of guests: 2

Guide Price
Venue hire only: **£40 – £450**

When to get married here: **All year round**

Mounting the famous stone steps from the King's Road couples move into a monochrome entrance hall to be met by great chandeliers and oak doors

As the most well-known register office in London, Chelsea Register Office needs little introduction. It forms part of the Chelsea Old Town Hall, a late-Victorian building prominently situated on the fashionable King's Road. Built in 1875 and designed by architect John McKean Brydon, this eminent building, with its imposing entrance, provides a memorable and illustrious setting for any ceremony.

Holding upwards of 1,500 ceremonies annually, this register office has been the venue for many famous weddings throughout its history, including the first marriage of Wallis Simpson, before she became the Duchess of Windsor through her second marriage to King Edward VIII in 1937.

Other people to be married here include Alfred Hitchcock, DH Lawrence, George Best, Honor Blackman, Roman Polanski, Richard Burton, Roger Taylor, Oliver Reed and Judy Garland.

The Royal Borough of Kensington and Chelsea was granted its royal status in 1901, in recognition both of Queen Victoria's love of the area (she was born in Kensington Palace) and its long association with royalty. Charles II created the King's Road in the 1660s. It was also in this decade that he founded the Royal Hospital with the unique Chelsea Pensioners, in the same area.

Modern changes in legislation licensing Approved Venues mean that couples are now free to choose exactly where they are married and are no longer restricted by their postcode. Thus any couple can now marry or register their civil partnership in the most prestigious register office in the country. With a reputation that sets it apart from all others, Chelsea Register Office offers some delightful rooms and strives to maintain the level of service it is so well known for.

Mounting the iconic stone steps from the King's Road, couples enter through the much photographed doorway, into a monochrome entrance hall where white and black tiling, two chandeliers and great oak doors greet you. Through the far doors, there is a waiting area from which wedding parties ascend the red-carpeted stairs to the upper ceremony rooms. This grand staircase is an ideal place to hold small group photographs – an alternative to the steps outside in unfavourable weather. This part of the building used to house part of the Old Town Hall's Library before becoming part of the Register Office.

The Register Office part of the building has two beautiful and atmospheric rooms, separately licensed, in which ceremonies are held.

The largest of the ceremony rooms is the Brydon Room, named after the building's architect. This room can hold up to 40 people for the ceremony and couples have use of the room for a full hour, allowing ample time for readings and music to accompany the vows. The room itself is beautifully decorated, with sweeping cream curtains and a striking dark wooden doorway.

The nearby Rossetti Room is smaller and can accommodate up to 14 people for a ceremony, surrounded by cream walls, chandeliers and a speckled green carpet. Ceremonies held in this room are more limited on time but can include one piece of music and one reading to personalise your ceremony.

There are two smaller rooms situated on the first and top floor of the Register Office, suitable for an intimate ceremony with only the couple and two witnesses present.

Once the formalities are over, the steps of the building are often used as a setting for photographs, where guests find themselves excellently positioned to throw confetti over the happy couple.

Adjoining to the Register Office, and accessed through the other entrance on the King's Road, lies the Old Town Hall providing a nearby space for wedding breakfasts and receptions.

Venue Details

Kensington and Chelsea Register Office
Chelsea Old Town Hall
King's Road
London
SW3 5EE
t 020 7361 4100
e chelsea.registeroffice@rbkc.gov.uk
w www.rbck.gov.uk

Licensed for ceremony: The Rossetti Room (14), The Brydon Room (40)
Outside space: ✗

SPECIAL NOTES

Car parking spaces: Metered parking in the surrounding streets
Confetti: ✓ (outside the building, preferably biodegradable or fresh rose petals)
Candles: ✗
PA system: ✗

De Morgan Centre

This building of great architectural merit boats stunning array of artwork including the largest collection of William De Morgan ceramics and paintings by William's acclaimed Victorian artist wife

Location: Wandsworth

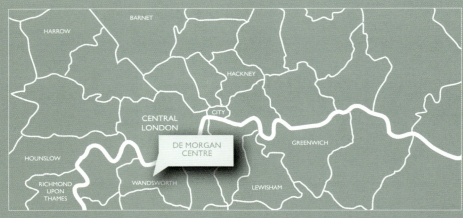

Capacity: Ceremony 100; Reception 100
Minimum number of guests: **None**
Guide Price Venue hire only: **£350**
When to get married here: **All year round**

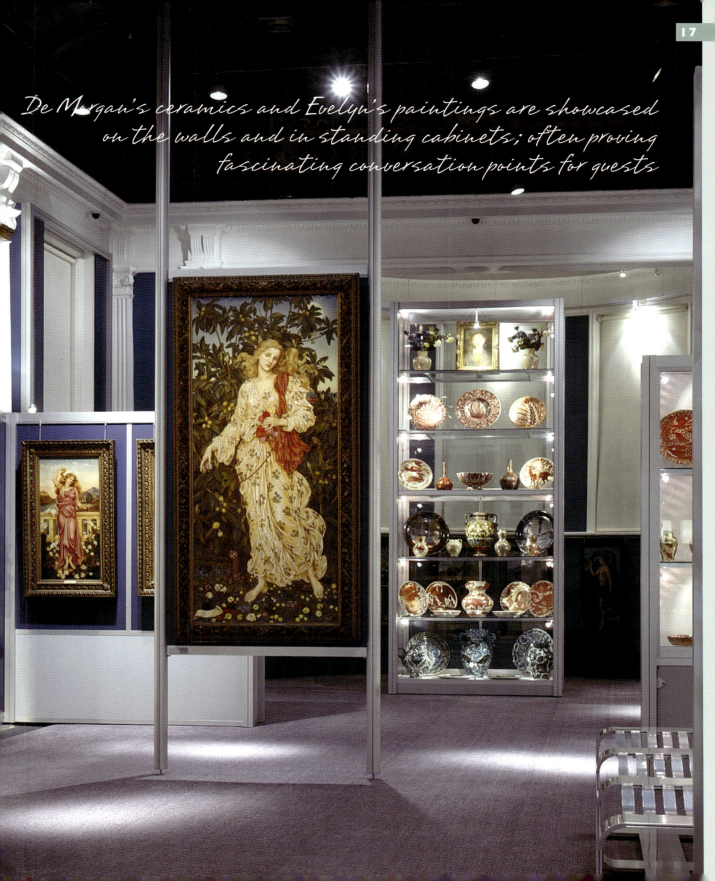

De Morgan's ceramics and Evelyn's paintings are showcased on the walls and in standing cabinets; often proving fascinating conversation points for guests

A wonderful backdrop for an art-lover's wedding with the building's Arts and Crafts architecture offset by the varying pieces in venue's collection

Named after the renowned art which it houses, the De Morgan Centre is a small museum nestled in the heart of south-west London. Home to the finest and largest collection of William De Morgan ceramics, it also features paintings by William's wife, Evelyn, who was herself an acclaimed Victorian artist. Having been granted a civil licence in 2005, this beautiful museum now provides marrying couples with a wonderful backdrop for their ceremony; with the building's Arts and Crafts architecture offset by the variety of pieces in the venue's unique collection.

William De Morgan and his wife Evelyn were highly respected Victorian artists. William De Morgan was one of the most important figures of the nineteenth-century Arts and Crafts movement with his greatest artistic legacy lying in his rich and beautiful ceramics. Initially inspired by William Morris, whom he worked with for many years, De Morgan also rediscovered the lost art of Islamic pottery; an art that boasted the rich and beautiful colours he had admired on a sixteenth-century Isnik work he had studied.

After an acclaimed career as a ceramic designer whose work decorated not only a number of P&O Liners and the Czar of Russia's yacht, but also the houses of the discerning public in this country, in 1907 De Morgan embarked on a career as a novelist. In the final years before his death he published seven novels and enjoyed the great success and financial security which had until then eluded him.

His wife, meanwhile, was a successful and prolific artist. The daughter of Percival Pickering QC and Anna Maria Spencer-Stanhope, Evelyn had wanted to become an artist from an early age. She was supported in her ambitions by her artist uncle John Roddam Spencer Stanhope and in 1873 entered the Slade School of Art as one of the first women students to attend. Having won many medals and awards at the Slade she was invited to exhibit at the inaugural exhibition of the influential Grosvenor Gallery alongside such established names as Burne Jones, Watts and Alma Tadema. Having studied the renaissance masters in Italy, Evelyn's own distinctive style was rich in use of colour, allegory and the dominance of the female form and her legacy is now often associated with the pre-Raphaelite artists of the nineteenth century.

After marrying in 1887, the De Morgans coupled their love for the fine and decorative arts with an interest in many of the leading issues of the day – including the suffragette movement, prison reform, pacifism and spiritualism. Producing a plethora of artistic work, their legacy was maintained by Evelyn De Morgan's sister, Mrs Stirling who devoted the last 40 years of her life to collecting together as much of their artwork as possible; donating the collection to the nation on her death in 1965. The collection has been housed in the De Morgan Centre's Longstaff Room since 2002 where their work is gloriously displayed for all visitors to see. It is this room, available for private hire, which provides the setting for weddings held at the Centre, allowing couples and their guests to immerse themselves in history and marry among unique works of art.

Part of a period building, the Longstaff Room, was built by a local philanthropist in 1887 to celebrate Queen Victoria's jubilee. The room is long and spacious and boasts a superb timber-roofed Arts and Crafts interior. It is a versatile space that can be made suitable for both intimate gatherings and larger ceremonies with up to 100 guests. A fascinating backdrop for any art-lover, De Morgan's ceramics and Evelyn's paintings are showcased on the walls and in standing cabinets around; often proving fascinating conversation points for guests.

Following the ceremony in the Longstaff Room, guests can move into the nearby Foyer and continue to view the tasteful artwork on display. It is possible to serve guests champagne and canapés in this room prior to the wedding party departing to continue the reception celebrations elsewhere.

Venue Details

De Morgan Centre
38 West Hill
London
SW18 1RZ
t 020 8871 1144
e info@demorgan.org.uk
w www.demorgan.org.uk

Licence authority:
Wandsworth Register Office
Wandsworth High Street
London
SW18 2PU
t 020 8871 6120/1
e registeroffice@wandsworth.gov.uk
w www.wandsworth.gov.uk

Licensed for ceremony: Longstaff Room (60)

Function rooms available: Foyer (100) for drinks reception and canapés only

Outside space: ✗

SPECIAL NOTES

Licensing hours: Throughout the period of hire

Corkage charge: £3

Catering: Recommended caterers

Complimentary menu tasting: Dependent on caterer

Car parking spaces: Two spaces available on the premises, further parking available in the surrounding streets and in an NCP 10 minute's walk away

Confetti: ✗

Candles: ✗

PA system: ✗ (a stereo is available for music)

Golden Hinde

Fabulous because...

This replica of Sir Francis Drake's ship that circumnavigated the world provides and exciting and intriguing venue by the side of the Thames. Stepping aboard this vessel, handcrafted with original tools, you move into another place and time

Location: **London Bridge, Southwark**

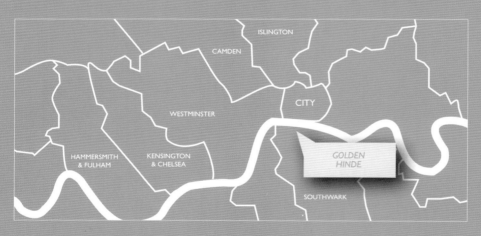

Capacity: **Ceremony 50; Drinks reception 120**

Minimum number of guests: **None**

Guide Price
Venue hire only: **£353 – £764**

When to get married here: **All year round**

The *Golden Hinde*, berthed in Bankside near London Bridge, is an exact reconstruction of the sixteenth-century warship in which Sir Francis Drake circumnavigated the world for three years from 1577. Today, it is used as an educational vessel and run by a charity. The ship is also licensed to hold wedding ceremonies aboard, for couples in search of a distinctly unique venue.

On its return, the original *Golden Hinde* lay docked for almost a century on the Thames at Deptford as a memorial to Sir Francis Drake. However, around 400 years ago, its timbers rotted beyond repair and it was broken up. Today the only memento is a chair, formed from the remaining sound timber, which was presented to the University of Oxford by Charles II.

In the early 1970s, Mr Albert Elledge, president of a San Francisco tugboat and harbour-tour company decided to reconstruct Drake's legendary flagship. A naval architect was commissioned to research the first historically authentic replica of the *Golden Hinde* and to draw up plans for a full-scale, working replica using the ship's original plans from the Pepys Library at Magdalene College, Cambridge. The research was completed in 1971 and the keel was laid in Devon in September of that year.

The reconstruction of the *Golden Hinde* was heralded a milestone in the history of naval architecture and was built with the same tools and techniques as the original. The replica has been interpreted as a small warship of the mid-sixteenth century having three masts, five decks and carrying 18 cannon typical of the period. The completed vessel weights a little over 100 tons.

After her launch in 1973 the new *Golden Hinde* sailed to San Francisco as a memorial to Drake's voyage. She then retraced Drake's route across the Pacific and Indian Oceans to England to complete her own circumnavigation of the world in 1980. She has circumnavigated Great Britain twice, and sailed nearly 140,000 miles in 30 years.

Today, the *Golden Hinde* Educational Trust uses the ship to educate and inspire, running workshops and events, as well as working closely with the community. Couples can now hold their ceremony on board the black, red and gold ship, as well as a drinks or buffet reception (standing) spanning the decks.

Ceremonies can be held amongst Tudor beams, a large, black capstan, replica chests and polearms mounted on the wall

To aid exploring the ship, couples can opt to hire guides dressed in traditional Elizabethan costume to explain the ship's history, using the full potential of this venue. These costumed staff can also serve drinks to guests and assist with receptions.

A gangplank leads from the footpath up onto the Main Deck of the ship, where rigging, timber and ropes abound. In the past, couples have created a bamboo walkway over the gangplank and entwined this with flowers to create a magical entrance. On the Main Deck, a drinks reception can be held, and a canopy can be erected over the area in case of bad weather.

On the Half Deck, accessed up some steps and past the ship's helm, the Captain's Cabin is found where Drake would have slept. This tiny room has views of the City and can be used as a cloakroom or by the bride as a private changing room. Alternatively it can be kept open as part of the tour. At the stern of the ship, the *Golden Hinde* and latin motto are inscribed, as is the Tudor Rose and ER (Elizabeth Regina).

At the bow of the ship there lies the Fo'c'sle, with block and tackle, long-range guns called falcons and bow chasers displayed. As well as passing through this room to descend the bow's stairway, small tables can be set up here, to serve drinks to guests milling on the deck.

A door from the main deck leads through to the Armoury, a surprising size considering its location. Ceremonies can be

Couples can opt to hire guides dressed in traditional Elizabethan costume to explain the ship's history

held in this space, amongst Tudor beams, a large, black capstan (used for hauling up the anchor), replica chests and polearms mounted on the wall. In keeping with the original purpose of the ship as a vessel for war, much of the floors are painted red. This is striking indeed, though the historical reason for this is more gruesome than grandeur; the red colour was chosen so that during warfare, when blood was spilt, other sailors would not be disheartened and be less aware of their uncertain fate.

In the middle of the Armoury, a stairwell leads to the floor below. Many brides choose to enter the Armoury from below, to make more of their entrance into the room. Wooden benches and seating are set up, facing inwards, for the guests watching the ceremony. As many as 40 people can be seated in this way.

At the back of the Armoury, and separated by a half-wall and small open door, lies The Great Cabin. Used by the officers and gentlemen for dining and strategy planning, this room contains a large, robust wooden chair that only Drake would have sat in (one of only two on the ship). This room is ideal for wedding photographs, with a painting of Drake and views out over the Thames.

Beneath The Great Cabin lies the Gun Deck, accessed either from the Armoury or the staircase at the port of the ship. This deck spans the length of the ship, and is around 4ft high, with space to stand in the centre. Along the deck are 14 minions positioned facing out of the portholes. While this space does not lend itself well to adults, it is an ideal area for children to explore, or adults to sit down in!

FOR A FABULOUS CEREMONY

Sunlight filters down through the wooden grills to The Hold below, creating a wonderful dappled effect

At the bottom of the ship is the Hold. This is the second space that is licensed to host a civil ceremony. Originally used for storage, the Hold is a more spacious area which can seat around 50 guests. Fairy lights can be strewn around the room to create a magical atmosphere and the base of the mast in the middle of the room can decorated with flowers.

The *Golden Hinde*, though already full of its own character and charm, can be decorated as couples wish. The big hatch on the Main Deck and a hatch in the Gun Deck can be uncovered, so that sunlight can filter down through the wooden grills to the Hold below, creating a wonderful dappled effect (although this does make the Gun Deck off limits for safety reasons unfortunately). Due to the ease of this task, couples can decide whether or not the weather is good enough for this on the day of the wedding.

After the ceremony, wedding parties can move on to begin the reception celebrations elsewhere, although it should be noted that the ship can be used for a standing reception, holding up to 120 people. In the Hold, large, upright barrels make excellent ledges to rest drinks on, but can also be cleared away and replaced with the ship's available tables. Some couples choose to display a buffet in the Hold, alongside one wall. Acoustic music is allowed anywhere below deck, and is especially appropriate in the Hold: since it is below water level the room is soundproof.

The *Golden Hinde* Educational Trust's main aims are to maintain the ship, finance restoration, and promote the education of children. There are plans to turn the ship around so that its bow faces out into the river and create an education centre at the back of the ship, although this work has not commenced yet.

This gem, hidden on the riverfront in Southwark, provides couples with a very memorable venue in which to be married.

Venue Details

Golden Hinde Ship
St Mary Overie Dock
Cathedral Street
London
SE1 9DE
t 020 7403 0123
e info@goldenhinde.org
w www.goldenhinde.org

Licence authority:
Southwark Register Office
34 Peckham Road
London
SE5 8QA
t 020 7525 7651
e registrars@southwark.gov.uk
w www.southwark.gov.uk

Licensed for ceremony: The Great Cabin (40), the Hold (50)

Function rooms available: Whole ship (drinks reception 120)

Outside space: The Main Deck

Option of a marquee: A canopy can be erected over the Middle Deck

Rooms available for overnight accommodation: ✗

Complimentary dressing room for bride available: ✓

SPECIAL NOTES

Licensing hours: Until midnight

Corkage charge: None

Catering: Recommended suppliers

Complimentary menu tasting: Dependent on caterer

Car parking spaces: Parking on Southwark Street and Tooley Street

Sound/noise restrictions: Acoustic music only, until 11.30pm

Confetti: ✗

Candles: ✗

PA system: ✗

Richmond Theatre

Fabulous because...

In front of a captive audience, couples can take centre stage to marry in this classic, richly decorated theatre which can prove to be a distinctly different venue depending on the theatre's season

Location: Richmond, Surrey

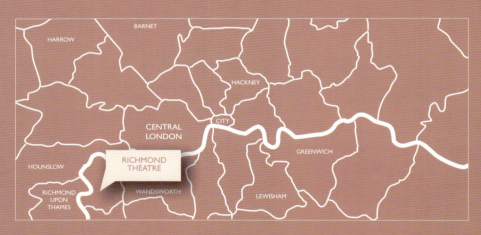

Capacity: Ceremony 800

Minimum number of guests: None

Guide Price
Venue hire only: £1,175

When to get married here: All year round

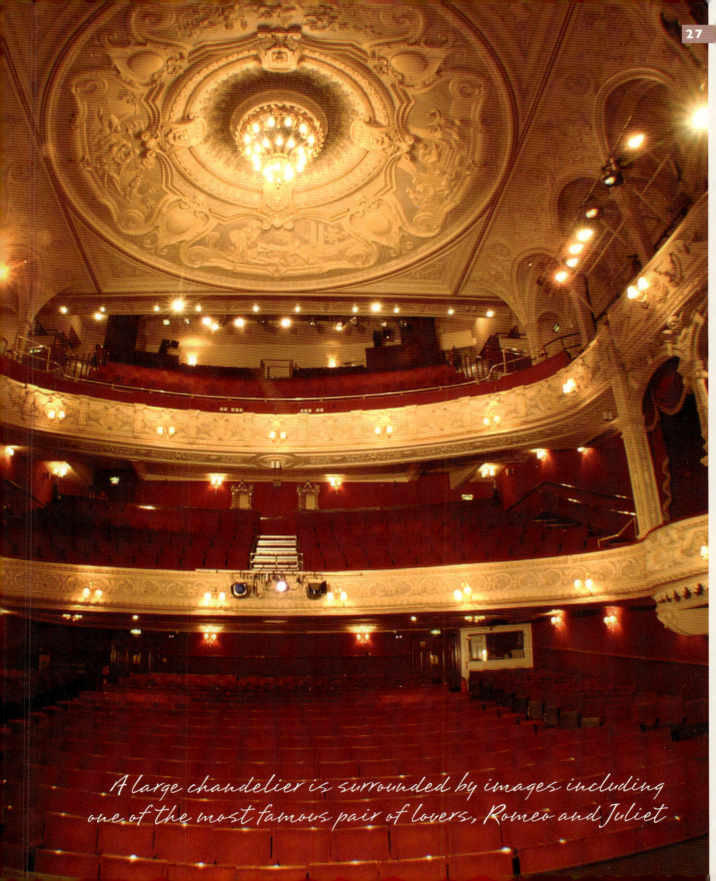

A large chandelier is surrounded by images including one of the most famous pair of lovers, Romeo and Juliet

Richmond Theatre is a truly spectacular setting in which to hold a ceremony. This classic theatre's outer façade facing the pretty Richmond Green, and the rich interior of the auditorium, bedecked in crimson with cream and gold cornicing and gilt detailing throughout makes this a picturesque location both inside and out.

The theatre was built in 1899 originally known as the Theatre Royal and Opera House and was designed by the renowned Victorian theatre architect Frank Matcham. After extensive refurbishment in 1991, this Grade II listed building has played host to a wide range of quality drama, record breaking musicals, opera, dance and family entertainment each year. Over the past century many legendary actors have performed at the theatre, including Judi Dench, Anna Pavlova, Ralph Richardson and Helen Mirren. These appearances have added to the theatre's reputation as one of the most respected drama houses in the country.

It has also been featured in many film and television productions, including *Finding Neverland* and *Evita*. Welcoming a quarter of a million theatregoers to over 40 outstanding productions a year the theatre is actively performing for about 49 weeks each year. For this reason, the venue is only able to hold a handful of weddings each year, making it a highly sought after and inimitable place to be married.

The main auditorium can hold up to 800 people, far more than most couples would consider inviting, and many choose to use only the stalls which can sit up to 400. The traditional theatre chairs are covered in plush red fabrics. A large chandelier suspends from the expansive ceiling, and is surrounded by images including one of the most famous pair of lovers, Romeo and Juliet. Beside the stage sit the four boxes, which can be used by the couple's families, or to create wonderful photograph opportunities after the ceremony. With stained glass doors and ornate cornicing around their edges, these boxes abound in traditional glamour.

The theatre's aisle becomes the wedding aisles and allows the bride to make a spectacular entrance. In true theatre style, the lighting can be dramatically dimmed before her big moment. While the stage lights are to remain set for the current performance, they can be all be used, and can spotlight the bride and groom on stage.

The couple can choose to either conduct the ceremony on the floor just in front of the stage, where the registrar table is set up, or to stand on the stage, in front of the grand red curtains and spotlights. This table can be decorated as the couple choose, and, after the vows, is also where the register is signed, so the newlyweds can continue proceedings in front of their guests.

For couples choosing to wed centre-stage, there is an alternative to the red curtains as a backdrop: they can choose to have the curtain up and marry on the set! Booking the theatre well in advance, couples have no way of knowing what production will be on, or what the set will look like. If they do choose to get married on the set, they must seek permission from the production running. The week of their wedding, couples are invited to visit the theatre and ascertain whether the set is appropriate for their ceremony – in the past, this has ranged from a beautiful country garden scene, with real grass laid out and bright summer lighting for the play *Entertaining Angels*, to a set for the First World War play *Journey's End*, complete with a muddy trench! The uncertainty of the set adds to the surprise of this unique, extremely unusual venue. Couples often choose to have the curtain down as the guests arrive and wait to unveil their unique set to their audience once seated.

One couple getting married during the pantomime season decided to make the most of their venue: the ceremony in front of the set of *Aladdin*, and afterwards the guests enjoyed a champagne reception before returning to the matinee performance of the show.

With use of the whole building, guests are free to roam the theatre, making the most of the impressive views of the stage from the upper circle and photographic opportunities alongside the theatre's nineteenth-century features.

The set has ranged from a beautiful country garden scene, with real grass laid out and bright summer lighting, to a set for a First World War play complete with muddy trenches!

Those who are beginning to imagine an all singing, all dancing wedding at the theatre are to be disappointed however. The set belongs to the production and so can only be used with permission (although this has never been refused so far) and restrictions. Small bands can, however, grace the stage and serenade the couple but this must be kept to a small number of people. Included in hire price is the use of a technician and the house manager's presence throughout the events.

Richmond Theatre is not a venue that offers large reception spaces. Its four bars accommodate around 40 people each, so it is likely that not all guests will be able to congregate in any one room. The Dress Circle Bar is an impressive room in its own right, with the original nineteenth-century bar still in place, a beautiful semi-circular stained glass window and access to two balconies overlooking Richmond Green. This room could also providing a fitting backdrop for some of the wedding photography.

Due to the nature of this unique venue, ceremonies can only be held on Fridays, from 10am until 4.30pm. Couples are given an hour to gather guests and partake in the ceremony, although time for photographs afterwards is welcomingly given.

FOR A FABULOUS CEREMONY

There is the facility for the bride to prepare in one of the small rooms in the theatre's building and there are ample additional private small rooms for both the bride and groom to meet with the registrar before the ceremony begins.

The exclusivity and uniqueness of this theatre is a testament to the unparalleled diversity of wedding venues that London has to offer.

Venue Details

Richmond Theatre
The Green
Richmond
Surrey
TW9 1QJ
t **020 8940 0220**
e **richmondtheatre@theambassadors.com**
w **www.richmondtheatre.net**

Licence authority:
Richmond Register Office
1 Spring Terrace
Richmond
Surrey
TW9 1LW
t **020 8940 2853 or 020 8940 2651**
e **registeroffice@richmond.gov.uk**
w **www.richmond.gov.uk**

Licensed for ceremony: Auditorium (800)

Function rooms available: Dress Circle Bar, Matcham Room, Upper Circle Bar, Stalls Bar (drinks reception 40 each)

Outside space: Richmond Green is immediately outside the entrance, though not available for hire

Complimentary dressing room for bride available: ✓

SPECIAL NOTES

Licensing hours: Only permitted after the ceremony

Corkage charge: Corkage not permitted

Catering: Recommended caterers

Complimentary menu tasting: Dependent on caterer

Car parking spaces: Street parking around Richmond Green

Confetti: ✓ (outside only)

Candles: ✓ (fire officer at additional cost)

PA system: ✓

Sutton House

Fabulous because...

The oldest domestic dwelling in east London, this sixteenth-century intimate Tudor house occupies a discreet position, steeped in history

Location: Hackney

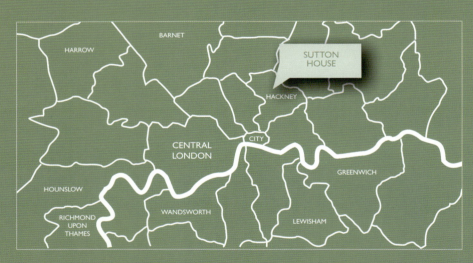

Capacity: Ceremony 100; Drinks reception 100

Minimum number of guests: None

Guide Price
Venue hire only: £655

When to get married here: February to December

The Wenlock Barn is accessed through the wisteria-adorned courtyard, a quiet stone-flagged area decked with foliage that offers guests a glimpse through a beautiful armada window

An unexpected treasure nestled in a leafy oasis close to London's centre, this sixteenth-century stone-bricked house is the oldest domestic dwelling in east London. Open to the public after a period of restoration by the National Trust, Sutton House is a building that is steeped in history. Maintaining many of its original features including oak panelling and exposed brickwork, it was once frequented by the secretary of state to Henry VIII and now provides a perfect backdrop for ceremonies. With royal affiliation and a wedding service that is hospitable and friendly, couples choosing to marry here will also revel in a warm interior that exudes traditional Tudor grandeur, complete with features such as polished redwood walls and open fireplaces.

Built in 1535 by Sir Ralph Sadleir, the principle secretary of state to Henry VIII, Sutton House is, at first appearances, a modest looking building. Beautifully deceptive in all its understated glory, features such as the building's secluded inner courtyard are hidden from the eye by those facing the property but can be accessed after the ceremony or drinks reception by descending wide stone steps leading from a large wooden door.

Sutton House closes annually for a month but is available for private hire from February to December. The venue offers couples the choice of three varying size rooms to hold their ceremony in and wedding parties are permitted open access round the remainder of the house.

The first room available for a ceremony at Sutton House, and the smallest of the three, is the Linenfold Parlour. Warmly decorated in deep oak, it seats up to 16 people and is perfectly suited for couples looking for an intimate ceremony in an authentic Tudor setting. Featuring rare linenfold oak panelled walls after which the room is named, a large window at the far end of the room is encased in double wooden doors and immerses the varying shades of brown and red wood in sunlight. Raised on a brick style platform, a wide centerpiece fireplace reaches deep into the building's

Featuring rare linenfold oak panelled walls, a large window at the far end of the room is encased in double wooden doors and immerses the varying shades of brown and red wood in sunlight

walls. An attractive feature in itself, winter ceremonies here may benefit here from the spectacular comfort of a real, blazing fire which provides a warm and cosy atmosphere.

The Marriage Suite incorporates two rooms which are hired together; the magnificent Great Chamber and its adjourning Little Chamber – the Great Chamber's exclusive waiting room. Suitable for up to 50 guests, the Great Chamber is a glorious ceremony room with original red-tinged oak fixed in square panels rising to greet a high ceiling. While gilded framed portraits line the walls, polished wooden floors in a paler hue meet another traditional open fireplace.

For larger ceremonies, Sutton House can offer couples the Wenlock Barn, which can accommodate up to 100 guests. Named after Lord Wenlock, the later title of the rector of Hackney, Algernon Lawley, the hall was built in 1904 and designed by the architect Lionel Crane, son of the notable Arts and Crafts designer, Walter Crane. This room is accessed through the wisteria-adorned courtyard, a quiet stone-flagged area decked with foliage that offers guests a glimpse through a beautiful armada window. The room itself is spacious and surprisingly modern, with a pale polished floor; tall red walls half-timber exposed beamed ceiling, large windows, and a balcony constructed in ash. Beautifully decked in cross panelled wood with deep brown beams, it was built as an Edwardian ground floor addition to the Tudor house and reveals carefully preserved original features in the Arts and Crafts style.

Venue Details

Sutton House
2 and 4 Homerton High Street
Hackney
London
E9 6JQ
t   020 8986 2264
e   suttonhouse@nationaltrust.org.uk
w www.nationaltrust.org.uk

Licence authority:
London Borough of Hackney
Hackney Town Hall
Mare Street
London E8 1EA
t   020 8356 3376
e   info@hackney.gov.uk
w www.hackney.gov.uk

Licensed for ceremony: Marriage Suite (50, drinks reception 80), Wenlock Barn (100, drinks reception 100), Linenfold Parlour (16, drinks reception 18)

Outside space: The courtyard area

Option of a marquee: ✗

Rooms available for overnight accommodation: ✗

Complimentary dressing room for bride available: ✗

SPECIAL NOTES

Licensing hours: Until 12.30pm

Corkage charge: £5 (minimum charge £30)

Catering: In-house (hors d'oeuvres can be provided for the drinks reception)

Complimentary menu tasting: ✗

Car parking spaces: Metered parking in surrounding streets, free on Sundays

Sound/noise restrictions: Music may be played, recorded or live, throughout the house. Reasonable amplification restrictions apply

Confetti: ✗

Candles: ✗

PA system: ✗

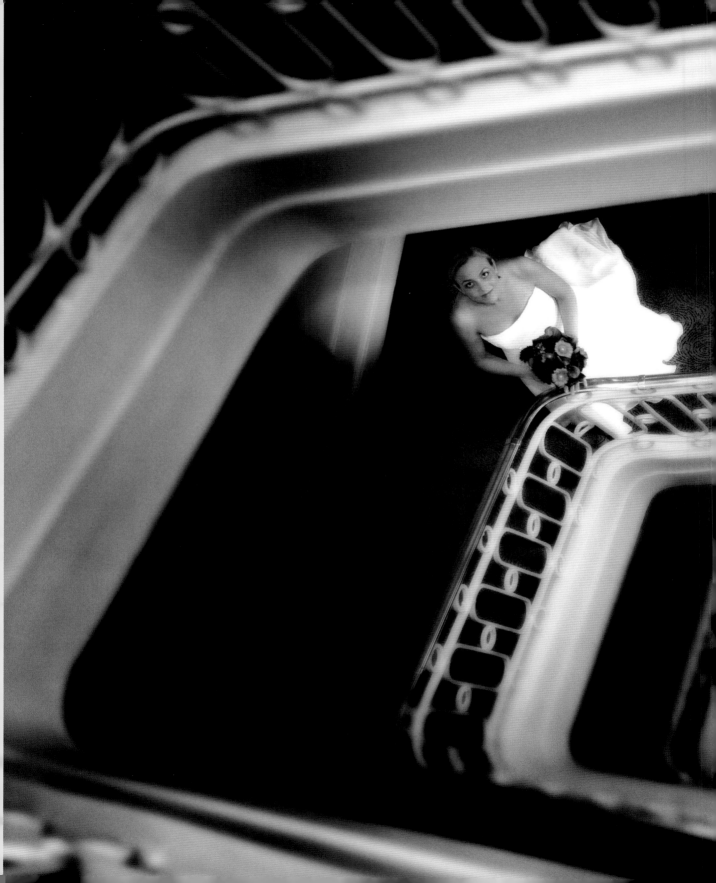

For a Fabulous

Reception

Chelsea Physic Garden

Fabulous because...

As the second oldest botanic garden in England, this garden has over 5,000 species of plants and provides a tranquil, yet central, adaptable marquee site in the midst of a horticultural haven

Location: **Chelsea**

Capacity: **Wedding breakfast 325; Evening reception 400**

Minimum number of guests: **None**

Guide Price
Per guest (including venue hire): **Not available**
Venue hire only: **Saturdays £6,000, weekday evenings £3,000 – £5,000**

When to get married here: **Spring/Summer**

Home of the largest outdoor fruiting olive tree growing in Britain and the world's most northerly fruiting grapefruit tree

Chelsea Physic Garden is one of the few truly 'hidden gems' remaining in London. It is the second oldest botanic garden in England, dating from 1673, and provides a wonderful space to erect a marquee, or enjoy an outdoor reception surrounded by the tranquillity of the Garden's landscape. Despite being located in the heart of the capital, just moments from the River Thames, the Garden's high walls give it a secluded and magical air. Entering through the 'secret' old iron gate on Swan Walk on the east side of the Garden, visitors are transported into a beautiful, tranquil space, away from the hustle and bustle of London.

The Garden was founded in 1673 by the Worshipful Society of Apothecaries, as the Apothecaries' Garden, with the purpose of training apprentices in identifying plants. The Garden has miraculously survived the centuries due to its peppercorn rent of £5 per annum, arranged in the 1720s by physician and philanthropist Sir Hans Sloane – after whom the nearby Sloane Square and Sloane Street were named and whose statue stands prominently in centre of the Garden. The location of the Garden was chosen due to its proximity to the river which created a warmer microclimate, allowing the survival of many non-native plants and, more importantly, to allow plants to survive harsh British winters.

This small Garden has had a significant effect on history: in 1848 Robert Fortune used Wardian cases, which are rather like miniature greenhouses, to transport seedlings of *Camellia sinensis* (tea) from China leading to the establishment of the tea industry in India.

At the end of the nineteenth century the trustees of the City Parochial Foundation agreed to take over the running of the Garden from the Society of Apothecaries. In 1983 the Garden became a registered charity and was opened to the general public for the first time. It is now patronised by HRH The Prince of Wales.

The four-acre Garden is home to 5,000 rare plants from across the globe, including the largest outdoor fruiting olive tree growing in Britain and what is believed to be the world's most northerly fruiting grapefruit tree. The collection concentrates on medicinal plants and those of ethnobotanical interest, as well as rare and endangered species. In addition to the plant collections, a large

Located moments from the River Thames, the Garden's high walls give it a secluded and magical air

number and variety of animals can be found in Chelsea Physic Garden, which is a Grade I Site of Borough Importance.

Environments for supporting different types of plants were built through the years, including the pond rock garden, next to Sloane's statue, which has been listed Grade II star and is the oldest rock garden in England on view to the public. Completed on 16 August 1773, this curious structure is constructed from a variety of rock types, namely masonry from the Tower of London, Icelandic lava (brought to the garden by Sir Joseph Banks in 1772) and giant clamshells brought back from Captain Cook's explorations.

The Garden is made up of different sections, including a woodland garden, a Garden of World Medicine, Britain's first garden of ethnobotany, and a main lawned area. Paths run geometrically through the areas and there is a Historical Walk, laid out along the western side of the Garden, planted to show the work of some of the best known people associated with the Garden's history, through plants introduced or first named by them. For example, the Phillip Miller Garden in the north-western corner houses beds arranged geographically, with plants introduced from Europe, Far East and the Americas.

Most events are centred on the lawn in front of the main building though couples are able to hire the whole Garden. The 80ft x 60ft lawn is a picturesque location for a wedding marquee. A large marquee here can seat up to around 325 guests for a wedding breakfast, or host for a drinks reception for 400 people (extended up to 550 with a special licence).

There are many idyllic spots for wedding photography with a fascinating collection of plants and ponds

Even once a marquee is in place though, a large proportion of the lawns are still exposed. There is also the option of an awning on the gravel area next to the building.

The main building at the northern end of the Garden is a marvellous red brick Edwardian house, clad with ivy. This building hosts a reception room which, in addition to the spacious lawn, can be used to seat around 80 guests for a wedding breakfast, or 130 for a standing reception, in case of bad weather. This building can also be used as a place where caterers prepare for an outside event. Hire of the Reception Room is free with hire of the Garden, although without hiring the Garden there is a fee. The room has a partition that can be drawn to separate the room in half if required.

The venue is available for hire on Saturday and weekday evenings throughout the year, as well as daytimes on some weekends.

Sunday daytime hire is occasionally available between November and March. Couples are welcome to have a classical or jazz band serenading the reception, before guests move into dinner.

As can be easily imagined, there are many idyllic spots for wedding photography to be taken throughout the Garden. Guests are welcome to explore the peripheries of the Garden, with its fascinating collection of plants and two ponds, during the reception. Access to the glasshouses is not permitted, and children need to be closely supervised around the ponds and some poisonous plants. A guide can be arranged to give those interested a tour of the Garden or to provide general Garden information.

In this botanical wonderland, wedding receptions are bespoke events, with a marquee holding any number of possibilities for décor and theme.

Venue Details

Chelsea Physic Garden
66 Royal Hospital Road
London
SW3 4HS
t 020 7352 5646
e hire@chelseaphysicgarden.co.uk
w www.chelseaphysicgarden.co.uk

Function rooms available: Garden (reception 325, evening 550), The Reception Room (reception 80, evening 130)

Outside space: Four acres of garden

Option of a marquee: ✓ (requisite supplier)

Rooms available for overnight accommodation: ✗

Complimentary dressing room for bride available: ✓

SPECIAL NOTES

Licensing hours: Until 10pm

Corkage charge: Dependent on caterer

Catering: Recommended suppliers

Complimentary menu tasting: Dependent on caterer

Car parking spaces: NCP car park $1/3$ mile away

Sound/noise restrictions: Amplified or non-amplified music until 10pm. No DJs, rock, pop or dance music. Classical, jazz and world music permitted.

Fireworks: ✗ (sparklers permitted)

Confetti: ✗

Candles: ✓ (external use only)
PA system: ✓ (requisite supplier)

Helicopter landing permission: ✗

Wedding options

A recent wedding reception at Chelsea Physic Garden was hosted in the style of a quintessential English Garden party, with a marquee in one area of the lawn. The couple hosted a reception and dinner for 150 people.

The wedding party had their pictures taken in various Garden locations before their guests arrived. Guests arrived after a service at nearby Chelsea Old Church, making the short walk along the Embankment to the Garden. They entered via the old iron gate and were offered a glass of champagne as they walked through the enchanting garden to the lawn.

A string quartet played as guests mingled on the lawn and wandered freely throughout the four acres of Garden. Throughout the afternoon guests were offered delicious canapés and a variety of soft and alcoholic drinks. A guide was on hand to give those interested a tour of the Garden. Padded chairs and benches lined the side of the lawn and cover was offered in a clear-sided marquee that was used for the evening dinner.

Later guests congregated on the lawn for speeches and the wedding cake was cut. Guests were then invited to take their seats for dinner and as daylight faded, the Garden was subtly illuminated.

Each table had been designed according to the bride and groom's taste and each guest was given a jar of the Garden's own honey and a packet of seeds for themselves. The food had been chosen with the guidance of the Garden's caterers and event organisers.

Towards the end of the dinner the jazz band started to play softly and continued when the bride and groom had their first dance.

At the end of the evening, as the couple left, guests waved them down the main pathway before they climbed into the car waiting for them on Royal Hospital Road.

Design Museum

Fabulous because...

At the cutting edge of design, the museum provides contemporary, adaptable spaces where there is ample room for couples to imprint their own style, overlooking the Thames and Tower Bridge

Location: Tower Bridge, Southwark

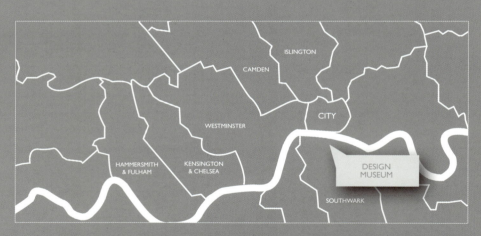

Capacity: Wedding breakfast 120; Evening reception 250

Minimum number of guests: None

Guide Price
Per guest (including venue hire): **Not available**
Venue hire only: **£3,525**

When to get married here: All year round

DESIGN MUSEUM

*From minimalist, sleek dinners
to themed, vibrant receptions, the
possibilities at the Design Museum are endless*

Imagine holding a wedding breakfast in a venue decorated exclusively to your tastes, overlooking the River Thames in one of London's most fashionable museums.

Situated beside Tower Bridge, the Design Museum blends an unparalleled location with contemporary and adaptable spaces. Creating a unique and memorable experience is imperative, capturing couples' creative desires for their wedding reception. At the museum, the 'blank canvas' is in place for couples to create, design and be inspired. From minimalist, sleek dinners to themed, vibrant receptions, the possibilities at the Design Museum are endless. And for those creatively minded, what better place to craft the perfect reception than at the heart of London design.

Founded in 1989, the Design Museum was the first museum in the world to be dedicated to modern and contemporary design, and holds critically acclaimed exhibitions on modern design history. The fashion designer, Sir Paul Smith, described this venue as 'the natural home for everyone who has ever enjoyed or appreciated design' and its unique function makes it ideal for a bespoke wedding reception. The stark white building is a former 1940s banana warehouse, which was renovated in the International Modernist style of the 1930s. Exhibitions at the museum are diverse and have ranged from retrospectives of Manolo Blahnik's shoe design and Philip Treacy's hats to E-type Jaguars and Saul Bass' classic film title graphics. The ever changing exhibitions contain many iconic pieces of design, from Dyson's DC01 vacuum cleaner, iPods, Le Corbusier chaise longues and Bic biros to Technics decks from Manchester's famed Hacienda night club.

The venue's layout and sparse design mean the couple's exact requirements can be met. In addition to this, remarkable views set this venue apart: from a contemporary cocoon, guests can gaze out over some of London's most famous landmarks.

There are three versatile spaces at the museum, brimming with potential and all are ideal to create a perfectly styled reception. The Riverside Hall is the largest of the spaces,

The Design Museum Space is inspired by infinity pools;
the walls and floor are a discreet shade of light blue

on the ground floor of the museum. It has floor-to-ceiling windows which open out onto the terraced area on the bank of the River Thames. The hall's white walls and floor to ceiling windows can be transformed or minimally accessorised to cater for a dinner for up to 120 guests, or a drinks reception for around 250 and with robust marble flooring the area is suitable for dancing. On warm evenings, guests can spill out onto the riverside terrace which looks out onto Tower Bridge and the nautical sculptures along the Shad Thames.

Up to 120 guests, depending on the exhibition, can dine amongst the Design Museum's collection of design classics and the latest design innovations in the Contemporary Design Gallery. This is one of London's most prestigious

galleries and is situated on the second floor of the Design Museum. The bright, naturally lit, modern space has panoramic views across the River Thames and contains design pieces which are rotated and themed periodically.

On a mezzanine, between the first and second floors of the museum, the Design Museum Space is found. With access from a private riverfront entrance the room enjoys spectacular views looking over Tower Bridge and Canary Wharf. A large balcony, spanning the length of the room, gives guests a breathtaking view. The room's décor is inspired by infinity pools; the walls and floor are a discreet shade of light blue. Wedding breakfasts in this room have the advantage of using the museum's classic modern chairs

From a contemporary cocoon, guests can gaze out over some of London's most famous landmarks

designed by Charles and Ray Eames. Screens can be erected to create up to five separate spaces, to divide into reception, dinner and dancing areas, if couples so wish.

The museum's galleries are also available during events at the venue, so that guests can enjoy exclusive private views of the museum's exhibitions and relish the true creativity of the venue, with gallery invigilators incorporated in the venue hire price.

The Design Museum's events team are on hand to work with the bride and groom, either to help piece together their imagined design ideas, or offer inspiration, suggest suitable creative ideas and bespoke ways of decorating the blank canvas – they can be as involved with arrangements as much as the couple wish.

Attentive to the needs of guests, modern facilities are included in the fee including audio, visual presentation and PA equipment and adjustable air conditioning systems.

The Design Museum has a lift to every floor and provides a lift operator and security staff included in the venue price. The museum offers dry hire rates and provides details of the museums accredited caterers for couples to choose from. For those looking for an inimitably stylish venue, the Design Museum amalgamates sleek sophistication with the flexibility of a clean space.

Venue Details

Design Museum
Shad Thames
London
SE1 2YD
t   020 7940 8262
e   events@designmuseum.org
w   www.designmuseum.org

Function rooms available: Riverside Hall (reception 120, evening 250), Contemporary Design Gallery (reception 120, evening 180), Design Museum Space (reception 80, evening 200)

Outside space: Ground floor roof terrace and second floor private balcony

Option of a marquee: ✗

Rooms available for overnight accommodation: ✗

Complimentary dressing room for bride available: ✗

SPECIAL NOTES

Licensing hours: Until 11pm (late licence available on application)

Corkage charge: Dependent on caterer

Catering: Recommended caterers

Complimentary menu tasting: Dependent on caterer

Car parking spaces: NCP on adjacent street

Sound/noise restrictions: Must be reduced to a background level after 11pm

Fireworks: ✓ (with council's permission)

Confetti: ✓

Candles: ✓ (naked candles not permitted)

PA system: ✓

Helicopter landing permission: ✗

Wedding options

The Design Museum's first ever wedding celebration was held with a distinctive 'Beach Bar upon Thames' theme. The reception for 120 people was organised during an eight-month period by an events team.

The total space was utilised, guests using both the outdoor and sleek interior areas of the Design Museum.

Against the dramatic backdrop of Tower Bridge, the large space directly outside the Riverside Hall was transformed into a smart urban club lounge. It was carpeted with natural sea-grass matting and bespoke seating areas were installed as well as a long club-bar providing cocktails. Awnings and linen parasols protected guests from unpredictable weather. The outdoor walls and entrance were washed with fuscia lighting. Large potted palms and brightly coloured scatter cushions created a smart and sassy, yet warm and friendly environment.

As the bride and groom made their entrance, the BBQs cooked up a variety of canapés before guests moved onto substantial bowled offerings for this non-traditional reception.

As dusk deepened the party moved inside for the speeches before dessert treats and funky confections were served. The DJ hit the decks and guests hit the dance floor. The Riverside Hall seems almost purpose-built for dancing with an indestructible marble floor.

Foundling Museum

Fabulous because...

Hidden in leafy Bloomsbury, this museum houses England's first public art collection and gives couples the chance to entertain in spectacularly historical surroundings

Location: Bloomsbury

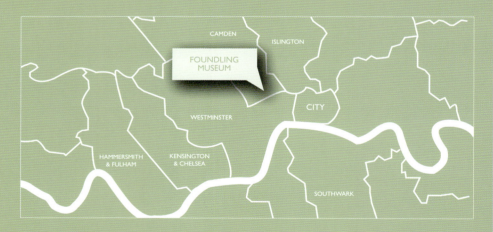

Capacity: Wedding breakfast 100; Evening reception 200

Minimum number of guests: **None**

Guide Price
Per guest (including venue hire): **Not available**
Venue hire only: **£3,500**

When to get married here: **All year round**

Titanium

Copper

Guests may revel in surroundings that were once enjoyed by both Hogarth and Handel

The Foundling Museum is situated in a leafy and secluded square in the heart of Bloomsbury, between the British Museum and the British Library. It is home to one of London's finest surviving Rococo interiors and London's first public art collection. A truly unique place in which to host a wedding reception, the museum's neo-Georgian style is matched with eighteenth-century interiors, taken from the original Foundling Hospital. Couples will delight in a venue that marries the historical with the contemporary; where the story of the building itself – and the inspiring social history it embodied – are brought to life in an atmosphere of celebration.

The award-winning Foundling Museum is located on the site of the same Foundling Hospital it commemorates. Established in 1739, the Hospital occupies a special place in Britain's cultural history as it was the country's first home for abandoned children as well as the nation's first public art gallery. The result of a tireless campaign by Captain Coram, the Hospital emerged from what has been referred to as 'a golden age of philanthropy' and provided a home for nearly 30,000 abandoned children in the two centuries following its foundation. Now a testament to history, it is an attractive setting for any wedding reception, twinning its contemporary exhibitions with lavish Rococo interiors linked by an original eighteenth-century stairway.

Couples entering the museum will pass through grand glass doors into a cool and airy space, perfect for a champagne reception. The clean lines of the entrance hall allow for floral displays in the reception area; the lacquered wooden floors and nearby staircase also highlight the building's stand-alone features of Georgian design. Guests are then able to wander through the Coram's Children Gallery; which tells the poignant story of England's abandoned children and displays, amongst other things, the Royal Charter granted by King George II. The Committee Room displays moving nineteenth-century works of art by Emma Brownlow King, the daughter of a

The museum's neo-Georgian style is matched with eighteenth-century interiors

former foundling. These highlight the links with Charles Dickens and his involvement with the Hospital. Guests are then able to continue on to explore the higher floors of the Museum.

The Foundling Museum offers three function rooms to couples wishing to hold either their drinks reception or a wedding breakfast here. Of these, the two most renowned are situated on the first floor, easily accessed by way of the grand oak staircase which is equipped with a low, wide handrail and covered in a deep red carpet. Guests will pass by gold framed portraits of former Governors and will also be presented with a number of religious paintings.

One of the principal attractions of the Foundling Museum, the Picture Gallery, is a large grand room modelled on the original building and houses works of art by some of Georgian London's great artists. The collection began with William Hogarth's donation of his portrait of Thomas Coram and now contains portraits by an array of artists including Gainsborough and Reynolds. The pale green and white hue forms a peaceful background against which to display the grand full length and smaller portraits in the Collection. The gracious room will seat up to 100 guests comfortably. This makes it an ideal dining venue for anyone requiring spacious surroundings and the allure of classic British art.

The Court Room, a breathtaking space, is a more intimate room which was designed by William Hogarth as the showcase for British Art. Guests will be impressed by the atmosphere created with the ornate white plaster Rococo ceiling against

*The atmosphere created by the ornate Rococo ceiling
against the dark green background will impress*

the dark green background and will feel privileged to be part of such a fascinating historical gem. With more breathtaking works of art guests may revel in surroundings that were once enjoyed by both Hogarth and Handel.

On the second floor a selection of Handel's music may be heard. The score of Handel's Messiah, bequeathed by the composer to the Hospital, is one part of the largest private collection of Handel memorabilia in the world. The Coke Collection is displayed in wooden cases alongside high back chairs creating an ambiance of tranquillity. Guests will be encouraged to explore the Collection and take advantage of the wider surroundings of the Foundling Museum.

The Museum's Temporary Exhibition Gallery is spacious and provides suitable space for 80 guests to mingle

during a drinks reception. A beautifully kept room, it is more modern in style; its fresh white walls and lacquered wooden floors balanced by the works of art on display.

Offering a bespoke wedding service to couples wishing to make independent choices about services such as catering, florists and musicians, the Foundling Museum is happy to cater for couples' personal preferences and is able to work within the confines of most wedding budgets.

FOR A FABULOUS RECEPTION

Venue Details

Foundling Museum
40 Brunswick Square
London
WC1N 1AZ
t   020 7841 3608
e   events@foundlingmuseum.org.uk
w   www.foundlingmuseum.org.uk

Function rooms available: Court Room
(reception 30), Picture gallery (reception100),
Temporary Exhibition Gallery (reception 80)
Outside space: Paved area outside museum
Option of a marquee: ✓
Rooms available for overnight accommodation: ✗
Complimentary dressing room for bride available: ✓

SPECIAL NOTES

Licensing hours: Until 11pm (late licence available
on application)
Corkage charge: Dependent on caterer
Catering: Recommended caterer
Complimentary menu tasting: Dependent on caterer
Car parking spaces: NCP car park nearby and limited
metered parking (free after 1.30pm on Saturdays)
Sound/noise restrictions: No restrictions
Fireworks: ✗
Confetti: ✗
Candles: ✗
PA system: ✓
Helicopter landing permission: ✗

Wedding options

Offering a venue bedecked with history, the Foundling Museum provides a unique place to hold a wedding reception. A typical wedding at the museum might begin with a champagne reception in the entrance of the Museum, decorated with flower displays.

Guests pass through the contemporary Coram's Children Gallery to the grand staircase. Musicians can be situated on the first landing and serenade the guests into dinner to be held in the Picture Gallery where they dine amidst classic British Art.

Dinner is created and served by one of the Foundling Museum's extensive list of recommended suppliers. The venue can also recommend florists, musicians and productions guaranteed to fit any taste and budget, all of which have worked with the museum before.

After dinner, the party is encouraged to explore the remaining treasures that fill the Museum. The Court Room serves as an excellent space for guests to take a step away from the excitement and marvel in the beautiful grandeur and architecturally stimulating design of Hogarth's Rococo ceiling. Surrounding corridors continue the story of the hospital, and at the top of the stairs, guests will find some of Handel's greatest treasures.

'It is the work behind the scenes that makes this type of event memorable. With your help we were able to bring together a truly remarkable location and amazing entertainment, ensuring that all invited were able to enjoy something distinctly different. Our feedback shows that this event will stand out as one of the favourites.'

'The venue was a real gem – we loved the amazing art collection, Handel's music and were moved by the poignant story of the children. What a wonderful party!'

Hush

Fabulous because...

Located in the heart of Mayfair, Hush is a stylish venue that offers couples an exclusive space for their wedding reception amidst distinctive North African décor

Location: Mayfair

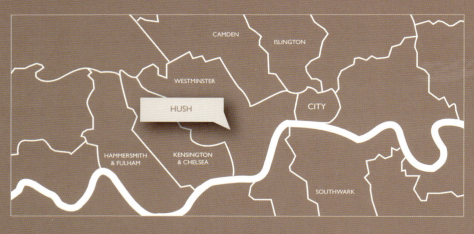

CAMDEN

ISLINGTON

WESTMINSTER

HUSH

CITY

HAMMERSMITH & FULHAM

KENSINGTON & CHELSEA

SOUTHWARK

Capacity: Wedding breakfast 85; Evening reception 180

Minimum number of guests: 8

Guide Price
Per guest (including venue hire): **£45 – £100**
Venue hire only: **Price on application**

When to get married here: **Autumn/Winter**

'Strictly' is an oasis of glamour with a gorgeous array of exotic and colourful drapes

Launched in 1999 to much acclaim, the stylish and savvy Hush, situated in the heart of Mayfair, is a popular dining and party destination that provides an exciting and innovative backdrop to a modern wedding reception. One of only a few bars in the UK to have been awarded the four-star *Class* magazine bar award, it is a chic venue that encompasses a vast array of contemporary, exotic and rich styles from classic French cuisine to original fruit and champagne cocktails.

As its name suggests, Hush is discreetly positioned in a quiet spot just off Bond Street. Located in a leafy courtyard in what was once a stable yard, this glamorous venue has in some ways retained a peaceful, village-like feel surrounded by century-old cobbles and garbled mews. With a welcoming air that is the result of the courtyard's enclosed yet spacious location, couples celebrating their marriage in Hush can relish the approach to the venue by way of its sloped cobbled pathway. Passing through the dark walkway, wedding parties can stop as they pass by the terrace and view the understated, contemporary décor of Hush's main entrance room situated on the second floor; the Brasserie. Decked in neutral shades, this room lies close to Hush's French restaurant, Le Club and makes for a pleasant entrance.

Hush offers couples a choice of wedding reception venues. La Cave is a stunningly ambient wine boutique and private room and is a popular choice for those looking for an intimate reception in a flexible and trendy space. La Cave has played host to presidents and pop stars alike, and is set back from the Hush courtyard with seating for up to 12 people. Specialising in rare and fine wines, it boasts a selection of highly sought-after vintages that are built in to the room's sophisticated décor. Decked in warm colours with the bottles prominently displayed, it is an excellent spot for connoisseurs to host an intimate post-wedding gathering.

For a larger space, Hush offer their private third-floor rooms, *Strictly*. These rooms are an oasis of glamour and sophistication, decked in deep oaken wood with rich brown flooring and overhead panelling offset by an array of exotic and colourful drapes framing a series of windows. Laced with a Moroccan

Located in a leafy courtyard this venue has in some ways retained a village-like feel surrounded by century-old cobbles and garbled mews

flavour the rooms can be decorated with candles and flowers, to individual couple's tastes, and confetti is allowed throughout.

The area is made up of three similarly decorated adjoining rooms suitable for both wedding breakfasts and champagne receptions. The rooms are named Zanzibar, Tangiers and Kenya. An extremely versatile space, they enjoy natural sunlight during the day, yet retain a spectacular, low-lit ambience at night. Well-suited to banquets, large, grandly decorated tables that reach the length of the room can host a extravagant spread with deep crimson tablecloths and candelabras creating a rich finish.

Couples here can make good use of the three inter-connecting rooms that allow up to 85 people to be seated for a dinner provided by Hush's competent catering team. These rooms are discreetly positioned aside from the rest of the building and have their own private entrance leading into a lift. For large parties of up to 400, a final alternative that can be made available for exclusive bookings is the possibility of hiring the whole venue, which would include La Cave, *Strictly* and the Brasserie.

Hush's experienced events team also offer a bespoke planning service. Whether couples desire a belly-dancer, DJ or ice luge, the team will endeavour to make it happen.

Laced with a Moroccan flavour, rooms can be decorated with candles and flowers

Venue Details

Hush
8 Lancashire Court
Brook Street
London
WIS IEY
t 020 7659 1500
e info@hush.co.uk
w www.strictlyhush.com

Function rooms available: Strictly (reception 85), La Cave (reception 12, evening 20), Le Club (reception 40, evening 70), The Cocktail Lounge (drinks reception 160)

Outside space: Terrace (only on total venue hire)

Option of a marquee: ✗

Rooms available for overnight accommodation: ✗

Complimentary dressing room for bride available: ✓

SPECIAL NOTES

Licensing hours: Until midnight

Corkage charge: £30

Catering: In-house

Complimentary menu tasting: ✗

Car parking spaces: Limited metered parking on surrounding streets. NCP on Grosvenor Street.

Sound/noise restrictions: Volume turned down after 11.30pm

Fireworks: ✗

Confetti: ✓

Candles: ✓

PA system: ✓

Helicopter landing permission: ✗

Wedding options

In October, *Strictly Hush* played host to a wedding breakfast and evening reception for 39 guests.

Arriving from the register office in Marylebone, the newly married couple were greeted by the venue's hostess and their wedding photographer in the private, leafy courtyard. After pictures were taken, the party proceeded upstairs to a champagne reception and harpist. With canapés circulating, guests stole the chance to say a few words of congratulations to the bride and groom, in the light filled exotic ambience.

After an hour the guests were seated for a lavish dinner in the Zanzibar room. The party then enjoyed a constant flow of North African themed dishes. From deep fried halloumi with grilled peppers and quail's eggs and Moroccan chicken cigars with almond and cinnamon to a choice of chicken tagine with sweet potatoes, honey and dried fruits or chermoulah marinated fillet of salmon, with delicious sides such as sautéed potatoes with garlic and rosemary.

The speeches followed and while this was taking place, guests were each presented the wedding book to sign. Finally, a chocolate and apricot tart with yoghurt and pistachio was served for dessert and made their selection of digestif between Port, Brandy and Whisky. Friends and family shared stories and basked in the sumptuous and inviting atmosphere.

Later on, tables then were cleared to make space for a dance floor and the band started to play. After the couple's first dance, guests took to the floor and continued the celebrations through until midnight.

Landmark Arts Centre

Fabulous because...

Formerly the Church of St Alban the Martyr, this is a magnificent Gothic building situated in a prime position in south London, and can hold up to 350 guests

Location: Teddington, Surrey

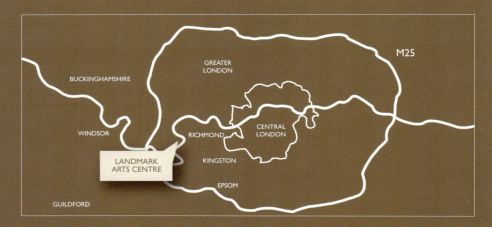

Capacity: Wedding breakfast 220; Evening reception 350

Minimum number of guests: 80

Guide Price
Per guest (including venue hire): **Not available**
Venue hire only: **£2,650 (from April 2008 – £2,750)**

When to get married here: All year round

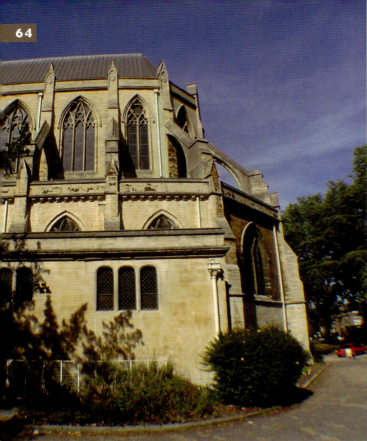

Located at the end of Teddington High Street lies a beautiful Gothic building. Formerly the Church of St Alban the Martyr, it is a stunning architectural feat that is now protected under a Grade II listing. Home to the Landmark Arts Centre, this towering building was once informally known as the 'cathedral of the Thames Valley' and is now available for private hire. A truly unique venue, it is the ideal backdrop for couples wishing to hold their wedding reception in an awe-inspiring church setting that comes complete with a magnificent history.

The Church of St Alban the Martyr was designed by architect William S Niven. A local man who had been a pupil of Sir George Gilbert Scott, his legacy includes involvement in the restoration of the Chapter House at Westminster Abbey. It was in fact this, as well as the sighting of a thirteenth-century French Church, that was said to have had a profound effect on his design and which led ultimately to a church infused with a European Gothic feel.

Erected in 1889, insufficient funds meant the building was never built to its full, original design and remained partially exposed; eventually neglected by dwindling congregational numbers. Saved by local campaigners who wished to turn the building into a community arts centre, it is now home to the flourishing Landmark Arts Centre; a registered charity that reverberates with an array of community clubs, classes and projects. The venue has also starred in films such as *Elizabeth*.

For couples wishing to hold their reception at the Landmark Arts Centre, there are a number of nearby options for the ceremony, including a church just opposite, or register offices in both Richmond and Kingston; some couples enjoy departing from a ceremony along the river and taking a boat ride to emerge near Teddington Lock just a few minutes from the Landmark.

Due to the vast expanse of the building, wedding parties of up to 350 can be accommodated, with catering arranged for up to 220. While couples are permitted choose their own caterer, the venue's staff are happy to recommend caterers

Couples approaching the building will note the traditional beauty of a church's soaring walls and stunning stained glass windows

they have worked with in the past. Offering savings by not charging corkage, the Landmark also leaves decision-making regarding drinks and alcohol up to the couple.

An unusual venue from the outset, couples approaching the building will note the distinctive party location by the traditional beauty of a church's soaring walls and stunning stained glass. Entering into the building they will be met with an expanse of space that is theirs to use as they wish. Although ideally suited to grand gatherings, the venue also caters for those in search of a more intimate reception and will screen off an area between two of the stone columns which couples can then decorate should this be a more suitable option.

On viewing the Arts Centre, the first thing to note is the striking versatility of the building. A central space by the pulpit

can be laid with carpet and set for dining, with a series of columns surrounding it which can be offset with dazzling lights. The sensation of grandeur is further enhanced by the walled archways which rise to meet high windows. Encompassing an array of features the building contains an ornate pulpit and canopy, which is unusually located halfway down the nave.

The Landmark is well equipped to facilitate a wedding breakfast and evening reception, courtesy of its purpose-built dance floor which is situated in another part of the church close to the stage, allowing guests to move directly to this area after dining. The Landmark place few restrictions on arrangements and welcoming live music or a DJ (with consideration to volume).

This austere building provides a functional yet grand setting where guests will enjoy dancing in truly original surroundings.

FOR A FABULOUS RECEPTION

Venue Details

Landmark Arts Centre
Ferry Road
Teddington
London
TW11 9NN
t   020 8977 7558
e   corrina@landmarkartscentre.org
w   www.landmarkartscentre.org

Function rooms available: Main Hall (reception 220, evening 350)

Outside space: ✗

Option of a marquee: ✗

Rooms available for overnight accommodation: ✗

Complimentary dressing room for bride available: ✓

SPECIAL NOTES

Licensing hours: Until 11pm

Corkage charge: No corkage

Catering: Recommended caterers

Complimentary menu tasting: Dependent on caterer

Car parking spaces: Four (additional free parking in surrounding streets)

Sound/noise restrictions: ✓

Fireworks: ✗

Confetti: ✗

Candles: ✗

PA system: ✗

Helicopter landing permission: ✗

Wedding options

The Landmark Arts Centre simply offers an elaborate venue without any wedding packages or events team. Making use of this spectacular gothic cathedral setting, couples can decorate and plan their celebrations as they wish. The centre does not charge VAT.

'The Landmark looked absolutely stunning and everyone commented on what an amazing venue it was. We can't thank you enough for all that you did and allowing us to hold an important part of the most wonderful day of our lives… It was truly perfect!'

'Everyone commented on how marvellous the celebrations were, the goodwill and happiness of all those present, and of course the beauty of the venue itself. Many, many thanks for your understanding and flexibility.'

'You have a magnificent building that can accommodate large numbers of people. There are only a few others in the west London area and none of them match the space and grandeur of the Landmark.'

Natural History Museum

Fabulous because...

Beautiful Victorian architecture is coupled with the museum's intriguing and contemporary interiors to create a lavish and spacious setting for a truly unique occasion

Location: Kensington

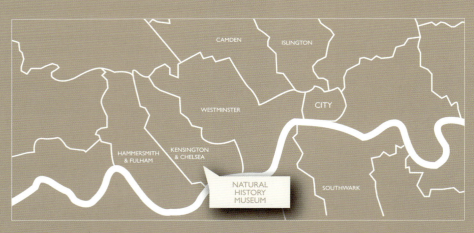

Capacity: Wedding breakfast 650; Evening reception 1200

Minimum number of guests: **None**

Guide Price
Per person (including venue hire): **Not available**
Venue hire guide price: **From £7,750**

When to get married here: **Autumn/Winter**

One of the most famous museums in London, the Natural History Museum is prominently situated in Kensington in a beautiful Victorian building and is world-renowned for the artefacts it holds. Its huge and intriguing interior spaces can be transformed to become the backdrop for a truly spectacular wedding reception. Couples wanting to leave a lasting impression on their guests can decorate either of the two main spaces with imaginative table decorations, dramatic lighting and spectacular entertainment.

The Central Hall at the Natural History Museum is without doubt one of the most prestigious settings for an evening event available in London. Its cathedral-like architecture features a soaring vaulted ceiling, intricately carved terracotta arches and a beautiful mosaic floor.

The huge arch in the Hall is decorated with birds and foliage, an example of the intricacy of the building's design. The wonderful stone staircase which leads down into the Hall makes a spectacular backdrop for the entrance of a newly married bride and groom and wedding photography. In the middle of this vast Hall, alongside the famous dinosaur skeleton, guests are seated for dinner. The 'wow factor' is all-important, and comes into its own when the Central Hall has been transformed by dramatic lighting.

An integral part of the Hall's framework, five iron arches span the room, each intricately decorated with gilt floral ornaments. Guests can climb the 'flying staircase', which surrounds the Central Hall and offers an excellent vantage point.

With the capacity to accommodate 100 to 650 guests for dinner and a flexible approach from the Museum staff make it an adaptable choice for any size and style of reception. Dinner and dancing for 450 can be accommodated in the Central Hall, and for larger wedding receptions for up to 650 guests, dinner can be held in the Central Hall, and dancing in the North Hall.

Under the same roof, yet a world apart, the Earth Galleries provide a dynamic, modern setting that has become an extremely popular venue since its opening in the summer of 1996.

FOR A FABULOUS RECEPTION

Its cathedral-like architecture features a soaring vaulted ceiling, terracotta arches and a beautiful mosaic floor

Passing through the gallery and up an escalator through a giant 'earth' suspended high above, guests can take their first drinks

First impressions count and arriving at the Earth Galleries entrance on Exhibition Road, guests enter a dramatic, soaring atrium with 18m high slate walls etched with the planets and depictions of the night sky. Passing through the gallery and up an escalator through a giant 'earth' suspended high above, guests can take their first drinks in Power Within; an exciting gallery where they can experience a recreation of the 1995 Kobe earthquake or stand under an erupting volcano.

Other galleries that can be made available include the stunning Earth's Treasury, on the first floor of the Earth Galleries, whose glittering collection of treasures includes fabulous jewels such as diamonds, emeralds, rubies and sapphires from around the world. This gallery can also be used for a pre-dinner drinks reception.

The wedding breakfasts in this part of the museum take place in the atrium on the ground floor, amongst the mystical star charts, where up to 200 guests can be seated beneath the suspended earth. Dancing is also permitted in this unusual space.

The sheer breadth of possibilities offered at the Natural History Museum is unsurpassed, from stilt walkers, fortune tellers and illusionists mingling with guests to giant exotic plants acting as table centre pieces and the Queen's guards band playing down the steps in the Central Hall. This is an impressive and awe-inspiring setting for a memorable wedding reception.

FOR A FABULOUS RECEPTION

Venue Details

Natural History Museum
Cromwell Road
London
SW7 5BD
t   020 7942 5434
e   exclusive-events@nhm.ac.uk
w www.nhm.ac.uk/exclusive-events

Function rooms available: Central Hall
(reception 650, evening 1200), Earth Galleries
(reception 200, evening 600)

Outside space: The museum's lawns

Option of a marquee: ✓

Rooms available for overnight accommodation: ✗

Complimentary dressing room for bride available: ✓(weekends only)

SPECIAL NOTES

Licensing hours: Until midnight (late licence available on application)

Corkage charge: Dependent on caterer

Catering: Recommended suppliers

Complimentary menu tasting: Dependent on caterer

Car parking spaces: 25 spaces for Central Hall guests only

Sound/noise restrictions: No restrictions

Fireworks: ✗

Confetti: ✗

Candles: ✓

PA system: ✗

Helicopter landing permission: ✗

Wedding options

When holding an event in either the Earth Galleries or Central Hall, the museum guarantees exclusive use of the space hired. Events managers are on hand to help organise every aspect of a wedding reception and can produce a detailed proposal tailored to couple's specific requirements and budget. The museum is exempt from VAT. Events must begin after the museum's closing time: hire charge starts from 6pm with guests able to arrive after 7pm.

The scope of decoration and entertainment at the museum is endless. The spaces are adaptable and the Central Hall can be split into sections depending on the number of guests. The Natural History Museum has a vast list of accredited suppliers – from theming specialists, entertainment agents and floral design companies to living foliage hire and ice carvings specialists. The galleries can be professionally lit with a plethora of lights, filling the room and highlighting the building's architecture. Past events have seen jazz bands, fire-eaters, magicians and stilt walkers entertain guests.

'Thanks for making our wedding day so special for us – I didn't expect to be upstaged by a building!'

'We had the most fabulous evening at the Museum… The front entrance and the Great Hall looked stunning to the thrill of both us and all our guests. Your staff were charming, very efficient and very professional and really made the evening run smoothly.'

Painshill Park

Fabulous because...

Situated on the outskirts of London, Painshill Park has been dubbed 'Surrey's best kept secret'. This eighteenth-century landscaped park is a beautiful rural retreat

Location: Cobham, Surrey

Capacity: Wedding breakfast 320; Evening reception 400

Minimum number of guests: 80

Guide Price
Per person (not including venue hire): **From £50**
Venue hire only: **£3,466 – £4,641**

When to get married here: All year round

A serene haven situated on the outskirts of London, Painshill Park is a stunning eighteenth-century landscaped park often referred to as 'Surrey's best kept secret'. Fully restored after its abandonment in the 1940s it is a unique wedding venue that allows couples to take advantage of picturesque outdoor surroundings whilst remaining in close proximity to the city. Set within walled gardens, the venue's Conservatory Marquee is a beautiful space which, well located within the grounds of the park, lends itself perfectly to dinner banquets and evening receptions.

Steeped in horticultural history, Painshill Park was created sometime between 1738 and 1773 by the Honourable Charles Hamilton — nineth son of the sixth earl of Abercorn. An imaginative designer who was also a painter and plantsman, he dedicated himself to the layout and composition of a landscape park unlike any other in Europe. Created as a romantic landscape to 'stimulate the senses and emotions of the visitor', the gardens

were divided into two parts. The ornamental parkland with its lake lies in the south while the open parkland sits in the north with the two connected by an array of changing vistas and areas that include The Gothic Temple and The Amphitheatre.

After selling the estate in 1773, it was held by a series of private owners and eventually began to suffer from neglect sometime in the mid-twentieth century. So severe was this that the painstaking restoration led to the park being awarded the Europa Nostra Medal in 1998 for 'the exemplary restoration from a state of extreme neglect, of a most important eighteenth-century park and its extraordinary buildings'. Now comprising 160 acres of landscaped gardens, it is a natural choice for those wanting a luscious and exclusive outdoor space.

The Conservatory Marquee is located in a discreet position at the heart of the park. Peeking out above the walled garden area, it is a sturdy structure that measures 25m by 29.5m and is capable of seating 320 guests for a grand meal. With a polished wooden floor, comfortable seating, coffee tables

Open parkland sits in the north with an array of changing vistas and The Gothic Temple

Spilling out onto wooden decking, couples can take advantage of the immaculately kept acre of private garden

and a handily placed bar, the reception space leads into the main dining hall. This carpeted space can seat guests around a series of 5ft round tables and can also be reduced by a quarter in order to give smaller parties a more intimate feel.

In a warm and airy space where light filters through the white covering in true marquee style, guests can also admire their outdoor surroundings through the marquee's clear front. The Conservatory is a well-equipped site that features a cloakroom, stage, dance floor and DJ booth as well as a fully functional kitchen. The venue does recommend preferred caterers but is happy to work with specialist caterers of the couple's choice at the incursion of a small fee.

With beautiful lighting that can adorn the interior of the Conservatory in a variety of shades to suit the mood, sumptuous table settings give way to a wonderfully versatile space suitable for dancing. Spilling out onto wooden decking that runs along the front of the marquee, couples marrying in the summer can then take advantage

of the immaculately-kept acre of private garden which runs up to the interior of the faded brick walls lined with flowers; a perfect setting for photography and drinks receptions.

While the team at Painshill Park are well-equipped in ensuring the Conservatory is decorated in a manner pleasing to the marrying couple, for couples seeking something a bit different, there is another alternative that can sometimes be made available. For exclusive bookings, Painshill Park also offers the option of a marquee to be erected in one of the park's two most idyllic locations; The Amphitheatre or The Lakeside. Suitable for the most highly lavish of celebrations, couples who are able to obtain permission direct from Painshill Park may use this site and will benefit from an expansive, manicured lawn in a sunny spot that permits truly spectacular views of the surrounding area.

With festivities able to continue until midnight, wherever couples celebrate their marriage at Painshill Park, they are invited to take in all of the park's stunning array of scenery.

Venue Details

Painshill Park
Portsmouth Road
Cobham
Surrey
KT11 1JE
t 01932 584 283
e events@painshillevents.co.uk
w www.painshillevents.co.uk

Function rooms available: The Conservatory (reception 320, evening 400)
Outside space: Landscaped parkland and private, lawned walled garden
Option of a marquee: ✓
Rooms available for overnight accommodation: ✗
Complimentary dressing room for bride available: ✗

SPECIAL NOTES

Licensing hours: Until midnight
Corkage charge: £2.35 per person
Catering: Recommended caterer, own caterer permitted for a fee
Complimentary menu tasting: Dependent on caterer
Car parking spaces: 400
Sound/noise restrictions: Bands can play until 11pm while a DJ can play until midnight
Fireworks: ✓ (in a meadow a two-minute walk from the Conservatory before 11pm)
Confetti: ✗
Candles: ✓
PA system: ✓
Helicopter landing permission: ✓

Wedding options

Part of the charm of the Conservatory at Painshill is that it allows each couple to put their own mark on their wedding – adding decoration to the venue and utilizing the tailored lighting provided by Painshill.

A wedding that was held in the conservatory lavishly decorated the dining area in reds and gold. The walls and ceilings were lined with strips of deep red organza, the chairs were dressed in ivory covers with the same red organza tied in bows around the chairs. The table centres added a floral and fresh look to proceedings. The lighting added the final touch to the venue, washing over the cream walls.

After dinner, speeches and a disco followed on the dance floor. Meanwhile the reception area had been transformed into a bar and chill-out area during dinner so people had a space to relax away from the music and dancing if they wanted. There was a selection of sofas, wicker chairs with coffee tables and the bar, which was now in place, lit in red to continue the theme of the evening.

At the end of the evening the guests left through the lit walled garden which encases the conservatory.

Painshill Park's chosen caterer and events planner can provide a range of food – from canapés and gourmet dinners to buffets and barbeques. After a traditional wedding breakfast, couples can choose to replace a buffet with a large cheeseboard, or even a hog roast. They also offer an events planning service, and can advise couples on flowers, entertainment, photographs and lighting.

Wellington Arch

Fabulous because...

An architectural landmark in central London, Wellington Arch combines grand architecture with contemporary spaces inside, providing couples with a distinctly different and memorable venue

Location: **Hyde Park Corner, Westminster**

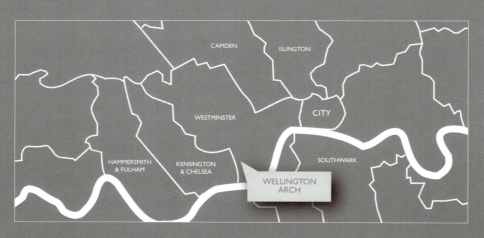

Capacity: **Wedding breakfast 36; Evening reception 80**

Minimum number of guests: **None**

Guide Price
Per guest (including venue hire): **Not available**
Venue hire only: **From £1,763**

When to get married here: **All year round**

Doors lead out onto two dramatic balconies either side of the Arch just below the spectacular bronze sculpture

Wellington Arch stands boldly in a green oasis in the centre of Hyde Park Corner, between Hyde Park and Green Park, with a bird's eye view across Westminster and Buckingham Palace Gardens. A iconic landmark to Londoners and visitors alike, it is a little known fact it is possible to hold a function inside the Arch. This surprising venue allows couples to host their wedding breakfast and reception in a signature London location with a theme to suit their individual tastes.

Commissioned by George VI and originally designed in 1825 by the architect Decimus Burton, it was intended as both a victory arch marking Wellington's defeat of Napoleon and as a grand outer entrance to Buckingham Palace. It marked what was then the western entrance into London. The Arch itself was completed in 1828, but soon after its completion was met with controversy when a colossal statue of the Duke of Wellington was added.

In 1883, the Arch was dismantled, moved 20m and rebuilt in its present location so that the surrounding roads around Hyde Park Corner could be widened. At the same time, the contentious Wellington statue was removed and later replaced with 'The Angel of Peace Descending on the Chariot of War', which remains the largest bronze statue in western Europe.

During the early twentieth century, the Arch was home to London's smallest police station but was abandoned in 1959 when the area became a traffic island. English Heritage has now restored the crumbling exterior to its former glory and the interior houses a modern exhibition space, offering a unique and spectacular setting for a drinks reception for up to 80 guests or a small dinners for up to 36 guests.

As guests arrive they are often surprised to be whisked up to the Arch's towering heights, where stylish rooms offer a sophisticated setting for daytime or evening events. Inside the Arch, three floors of exhibits tells the fascinating history of the building and on reaching the top, guests

As guests arrive they are often surprised to be whisked up to the Arch's towering heights

enter the Ante Room to be served drinks. This room, with its whitewashed walls and wooden floors, can be colour lit to coincide with the colour theme of the reception and its arches are accentuated with this up lighting.

The Ante room leads directly into the Burton Room, at the heart of the Arch. The two inter-linked rooms provide a good space, with the Ante room serving as a reception space if dinner is held in the Burton Room. Originally the sleeping quarters of the smallest police station in London, it now houses a modern exhibition and has a mezzanine gallery, perfect for drinks, or as an additional space for guests to mingle before or after dinner is served. This extra level gives the Burton Room height, and it is surprisingly spacious.

A more informal standing reception can readily be held here for 80 guests. In this room also, the lighting can be changed to complement the couple's chosen colour scheme.

Guests can enjoy spectacular views from the top of Wellington Arch. Doors from the mezzanine level lead out onto two dramatic balconies either side of the Arch just below the spectacular bronze sculpture which tops the imposing monument. One faces the neighbouring Apsley House and the expanse of Hyde Park, the other looks out over the gardens of Buckingham Palace, Westminster and the City of London beyond. The Arch is available to hire during the day and guests may be lucky enough to witness the Household Cavalry

At night the exterior of Wellington Arch
is dramatically swathed in light

passing beneath on their way to and from the Changing of the Guard at Horse Guards Parade.

Although at the very heart of the city, guests are privileged onlookers, rather than participants in the hustle and bustle of London life.

At night the exterior of Wellington Arch is dramatically swathed in light, highlighting the columns and architectural beauty of this venue. Couples holding their wedding reception at the Arch also have the opportunity to coordinate the colour of these lights to match the colour scheme of those inside.

Apsley House stands just yards away and can be hired for impressive private evening tours in conjunction with events at Wellington Arch. The House is the first Duke of Wellington's London home, also known as 'Number One London', as it

was the first house to be encountered after passing the Knightsbridge tollgates. The elegant mansion has sumptuously finished interiors: the walls of the 90ft long Waterloo Gallery display the Duke's superb art collection including masterpieces by Velazquez, Goya, Rubens and Van Dyck. This added option could make a pleasing prelude to a reception at Wellington Arch and add another dimension to an already unusual reception.

Couples have exclusive use of Wellington Arch during their event, and can choose from English Heritage's list of accredited suppliers. Its imposing position in the centre of London makes it an inimitable and distinctive venue in England's capital.

Venue Details

Wellington Arch
Hyde Park Corner
London
W1J 7JZ
t 020 7973 3292
e hospitality@english-heritage.org.uk
w www.english-heritage.org.uk/hospitality

Function rooms available: The Burton Room (reception 36, evening 80)

Outside space: Two balconies

Option of a marquee: ✗

Rooms available for overnight accommodation: ✗

Complimentary dressing room for bride available: ✓

SPECIAL NOTES

Licensing hours: Until 11pm

Corkage charge: Dependent on caterer

Catering: Recommended caterers

Complimentary menu tasting: Dependent on caterer

Car parking spaces: Free parking on nearby streets after 6.30pm on weekdays, after 1pm on Saturdays and all day Sunday

Sound/noise restrictions: No dancing or amplified music

Fireworks: ✗

Confetti: ✗

Candles: ✗

PA system: Not necessary

Helicopter landing permission: ✗

Wedding options

At Wellington Arch, couples can to hold informal cocktail receptions following a ceremony elsewhere. The two balconies are popular locations for drinks and canapés in fine weather, allowing guests to take in the fabulous views across London, elevated from the bustling streets below.

One couple recently had a blessing at the Arch, followed by a drinks reception. Another couple decided to keep the reception venue a surprise from their guests, so after the ceremony, the wedding party boarded a red London bus and had a 'mystery' tour of London's attractions. After touring various sights, the bus stopped at the Arch – guests thought it was just another sight on the tour and were amazed when they were actually taken inside for the reception!

The Arch is available to hire for exclusive use during the day as well as in the evenings. Depending on the time of the reception, guests can watch colourful mounted troops from the Queen's Lifeguards pass through the Arch from the balconies above – as they ride to and from Buckingham Palace to change the guard, providing very unusual and unique live entertainment.

Wilton's Music Hall

Fabulous because...

The last surviving grand music hall in the world, Wilton's is a nineteenth-century gem offering couples a versatile space for dancing and dining, complemented by a circular balcony

Location: Whitechapel

Capacity: Wedding breakfast 160; Evening reception 250

Minimum number of guests: 80

Guide Price
Per guest (including venue hire): **Not available**
Venue hire only: **£4,113**

When to get married here: Autumn/Winter

As the last surviving grand music hall in the world, Wilton's has a heritage of which to be proud. Once alive with the sounds of classical overtures, opera and music hall songs, it also bathed in the allure of the burlesque shows, circus acts and comedy it showcased prior to its change in direction in 1884. Picking up where it left off, this beautiful venue has, in recent years, played host to some of theatre's most acclaimed plays including Shakespeare's *The Taming of The Shrew* and Ben Jonson's Jacobian comedy *Volpone*.

Now open to the public, Wilton's Music Hall provides a stunning backdrop in which to hold a wedding reception whilst it also remains true to its history; with the high, arched ceiling and stage area in the venue's auditorium making it an ideal spot in which to host contemporary musical acts and theatre. Reviewed as 'London's most beautiful "lost" theatre', the years of neglect serve only to heighten its atmosphere and couples who wish to hold their

wedding reception here revel not only in the beauty of the venue's interior but also in the history within its walls. With all hire fees going towards rescuing the building, such history is far from an impersonal fact as couples actively contribute to and are therefore inextricably linked with the building itself.

Built in 1859 by John Wilton, Wilton's Music Hall's reputation for showcasing the greats began early. While George Leybourne (Champagne Charlie) sang in a mirrored hall that featured decadent designs including a crystal cut sun-burner chandelier, it is also rumoured that it was at Wilton's that the first ever cancan dance was performed.

After closing its doors on music in 1884, the hall served a strong social purpose housing a Methodist mission and provided 2,000 meals a day to Dockers in the first ever strike of 1889. It has also stood firm in the fight against fascism and provided shelter to a blitzed community during the Second World War before eventually gaining rightful protection as a Grade II star listed building. This old, dusty, yet highly

The long-standing front entrance is deliberately unassuming with a quaint charm that gives little away

atmospheric building, in need of repair, is a unique venue, ideal for couples seeking an unusual setting with ambiance. Encompassing modern decorative elements such as delicate dropped fairy lighting and faux candles, it also retains many of its original features including areas of exposed brickwork, intricate bordered designs and a network of connected spaces.

Approaching the hall down Graces Alley, the long-standing front entrance is deliberately unassuming with a quaint charm that gives little away. Weathered double doors beneath a partial archway sit alongside two built-in pilasters with raised relief and allow for an impressionable entrance into the venue's spectacular interior. Once inside, guests are transported back in time courtesy of the beautifully lit foyer and the stone staircase, framed by the original brick walls. Here is the perfect location for couples to greet their guests while doormen stand by and direct guests up to the mezzanine level and balcony.

With a slim handrail leading the circular design, the balcony is the perfect place from which to glimpse the sheer beauty of the auditorium whilst also basking in the sense of space obtained from being so high up. White walls are offset by a colour scheme of brown and gold and are favourable to a flexible decorative scheme, while the curvature of the ceiling with its dark, paisley-like print is just one example of the venue's attractive architecture. Ideally located for pre-dinner canapés and drinks, couples are also welcome to use the balcony to seat a few selected guests

Years of neglect serve only to heighten its atmosphere and couples may revel in the history within its walls

who, when they are not watching the world below, can also marvel at the three pictures modestly framed in one of the far apse. The majority of guests, meanwhile, can be seated in Wilton's main room, The Music Hall.

The spectacular Music Hall is the predominant feature of Wilton's, with wooden floorboards and twined sugar barley columns that support the base of the balcony. A versatile space, it is the central venue for both dining and dancing and after guests have dined on a three course dinner, staff will clear the tables to one side, creating an instant dance floor. Live music can be set up on the hall's glorious stage which is situated at the forefront of the room and faces outwards towards guests. Softly lit by fairy

lights, it is elevated close to The Hall's grand piano and is also place to hold any speeches, taking full advantage of The Hall's excellent acoustics. Guests wishing to hunt out more of the venue's older features can enjoy this show from one of the wooden benches which, dating from 1888 and originally used by the Methodist mission, sit at the back of the room. Adding interesting character to an already vibrant venue, these benches can also be used as extra seating alongside the long rectangular tables. This is representative of the flexibility of Wilton's in catering to the individual wedding.

A quirky and eclectic setting for a spectacular show of a reception.

Venue Details

Wilton's Music Hall
**Graces Alley
Off Ensign Street
London
E1 8JB**
t 020 7702 9555
e info@wiltons.org.uk
w www.wiltons.org.uk

Function rooms available: The Music Hall (reception 160, evening 250), Old Mahogany Bar (drinks reception 80), Mezzanine (reception 25, evening 25)

Outside space: ✗

Option of a marquee: ✗

Rooms available for overnight accommodation: ✗

Complimentary dressing room for bride available: ✓

SPECIAL NOTES

Licensing hours: Until 11pm

Corkage charge: Dependent on caterer

Catering: Recommended caterers

Complimentary menu tasting: ✓

Car parking spaces: On-street parking on streets either side of Graces Alley and car parks on other nearby streets

Sound/noise restrictions: No restrictions

Fireworks: ✗

Confetti: ✓

Candles: ✗

PA system: ✓

Helicopter landing permission: ✗

Wedding options

Wilton's Music Hall provides a quirky venue that couples can make their own. Last year, a bride and groom held a winter wedding at The Music Hall.

Guests arrived at 7pm after the church service and gas heaters and a red carpet lined a quarter of Graces Alley to welcome them, providing an elegant path to the building. They entered Wilton's through the main doors and were greeted by doormen. The exposed brickwork of the foyer was enhanced by drapes and ivy decked the staircase.

Guests were directed upstairs to the mezzanine level and through to the auditorium balcony for champagne and pre-dinner canapés. The balcony overlooks the auditorium and was romantically lit with fairy lights and faux candles.

A three-course dinner was then served in the auditorium as a jazz musician played the grand piano on stage. Tables were set up as rectangular trestle tables with the option of mission benches.

Speeches were given from the stage and after, guests adjourn to the Old Mahogany Bar for post dinner cocktails while the musicians set up on the stage. At this point catering staff cleared away the dining tables to create a dancefloor for the guests to return to. to tunes of a full live band. Guests were also welcome to sit in the mezzanine level. The dancing and music ended at 11pm and guests left Wilton's at around midnight.

For a Fabulous

Ceremony and
Reception

Andaz Liverpool Street London

Fabulous because...

Once a prominent railway hotel and well located in the heart of the City, this prestigious venue offers a number of spaces, each with a distinctive style

Location: The City

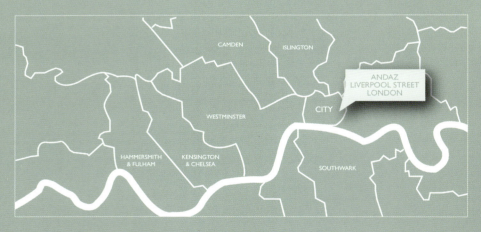

Capacity: **Ceremony 170; Wedding breakfast 170; Evening reception 400**

Minimum number of guests: **50**

Guide Price
Per head (including venue hire): **£120 – £210**
Venue hire only: **£7,000**

When to get married here: **All year round**

The newly opened Andaz Residence, with its suspended bar, focuses on effortless luxury

A grand Victorian building that is located on the infamous Liverpool Street, Andaz Liverpool Street London is gloriously situated amid some of Britain's most influential and cultural landmarks. Having started life as a railway hotel, it is now a living testament to traditional Victorian architecture; with features such as its red brick façade and elegant public rooms merging with spectacular contemporary design. Formerly named the Great Eastern Hotel and well known among City dwellers as one of the best luxury hotels, Andaz Liverpool Street London is also home to Aurora; the venue's main dining space renowned for its excellent cuisine and décor. This room leads the way in the style stakes and its gorgeous historical-stained glass dome makes dining a real treat.

Built in 1884, the main body of the hotel is listed; a tall, sweeping building that dominates the street and stretches towards the sky. Having been a prominent fixture among railway hotels for many years, the hotel re-opened its doors in 2000 after undergoing a £70 million refurbishment. Retaining many of the original features it recalls the glamour of travel in the Victorian era when hallways had to be wide enough to take cabin trunks. Carefully crafted to both preserve and instigate styles, it now sits among some of London's greats in its masterful reputation as a luxurious haven.

Offering a bespoke wedding service, Andaz Liverpool Street London is also one of the great innovators and is happy to welcome alternative ideas to the traditional

*The modern six-storey, glass-roofed Gallery is the
perfect venue for couples to greet their guests*

wedding party. Making available a number of different suites, there is ample choice and Chinese tea ceremonies, buffets or even burlesque dancers can all be arranged. With a total of six spaces licensed for ceremonies, couples are encouraged to tour the venue with the Andaz's wedding planner who will help them pick out the perfect space.

Of the many options available to choose from the Fenchurch room, named after one of the oldest streets in London, is able to hold up to 90 for a ceremony. Boasting high ceilings, intricate plasterwork, pale walls and stunning decorative brass chandeliers, this room is a versatile space that can be made the couple's own.

For couples in search of something a little more unusual, there are restaurants that can be hired out exclusively. Along with

Aurora, Catch and the Champagne Bar create alternative private reception venues. Accessed via an elaborate marble staircase, guests can celebrate with crustecea and cocktails. There is also the newly opened Andaz Residence, a luxurious, exclusive and bespoke private room, for up to 48 guests. With a suspended bar and show kitchen where guests can watch the chefs create, its focus is on effortless luxury and personalised service.

For the large wedding parties, The Great Eastern room with adjoining Gallery is the biggest space licensed for ceremonies in the hotel, able to accomodate 170 for a ceremony and dinner dance. Couples can greet their guests in the modern six-storey, glass-roofed Gallery before the party moves into the Great Eastern Room next door. Having

Picture caption to

The breathtaking white rotunda, a Guggenheim-inspired spiral through the floors of the hotel, is a wonderful location for photography

undergone a recent refurbishment, this is a wonderful contemporary room; minimalist in style with dark chocolate coloured carpet and white walls. Home to a state-of-the-art lighting system which gives couples the opportunity to choose which colour the room may be lit in. Table settings glow in the light, then the colour settings may be changed to create a different atmosphere later in the evening.

The final three rooms available for celebrations are the Minories, Chancery and Bishopsgate, all named after famous London landmarks. While the wedgewood blue Minories is ideal for an intimate wedding breakfast for up to 40 guests, the Bishopsgate and Chancery can seat 70 and 24 respectively. Part of the original building, the latter are airy spaces with huge windows, ornate wood panelling and magnificent fireplaces.

Whichever room couples decide to use for their ceremony, they are free to make full use of the venue for photographs. With a variety of beautiful settings and backdrops the choice is ample and ranges from the breathtaking white rotunda, a Guggenheim-inspired spiral through the floors of the Hotel, to the London sights nearby.

Following the evening celebrations guests taking one of the 267 rooms available can extend their stay further and enjoy the luxury of the hotel's facilities. Each room bearing a distinctive design, no two are the same and options range from those with period features and high ceilings to a light and airy 'loft' style space. And perhaps the party would like to enjoy a private breakfast, a chance to re-live the moments of the memorable event in style.

Venue Details

Andaz Liverpool Street London
Liverpool Street
London
EC2M 7QN
☎ 020 7618 5000
✉ charley.ewbank@london.liverpoolstreet.andaz.com
🖥 www.londonliverpoolstreet.andaz.com

Licence authority:
Islington Town Hall
Upper Street
London
N1 2UD
☎ 020 7527 6350
✉ registrars@islington.gov.uk
🖥 www.islington.gov.uk

Licensed for ceremony: Great Eastern Room and Gallery (170), Fenchurch (90), Chancery (40), Bishopsgate (80), Aurora Restaurant (120), Minories (50)

Function rooms available: Great Eastern Room and Gallery (reception 170, evening 400), The Temple (reception 22, evening 70), Minories (reception 40, evening 70), Fenchurch (reception 70, evening 100), Chancery (reception 24, evening 60), Bishopsgate (reception 70, evening 100), Aurora Restaurant (reception 100, evening 180), Residence (reception 48, evening 100)

Outside space: ✗

Option of a marquee: ✗

Rooms available for overnight accommodation: 267

Room rates: From £141

Complimentary dressing room for bride available: ✓

SPECIAL NOTES

Licensing hours: Until 1am

Corkage charge: Wine £23, champagne £25

Catering: In-house

Complimentary menu tasting: ✓

Car parking spaces: Valet parking available

Sound/noise restrictions: Noise restriction in Gallery after 10.30pm

Fireworks: ✓ (indoor)

Confetti: ✓

Candles: ✓

PA system: ✓

Helicopter landing permission: ✗

Wedding options

Andaz Liverpool Street London offers couples three wedding packages to choose from. Each package includes the hire of a ceremony, reception and dinner room. These useful frameworks can be tailored to couples' specifications.

Petticoat Lane

- Selection of four canapés and two glasses of Prosecco
- Unlimited soft drinks, water and juices during reception
- Three course menu from chef's selection
- Half a bottle of house wine and a bottle of mineral water during dinner
- A glass of champagne for toast
- Printed menus
- Package not available for weddings held in Aurora

Finsbury Square

As Petticoat Lane with additions:

- Selection of eight canapés and two glasses of champagne or two cocktails
- Four course menu from chef's selection
- Table plans, table numbers and place settings
- Complimentary room to host a private breakfast the following morning
- For weddings held in Aurora, a charge of £2,500 in addition to the package

Liverpool Street

As Finsbury Square with additions:

- Champagne breakfast on wedding morning for bride and three bridesmaids
- Massage and manicure for the brides, discount for bridesmaids
- Five course menu from chef's extended selection
- Tailored menu for wedding party
- A glass of dessert wine or port per guest
- Cake designed by pastry chef (with consultation and tasting) OR flowers designed by in-house florist (with consultation)
- DJ for evening entertainment
- Complimentary late bar license
- Party food – from a selection of three menus

The Bentley Kempinski

Fabulous because...

Situated in a discreet area of Kensington, the five-star Bentley Kempinski is a luxury hotel with a variety of exquisite suites available

Location: South Kensington

CAMDEN

ISLINGTON

CITY

WESTMINSTER

KENSINGTON & CHELSEA

THE BENTLEY KEMPINSKI

HAMMERSMITH & FULHAM

SOUTHWARK

Capacity: Ceremony 70; Wedding breakfast 60; Evening reception 150

Minimum number of guests: None

Guide Price
Per guest (not including venue hire): From £19.50
Venue hire only: From £500

When to get married here: Autumn/Winter

Part of the prestigious Kempinski hotel chain, The Bentley Kempinski Hotel is one of the most opulent hotels to have opened in the capital in recent years. Situated in a discreet residential area of Kensington, a stone's throw from the famous King's Road, it offers couples a great location for a city wedding matched with a service team who specialise in organising such events. Proclaiming that 'weddings are made in heaven and held at The Bentley Kempinski', the hotel is well versed in the intricacies of wedding planning and offer such extras as honeymoon suites and an exclusive Hen Package for the bride-to-be.

The Bentley is located in a stunning nineteenth-century property which began life as four grand private residences. Tastefully restored behind the original façade, the hotel now offers a series of modern luxuries which include a range of sumptuous suites and the venue's own authentic Turkish bath. With a grand marbled interior, The Bentley is proud to state that this Hamam is the only traditional Turkish bath in a London five-star hotel.

For couples drawing up in front of the hotel, they will see a tall white Victorian building in the same style of timeless chic replicated elsewhere in Knightsbridge. Entering the lobby, guests will note the beautiful marble floor that sits beneath the white ceiling with gilded detail. Making a good first impression, guests will then move towards one of The Bentley's three licensed spaces. Each with a distinctive style, they range from Alexander, the grand reception space, to the venue's ground-floor brasserie, Peridot, and its acclaimed restaurant, 1880.

The largest of the three rooms is the Alexander Room, capable of holding up to 70 people seated theatre style. Named after Alexander Estates, who were the original owners of The Bentley's Harrington Gardens, it is a versatile space which doubles as an attractive pre-function room. Angular and long with a white and pale green colour scheme, matching silken chairs can be arranged beneath glittering circular lights to the couple's taste. Benefiting from natural light which pours through windows, the room allows guests to enjoy the view of the hotel's beautiful gardens where

Tastefully restored behind the original façade,
the hotel offers a series of modern luxuries

after the ceremony the couple may move for their photographs. The second largest room is the Peridot; a fresh and airy conservatory-style restaurant situated on the ground floor. Decorated in white marble and mosaic tiles, Peridot looks out towards the gardens and is typically used for serving refreshments and afternoon teas but makes an interesting ceremony venue thanks to its unusual design. Wonderfully spacious, chairs can be arranged in arched rows facing the far window where the couple may stand beneath unusual sun-roof style panelling. With white pillars and a raised balcony-style area, it also makes a good reception space with a capacity of 100.

The last room licensed for marriage ceremonies is 1880, The Bentley's restaurant. Named after the original year of the building, it is a grand setting for both ceremonies and banqueting and is also famed for its role in playing host to cocktail receptions and luxury jewellery showcases. With the capacity for 60 people, it is a spacious room with yellow silk walls and a delicately embossed panelled ceiling. Complete with a cream, yellow and pink carpet underfoot and crystal chandeliers above, the overwhelming sensation is one of timeless grandeur.

Wherever couples decide to hold their ceremony, a wonderful dining experience awaits them afterwards. With catering provided by an experienced head chef, couples can be guided through a myriad of menu choices from Indian, Italian or English in up to six different function rooms that double as reception spaces. As well as the three rooms licensed for ceremonies, the wedding

The Bentley is located in a stunning nineteenth-century property which began life as four grand private residences

breakfast can also be held in three smaller rooms; Malachite, The Daniel Room and the private dining room, The Gilbert Room.

Swathed in burgundy velvet, The Gilbert Room is a small space that can seat up to 12 diners for an intimate wedding breakfast. Complete with its own private entrance from Ashburn Place, it is a hidden gem full of rich colours and beautiful fabrics.

Malachite has some similarities in colour and is an opulent, curved space sumptuous in deep red and maroon. A cocktail lounge whose entrance is marked by a piano, it is ideal for pre-dinner drinks or dining, while its versatility is marked by a removable dance floor which makes it more than suitable for a modest evening reception.

Finally, the intimately-sized Daniel Room is primarily an elegant meeting space, able to seat 12 diners. Ideal for more modestly sized wedding parties, it is so named after the site of the hotel which used to be part of Daniel's Fields in 1773. Home to a mahogany table where guests dine with silverware and prime service, it can also host small drinks receptions of up to 20 people.

Whatever combination couples choose, after the celebrations they can retire to one of a number of luxurious rooms. The Bentley is also one of the few hotels in the world to offer a variety of honeymoon suites for those wishing to extend their stay. With 64 rooms for guests, the whole wedding party can take full advantage of the hotel's grandiose facilities.

FOR A FABULOUS CEREMONY AND RECEPTION

Venue Details

The Bentley Kempinski
Harrington Gardens
London
SW7 4JX
t 020 7244 5555
e info@thebentley-hotel.com
w www.thebentley-hotel.com

Licence authority:
Kensington and Chelsea Register Office
Chelsea Old Town Hall
Kings Road
London
SW3 5EE
t 020 7361 4100
e chelsea.registeroffice@rbkc.gov.uk
w www.rbkc.gov.uk

Licensed for ceremony: Alexander Room (70), Peridot (50), 1880 (60)

Function rooms available: Alexander Room (reception 70, evening 150), Peridot Room (reception 40, evening 100), 1880 (reception 60, evening 100), Gilbert Room (reception 12, evening 50), Malachite (reception 30, evening 50), Daniel Room (reception 12, evening 20)

Outside space: ✗

Option of a marquee: ✗

Rooms available for overnight accommodation: 64

Room rates: From £195

Complimentary dressing room for bride available: ✓

SPECIAL NOTES

Licensing hours: Until 11pm (late licence on application)

Corkage charge: Wine £15, champagne £20

Catering: In-house

Complimentary menu tasting: ✓

Car parking spaces: Paid parking two minute's walk away and metered parking in surrounding streets

Sound/noise restrictions: Hotel will have control over all levels of music

Fireworks: ✗

Confetti: ✗

Candles: ✓

PA system: ✓

Helicopter landing permission: ✗

Wedding options

The Bentley Kempinski events team are dedicated to creating tailor-made receptions for each couple. They promise to provide a 'complete' service with guidance on flowers to invitations, photography to wedding favours.

The hotel's executive chef will help create a personalised menu and guide couples through the intricacies of their dining experience while the executive pastry chef compliments this with his cake design and decoration. In close consultation with the couple he can advise on the creation of a classic, traditional or contemporary style wedding cake.

Once the wedding ceremony has taken place, The Bentley has a variety of honeymoon suites to select from. The Imperial Suite not only has its own steam room and Jacuzzi but there is also a private lift to Le Kalon Spa, where couples can experience the Hamam (an authentic Turkish Bath) or enjoy a range of beauty and massage treatments.

Before the wedding, The Bentley offers brides a Hen Package, to enjoy their pre-nuptial party in style and luxury.

From £144.50 per person, the Hen Package includes:

- One night's accommodation including continental breakfast
- Group booking of the turkish Hamam in Le Kalon Spa
- Complimentary fruit smoothies in the spa relaxation area
- 15% off list price of any spa treatments on the day
- Champagne and chocolate, afternoon tea

Parties also have the option to build into this package: a chauffeur driven shopping trip; theatre or concert tickets; cocktails in the Malachite Bar before dinner in the hotel; or perhaps a pyjama party with champagne and canapés in their room.

Bingham

Fabulous because...

This boutique hotel works with its period roots to exude style. The neutrally decorated Garden Rooms open out onto the hotel's gardens, and enjoy fantastic views of the Thames

Location: Richmond, Surrey

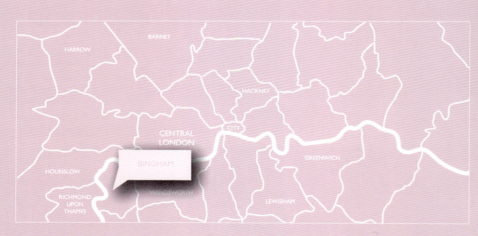

Capacity: Ceremony 50; Wedding breakfast 90; Evening reception 150

Minimum number of guests: 50 on Saturdays

Guide Price
Per guest (not including venue hire): From £70
Venue hire only: From £3,500, exclusive hire of Garden Rooms

When to get married here: All year round

Steps lead down to a Zen inspired Garden, a white gravelled lower terrace with angular black stone tables

Poised on the banks of one of the most picturesque parts of the River Thames, the Bingham offers wedding couples a boutique riverside retreat.

The perfect place to host a stylish and intimate wedding, large or small, formal or informal, a wedding at the Bingham will definitely be remembered, for the right reasons. Originally built as two Georgian townhouse dating back to the 1700s, the Bingham's rich history has shaped the property. One of the two houses was home to poets Katherine Harris Bradley and Edith Emma Cooper at the turn of the last century. In 2004, the property began its transformation from a B&B into the stylish boutique hotel it is today.

The Bingham's deceptively understated façade on a road out of Richmond gives way to a truly breathtaking interior. Using a dramatic monochrome palate to highlight the building's original features, a homage to elegance is created by contemporary finishes including bespoke mahogany mirrored furniture. In the bar, expansive windows, floor to ceiling French doors and over-sized mirrors draw the outside in, flooding rooms with natural light and making the most of the pretty river vistas.

The Bingham's Garden Rooms are a beautifully designed riverside event space, dramatically different from others making similar claims, and bestowing contemporary luxury living with a vintage twist. With their own private entrance through the garden at the hotel, the rooms are accessed either by a lift or down a wrought iron staircase onto an outside terrace area. The three interconnecting rooms open into one breathtaking, long space seating up to 90 guests, with up to 150 accommodated for a standing evening reception. The rooms can be hired individually for smaller weddings, or as one exclusive space; and must be hired as such on a Saturday. Each room has honed limestone flooring, neutral wallpaper and French doors leading out on to an expansive private terrace that overlooks the landscaped garden and the River Thames.

The impressive slate terrace, covered with giant umbrellas can seat up go 60 guests. The look is very striking with cool ivory Phillip Stark 'Dr No' chairs and is the perfect way to make the most of this beautiful riverside space. There are heaters so the terrace can be used throughout the year, and subtle lighting at night creates a wonderful atmosphere. Steps lead down to a Zen inspired garden, a white

The hotel's alluring mix of old glamour and contemporary chic can be enhanced by simple decoration

gravelled lower terrace with angular black stone tables and block seats. Contemporary planting and squares of thyme fill the air with scent. Further steps lead down to the lawn. Brides can make a picturesque entrance to their wedding arriving by boat, alighting at the mooring point just steps from the Bingham's riverside entrance from the towpath.

Each of the Bingham's bedrooms has recently been refurbished to embody tranquility with sensuous style. Quietly glamorous, each room has its own character and is named after the works of Michael Field – the pseudonym of poets Katherine Harris Bradley and Edith Emma Cooper who lived in one of the houses at the turn of the last century. Biscuit shades combine with rich chocolates against art deco inspired furniture by Nigel Carew Jones and handmade blinds and curtains commissioned by Green Hutchings Design. River and Superior River rooms make the most of timeless views over the Thames and landscaped gardens.

Duck and goose feather duvets cosset guests, whilst state of the art air-conditioning, digital TVs, wireless access and state-of-the-art

built-in music systems with music library ensure a very comfortable stay. Two rooms boast antique four-poster beds, and River and Superior River bedrooms benefit from the additional indulgence of Whirlpool baths. In-room 'Bliss Beauty' treatments, same day laundry, room service and complimentary newspapers are all available for a well-deserved pampering.

The hotel's alluring mix of old glamour and contemporary chic can be enhanced by simple decoration such as candle light, flowers and themed decorations, all of which can be arranged by the events team at the Bingham. The team can organise every aspect of the wedding, from suggesting photographers to arranging a boat to transport the couple to the event. Couples desiring ultra exclusivity have the opportunity of hiring the entire hotel for their occasion, reserving all 15 bedrooms for their guests.

The Bingham is renowned for its cosy, chic and contemporary interior and combined with divine food and exceptional service to provide a flexible and highly desirable venue to enjoy a unique wedding day.

Venue Details

Bingham
51–63 Petersham Road
Richmond Upon Thames
Surrey
TW10 6UT
t 020 8940 0902
e events@thebingham.co.uk
w www.thebingham.co.uk

Licence authority:
Richmond Register Office
1 Spring Terrace
Richmond
Surrey
TW9 1LW
t 020 8940 2853/2651
e registeroffice@richmond.gov.uk
w www.richmond.gov.uk

Licensed for ceremony: The Garden Rooms (50)
Function rooms available: The Garden Rooms
(reception 90, evening 150)
Outside space: Terrace and garden
Option of a marquee: ✗
Rooms available for overnight accommodation: 15

Room rates: £160–£250 (discounted rate)
Complimentary dressing room for bride available: ✓

SPECIAL NOTES

Licensing hours: Until midnight (late licence available
on application)
Corkage charge: Wine £20, champagne £25
Catering: In-house
Complimentary menu tasting: ✓
Car parking spaces: 20 car parking spaces available
at the Poppy Factory, across the road from the hotel
(included in hire)
Sound/noise restrictions: Until 11pm for live/amplified
music, below 85 decibels, background music thereafter
Fireworks: ✗
Confetti: ✓ (outside)
Candles: ✓
PA system: ✓
Helicopter landing permission: ✗

Wedding options

The Bingham recently won the Wrapit Award 2007 for best wedding venue – the first wedding industry awards. This is a testament to their pursuit of excellence and the popularity of this venue.

The Bingham's experienced events team offer a dedicated and personal service, to ensure that each aspect of the day is arranged. The events team can coordinate every aspect, from stationery to the entertainment, photographer, florist, and more, or leave you to arrange the finer detail and simply coordinate the catering.

Additional to the room hire, there are various options including more formal traditional wedding breakfasts which start from £42 per head, to more informal BBQs, and bowl food or canapés parties.

Minimum numbers for Friday and Saturday from May to September are 50 guests, and the minimum room hire is £3,500. On other days, there are no minimum requirements.

Exclusive hire of the Bingham is possible and is a wonderful way to make use of the whole venue. This would include the 15 bedrooms, restaurant, bar, and gardens. This is possible from 3pm to 11am the following morning and provides complete privacy and exclusivity for a wedding.

'Thank you so much for your help and advice, we appreciated your friendliness and understanding. All that you did made us have a wonderful day.'

'We just wanted to express our thanks for all your help in making our wedding such a special day… The actual reception was fantastic – everything that we would have wanted. The guests were all very complimentary and certainly enjoyed themselves. The food and staff were excellent.'

Brown's Hotel

Fabulous because...

Offering outstanding service in the heart of London, this is a venue at the cutting edge of style while remaining quintessentially English

Location: Mayfair

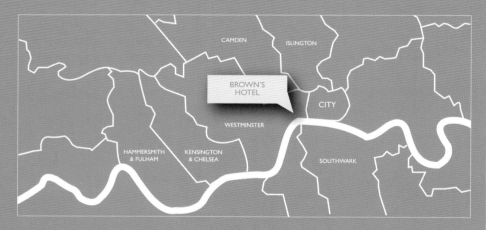

Capacity: Ceremony 70; Wedding breakfast 72; Evening reception 120

Minimum number of guests: None

Guide Price
Per guest (including venue hire): From £120
Venue hire only: From £1,000

When to get married here: All year round

Rocco Forte's Brown's Hotel is one of the most historic hotels in London: merging style with sophistication, the newly refurbished hotel offers a wonderful location for wedding ceremonies, dinners and receptions. Located on a peaceful street in the heart of Mayfair, this luxurious hotel was founded in 1837 to provide decorous accommodation for the fashionable people visiting London. Brown's has always had an air of exclusivity and refinement, which it has retained following its extensive £24 million refurbishment overseen by one of the world's leading hotel designers, Olga Polizzi. At Brown's, every wedding is created on a bespoke basis, and the venue ensures yours is the only wedding being held on one day.

Voted 'Best Hotel in Europe' at the prestigious Prix Villégiature Awards in Paris in October 2006 and named one of 60 'hottest, newest hotels' in the world in *Condé Nast Traveller UK*'s Hot List 2006, these early credentials forge a place for Brown's as one of London's top hotels. This venue offers a fresh and exciting place to hold a wedding celebration, creating a delightful occasion for the couple and their guests.

With a rich history, guests can revel in the idea of sharing the venue with past royal guests including Queen Victoria and Napoleon III, as well as Princess Eugenie and King George II of the Hellenes. Esteemed patrons include Sir Winston Churchill, Agatha Christie and Rudyard Kipling (who completed *The Jungle Book* here). Brown's was also the place where Alexander Graham Bell made the UK's first telephone call in 1876.

The designer, Olga Polizzi is Sir Rocco Forte's sister and has created a timeless look for the renovated property. The contemporary interiors have a real sense of style, while retaining much of their original, quintessentially English elegance. Fresh colour schemes and many natural materials are carefully juxtaposed with original wood panelling, gilt mirrors, mosaic floors and antique furnishings to create a fresh and comfortable style, still maintaining the refined English charm for which the hotel is reputed. The hotel itself is made up of eleven Georgian town houses merged together.

Brown's Hotel is home to six elegant, private dining rooms, of which three have marriage and civil licences. Each of these rooms offer a great deal of flexibility when deciding which room is right for your occasion, be it the actual marriage, the wedding breakfast or the evening reception.

Each room presents its own history and unique features and all are flooded with natural daylight, with traditional high ceilings, fabulous antiques and fireplaces.

Aptly named, The Roosevelt Room's unique history is displayed as former American President Theodore Roosevelt's marriage certificate to his second wife Edith Kermit Carow hangs in the room after they first stayed at Brown's Hotel in 1886. Franklin Delano and Eleanor Roosevelt were also guests on their honeymoon in 1905. The Roosevelt Room, which is situated on the first floor of the hotel, can be interconnected with the Niagara Room, creating a large space accommodating up to 70 guests for a wedding ceremony. Decorated in neutral colours, this elegant room's stunning mirror, ornate ceilings, opulent chandeliers, high windows and antique furnishings provide a truly regal experience.

The adjoining Niagara Room is similar in style and decoration and has also been used for many high-profile parties and events: this room was the room in which the Niagara Commission agreed that the power of water would be used to conduct electricity in June 1890.

The largest of the rooms, The Clarendon Room, is situated on the ground floor, and is also a licensed venue, perfect for festive banquets and evening receptions. Accommodating 120 guests for a reception or 72 for a seated dinner, The Clarendon Room is named after the Earl of Clarendon, who resided here during the 1660s. Boasting tall windows over Dover Street and crystal chandeliers, this sophisticated room is perfect for exclusive events, with a private entrance on Dover Street.

Due to the ornate flooring, the venue does not permit dancing in the private dining rooms; however Brown's can arrange for a string quartet, a jazz trio, a harpist or even an opera singer to perform for guests.

For a more intimate gathering, such as a candlelit dinner for 10 people, The Lord Byron, The Graham Bell and the St George's Room provide the perfect setting.

Each room has been individually furnished, while maintaining the refined English charm for which Brown's is famous

Offering a bespoke service, the hotel provides a wedding coordinator to guide couples through every detail of their celebrations; assisting with everything from chauffeurs and name-place designs to flowers and dress designers. The hotel's entrance on Dover Street can be used as an exclusive entrance for the bride and groom, with red carpet and their own personal doorman.

The celebrations do not need to end when the party finishes, as Brown's is also home to 117 elegant rooms and suites. Each room has been individually furnished in contemporary and comfortable style, whilst maintaining the refined English charm for which Brown's Hotel is famous.

The 29 magnificent suites, of which there are two royal and two presidential suites, offer the perfect place to retire at the end of this special day. Each suite is elegantly decorated whilst still being home to state-of-the-art technology. From the moment of arrival each guest is treated uniquely and Brown's even offers them a choice of pillows and a choice between Egyptian cotton sheets or Irish linen bedding. Suite bathrooms are decorated in the finest Italian mosaic and bush-hammered limestone and boast luxury walk-in showers with large 'Rain Forest' showerheads and baths with Bang & Olufsen TV tiles at the end, coupled with waterproof remote controls.

One statement that truly represents the feel of Brown's came from a notable individual when he was once asked which hotel he stayed in when he was in London. His response was, 'I don't stay in a hotel, I stay at Brown's'.

Venue Details

Brown's Hotel
Albemarle Street
Mayfair
London
W1S 4BP
t 020 7493 6020
e sales.browns@roccofortecollection.com
w www.roccofortecollection.com

Licence authority:
Westminster Register Office
Westminster Council House
Marylebone Road
London
NW1 5PT
t 020 7641 1161
e registeroffice@westminster.gov.uk
w www.westminster.gov.uk

Licensed for ceremony: The Clarendon Room (70),
The Niagara Room (40), The Roosevelt Room (40)

Function rooms available: The Clarendon Room
(reception 72, evening 120), The Roosevelt Room
(reception 40, evening 60), The Niagara Room
(reception 40, evening 60)

Outside space: ✗

Option of a marquee: ✗

**Rooms available for overnight
accommodation:** 40 subject to availability

Room rates: From £358

Complimentary dressing room for bride available: ✗

SPECIAL NOTES

Licensing hours: Until 1am

Corkage charge: Wine £20, champagne £25

Catering: In-house

Complimentary menu tasting: ✓

Car parking spaces: Valet parking service

Sound/noise restrictions: Music until
midnight, no amplified music

Fireworks: ✗

Confetti: ✗

Candles: ✓

PA system: ✓

Helicopter landing permission: ✗

Wedding options

At Rocco Forte's Brown's Hotel, each wedding couple has a dedicated private wedding coordinator who is on hand to tailor-make every aspect of their wedding to their specific requirements. No two weddings take place at Brown's on the same day.

The wedding coordinator is delighted to organise everything from table linen and chair covers to match any colour scheme, flowers to meet any style and menus for any specific food requirements. They will also be pleased to arrange a toastmaster to introduce the guests and a band to play them away. Wedding photographs can either be taken within the hotel, or with the leafy backdrop of nearby Green Park.

Each menu is specifically created and prepared by a team of talented chefs, who use only the finest seasonal ingredients. The hotel's sommelier has carefully compiled a list of over 40 wines and champagnes from which to choose. Should couples wish, a bar offering speciality cocktails such as Champagne Bellinis and Brown's signature champagne cocktail, the Box Brownie, can also be arranged. Each couple is invited to the hotel before the event, not only to sample some of the dishes available, but also to personally meet the chef.

Brown's sumptuous rooms and suites provide the perfect place to retire to at the end of the wedding day. The couple's room will have been lovingly prepared with rose petals, candles and bath salts and they will also receive, as a gift from the hotel, personalised monogrammed Egyptian cotton bed linen.

The Spa at Brown's provides a haven of tranquility from which to escape and enjoy luxurious treatments. Decorated in relaxing colours, with peaceful music and scented candles, it really does offer the ideal place to unwind, relax and indulge. The Spa is home to three private treatment rooms, including one luxury suite for two, providing the ideal location for couples to enjoy a magical treatment together.

With a marriage licence, six elegant private rooms, wonderful location and outstanding service, Brown's really does offer the perfect address to ensure a truly memorable day.

The Cadogan

Fabulous because...

Excellently situated near Hyde Park and Sloane Square, this decadent Edwardian hotel offers intimate luxury while maintaining the grandeur of its history

Location: **Knightsbridge**

Capacity: **Ceremony 38; Wedding breakfast 42; Evening reception 100**

Minimum number of guests: **12**

Guide Price
Per guest (including venue hire): **£150**
Venue hire only: **Not available**

When to get married here: **All year round**

Found half way between Sloane Square and Knightsbridge, this essentially London venue is swathed in history and unites modern chic with eighteenth-century style, making this venue one of the most decadent Edwardian hotels in London. Perfect for intimate ceremonies and receptions, the red-bricked Cadogan provides an idyllic setting from which to enjoy this memorable occasion with a select group of family and friends, in one of the most romantic parts of the capital.

Having undergone a recent renaissance, the contemporary elegance of the townhouse hotel is offset by antique features which whisper of its seductive past; its corridors are decorated with William Morris's willow pattern and a glorious iron-grille lift runs up the centre stairwell. In the restaurant part of the hotel, the original robust oak staircase sits, juxtaposed with a delicate floral floor mosaic.

The Cadogan Hotel differentiates itself from other London venues by its fascinating place in history, namely at the heart of some of Victorian society's most infamous indiscretions. History and literature lovers alike will appreciate the names associated with The Cadogan from its inception as a hotel in 1887. Within the walls of one of the stateliest of West End London hotels, some of society's most prominent figures came together in a furore of controversy. Society beauty, courtesan and actress Lillie Langtry lived in a house adjoined to – and eventually incorporated into – the hotel and from here, courted the future King Edward VII. In 1895, The Cadogan was the scene of playwright Oscar Wilde's arrest, immortalised by John Betjeman in his poem, *The Arrest of Oscar Wilde at The Cadogan Hotel*. Proud of its heritage, The Cadogan is now a more decorous venue, its risqué past a faint memory; remembered only by the two private dining rooms which are named after these renowned characters.

From the grand reception, guests are lead through the drawing room and luxurious bar area to a cream corridor, where a hidden door leads to two very private rooms.

The inter-connecting rooms, Salon Lillie and Salon Oscar, exude elegantly modernised Edwardian beauty and share the

*The Cadogan's risqué past is a faint memory;
remembered only by the two private dining rooms
which are named after renowned characters*

traditional atmosphere of the rest of the hotel: decorated in mellow clotted cream and pale-blue tones, natural light pours in through lead-crossed stained glass windows. Beneath stunning cornicing and ornate plasterwork, couples are invited to hold their ceremony and dinner reception. Unlike larger London venues, The Cadogan offers the archetype of intimacy with rooms perfect to hold a small gathering in an atmospheric setting. Should couples choose to hold their ceremony in these rooms, after the nuptuails guests can move through to the bar, with its red sofas, inviting feel and marble bar, for a champagne reception with the newly married couple.

An intimate venue, the Salon Lillie can accommodate 38 guests for a wedding breakfast, or the more intimate Salon Oscar can host up to 12 guests who will enjoy a delectable, bespoke wedding breakfast seated on original, newly upholstered hounds tooth tweed chairs.

The hotel's internal catering service creates a menu for every occasion and provides discreet, attentive staff to ensure the smooth running of the day. Salons Lillie and Oscar can also be opened up to accommodate 70 guests for an evening reception.

With a separate entrance on Pavilion Road, Langtry's, the hotel's restaurant, can also be used as a venue for a dinner.

Decorated in mellow clotted cream, natural light pours in through lead-crossed stained glass windows

Enticingly, there is no hire cost for the restaurant, only a minimum spend. Its purple and red upholstered chairs, large gilted mirrors and a light but luxurious feel make this a delightful venue for dinner, and seats up to 42 people.

The wedding service The Cadogan provides encompasses all areas of a wedding, to create a memorable and relaxing day. The staff are available to organise every aspect of the day, even the ceremony itself at the hotel or nearby church or register office.

A magnificent addition to this venue is the manicured Cadogan Place Gardens, just across the street from the hotel. This leafy sanctuary is a welcome escape from the bustle of London and provides an ideal place to take wedding photography, only moments away from the reception venue. With prior arrangement, there is the possibility of having a drinks reception here between the ceremony and reception.

Guests are also welcome to explore the garden and those who chose to stay at The Cadogan can enjoy a game of tennis.

When the celebration is over, guests have the pleasure of choosing from a combination of Edwardian and contemporary style rooms and the bride and groom enjoy a complimentary suite on their wedding night. They can stay in the room where Wilde was arrested, in its historical kept style, or enjoy the newly renovated rooms on the upper floors, pristinely decorated in individual colour schemes and bedecked with plush furnishings.

Distinguishing The Cadogan from other West End contemporary hotels is undoubtedly its ability to retain its historical attachments while being an esteemed stylish hotel. A truly boutique hotel, this venue provides a luxurious space in which to host intimate wedding celebrations.

FOR A FABULOUS CEREMONY AND RECEPTION

Venue Details

The Cadogan
75 Sloane Street
Knightsbridge
London
SW1X 9SG
t 020 7235 7141
e info@cadogan.com
w www.cadogan.com

Licence authority:
Kensington and Chelsea Register Office
Chelsea Old Town Hall
Kings Road
London
SW3 5EE
t 020 7361 4100
e chelsea.registeroffice@rbkc.gov.uk
w www.rbkc.gov.uk

Licensed for ceremony: Salon Lillie (38), Salon Oscar (12)

Function rooms available: Salon Lillie (reception 32, evening 50), Salon Oscar (reception 12, evening 20), interconnected (evening 70), Langtry's (reception 42)

Outside space: Private Cadogan Place Gardens across the road

Option of a marquee: ✗

Rooms available for overnight accommodation: 65

Room rates: From £300

Complimentary dressing room for bride available: ✓

SPECIAL NOTES

Licensing hours: Until 12.30am
Corkage charge: Wine £20, champagne £25
Catering: In-house
Complimentary menu tasting: ✓
Car parking spaces: NCP located next to the hotel
Sound/noise restrictions: Music until 12.30am
Fireworks: ✓ (on application)
Confetti: ✗
Candles: ✓
PA system: ✓
Helicopter landing permission: ✗

Wedding options

The Cadogan's events team are well versed in organising bespoke weddings, and can guide couples from their ceremony in a nearby church or in hotel through to their wedding breakfast, evening reception and overnight stay.

The Cadogan offers a basic wedding package, which couples can embellish with their own choices of flowers, entertainment and menus.

WEDDING PACKAGE

(Available for 12–50 guests)

- £150 per person
- Room hire for drinks reception and wedding breakfast
- Three course dinner menu
- Half bottle of wine per person during meal
- Champagne reception including two glasses per person
- Glass of champagne for the toast at speeches
- Wedding event organiser
- Menus
- Table plan and place cards
- Wedding menu tasting

Additional costs can include the ceremony fee, room hire for the ceremony, an evening buffet and canapés, wedding cake, and a photographer.

The bride and groom receive a complimentary stay in one of The Cadogan's newly renovated suites for the night of the wedding.

The Cadogan also has its own chauffeur service and can arrange car and coach transfers on the couple's behalf, as well as an in-house florist, which can assist if couples wish. A wide range of special entertainment and themed events have been held at The Cadogan, including a harpist on arrival, musical interludes and function bands.

Carlton Club

Fabulous because...

This private members' club marries the intimacy of a townhouse with the splendour of a rich interior, nestled moments from Buckingham Palace

Location: **Mayfair**

Capacity: **Ceremony 90; Wedding breakfast 90; Evening reception 150**

Minimum number of guests: **None**

Guide Price
Per guest (including venue hire): **From £130**
Venue hire only: **Not available**

When to get married here: **All year round**

The Carlton Club is one of London's foremost private members' clubs and provides an exclusive venue for couples to get married in a setting of stylish opulence and splendour. Originally founded as a Conservative party club in the 1830s, this Georgian clubhouse is delightfully situated between St James' Park and Green Park, in an area steeped with history and in close proximity to both Buckingham Palace and St James' Palace. The unique charm and elegance of the Carlton Club combine the style and traditions of yesteryear with modern facilities to create one of the most prestigious venues in the West End.

The Carlton Club was formed in the aftermath of the victory of the reforming party, and began with a small number of Tory Members of Parliament at an address in Charles II Street, off St James's Square, in 1831. By March 1832, the club had grown and appointed a committee to arrange the housing and management of new premises in Carlton Terrace. The name 'Carlton Club' was adopted on 17 March that year.

After its Pall Mall premises were destroyed in an air raid during the Second World War, the club moved to its current venue in St James' Street in 1940. The Club is full of historical items reflecting its close association with the Conservative party to date.

The Club's magnificent rooms all boast high ceilings graced by stunning chandeliers. With an array of rooms to choose from, holding anything from 16 people for an intimate dinner to a more lavish banquet for up to 150, couples can enjoy the exclusive use of the Club for the day.

These rooms are accessed by the most spectacular, lavish mahogany stairway with a royal blue carpet, which sweeps down into the entrance hall. This stairway can be lit with candles and the fireplace in the entrance hall lit to create a romantic ambience throughout the Club.

There are two rooms licensed for civil ceremonies each with its own individual character. The Churchill Room is the larger of the two rooms and can hold up to 90 guests. It has a magnificent high ceiling, large windows which bathe the room in natural light, and, adding to the ambience, two fireplaces with marble surrounds. The Cabinet Room

The Wellington Room has been returned to its former glory as a beautiful Regency dining room

hosts ceremonies for smaller groups of 30 guests, and has warm red surroundings and splendid silver display cabinets.

After the ceremony, couples can either hold a drinks reception in the candle-lit foyer, or lead their guests up into the Drawing Room, which can hold up to 150 guests for a reception. The Drawing Room overlooks St James' Street and the views from the large windows are very picturesque. In this room guests can enjoy the warmth of two fireplaces at either end. This room can also be used to host a wedding breakfast for up to 82 guests. A stunning chandelier lights the room and the pale blue walls are hung with a selection of fine portraits and gilded mirrors.

On the ground floor, the Morning Room makes an intimate and stylish backdrop to formal wedding photographs, with its large leather seats and fireplace. This room has been decorated in sympathy with the age of the building and is a typical Clubroom with a combination of highly polished mahogany and comfortable furniture upholstered in red leather.

For the wedding breakfast, the richly decorated Wellington Room is an idyllic choice; this room can accommodate up to 90 guests. The room has recently been restored and returned to its former glory as a beautiful red Regency dining room. Decorated in rich reds and gold hues, with the most elaborate ceiling and chandelier, this provides a lavish setting in which guests can enjoy and fully appreciate the highly regarded cuisine of the Carlton Club. On the walls are a series of full-length portraits of historical figures including The Duke of Wellington, the founder of the Club, after whom the room has been named.

With an array of rooms to choose from, couples can enjoy exclusive use of the Club for the day

The Churchill Room is also available for couples to use for their wedding breakfast, and again seats up to 90 guests, but has a distinctly different feel. Its cream walls and Georgian ceiling, dark wood furnishings and olive carpet take a step away from the grandeur of the Wellington Room and provide a light and bright banqueting space. Again the walls are hung with portraits of historical figures, the beautiful gilt frames adding to the splendour of the room. Just outside the Churchill Room is an area known affectionately as 'Cads' Corner', a cosy reception area with an inviting fire.

The Club's extensive rooms broaden further on the ground and first floors; the exquisite deep blue Disraeli Room, originally designed as a smoking room, or the Macmillan Room, which benefits from natural light, with a high ceiling decorated in natural tones, are ideal smaller settings for a dinner for up to 20 guests or a reception for 40. The Library, situated on the Lower Ground Floor of the Club, is filled with historic copies of Parliamentary Debates and Hansard going back to 1826 and its walls are lined with these aged books, providing an unusual setting for a drinks reception for up to 30 guests.

The Carlton Club has 24 en suite, air conditioned bedrooms, including two superior double rooms, each individually decorated to offer guests maximum comfort after the day's events.

Tailored to each couple's personal requirements, the Carlton Club offers a bespoke planning service for each wedding to ensure that the bride and groom enjoy to the full the experience of hosting their wedding at this prestigious and exclusive venue. The Carlton Club's executive chef can cater to suit each couple's individual requirements, as well as providing a selection of seasonal ideas to inspire choices, while the club's sommelier can pair this menu with a selection from the Club's extensive vintage wine list.

FOR A FABULOUS CEREMONY AND RECEPTION

Venue Details

Carlton Club
69 St James' Street
London
SW1A 1PJ
t 020 7493 1164
e weddings@carltonclub.co.uk
w www.carltonclub.co.uk

Licence authority:
Westminster Register Office
Westminster Council House
Marylebone Road
London
NW1 5PT
t 020 7641 1161
e registeroffice@westminster.gov.uk
w www.westminster.gov.uk

Licensed for ceremony: Churchill Room (90)

Function rooms available: Churchill Room (reception 90, evening 150), Wellington Room (reception 90, evening150), Cabinet Room (reception 36, evening 70), Disraeli Room (reception 20, evening 40), Macmillan Room (reception 20, evening 40), Library (reception 16, evening 30)

Outside space: ✗

Option of a marquee: ✗

Rooms available for overnight accommodation: 24

Room rates: From £171 double including breakfast

Complimentary dressing room for bride available: ✓

SPECIAL NOTES

Licensing hours: Until 1am

Corkage charge: Wine £11, champagne £16

Catering: In-house

Complimentary menu tasting: ✓

Car parking spaces: 10% discounted parking on Jermyn Street

Sound/noise restrictions: Music until 1am

Fireworks: ✗

Confetti: ✗

Candles: ✓ (in designated areas)

PA system: ✓ (supplier recommended)

Helicopter landing permission: ✗

Wedding options

A wedding held at the Carlton Club with 80 guests saw the venue decked with flowers and candles placed on mantles. The fireplaces were on in Cads' Corner and the Drawing Room.

The wedding ceremony for 80 took place in the Churchill Room. Chairs faced the large marble fireplace with an aisle down the middle. A string quartet played in a corner of the room facing guests. Large white and green pedestal flower arrangements framed the fireplace.

After the ceremony, the bride and groom received guests in the Drawing Room. Champagne and canapés were served on the staircase after guests left the ceremony. After mingling, the bride and groom had formal photographs on the staircase and in the Morning Room.

The banqueting manager announced dinner, and the party moved to the Wellington Room which was set up with eight round tables, covered in white linen tablecloths with flower centre pieces of red amaryllis and silver candelabras.

Guests enjoyed timbale of Cornish crab and brown shrimps followed by tournedos of macduff fillet of beef. To finish, passion fruit cream profiteroles were served followed by coffee and club mints.

During the dinner, additional evening guests arrived and had drinks in the Morning Room. A continental cheese platter with assorted cold meats was available.

At the end of the wedding breakfast the bride and groom officially cut the wedding cake – a three-tiered square chocolate mud cake with white chocolate icing. Speeches were held with the additional guests also gathering.

Guests then moved into the Morning Room for entertainment and bride and groom's first dance. The room had a dance floor with large red leather seats located around it for guests. A full bar was available throughout the night and wedding cake was served canapé style.

Chiswick House

Fabulous because...

Designed in 1728 by Lord Burlington and containing original period furnishings, this Palladian villa is surrounded by Italianate gardens and is a remarkable example of English architecture

Location: Chiswick

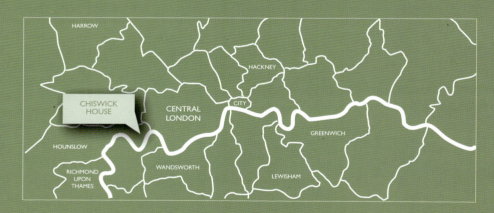

Capacity: Ceremony 100; Wedding breakfast 150; Evening reception 185

Minimum number of guests: None

Guide Price
Per guest (not including venue hire): **From £70**
Venue hire only: **From £4,113**

When to get married here: Summer

One of west London's most sought-after locations for wedding parties, Chiswick House is an eighteenth-century English Heritage property designed in the Palladian style and renowned as a remarkable example of English architecture. Once a society home and witness to countless glamorous events, it is now an ideal location for ceremonies and receptions alike. With couples choosing to marry having exclusive use of the whole venue, guests are welcome to explore its many sumptuous delights. Basking in its extravagant décor, they will enjoy the paintings hung in gilded frames before walking out into the landscaped Italianate gardens which surround the property.

Designed in 1728 by Lord Burlington, Chiswick House is neo-classical in style, inspired by the architecture of both ancient Rome and sixteenth-century Italy. Once a gallery showcasing Lord Burlington's fine art collection, it was also a glamorous party location; two roles that the venue can still attest to now.

On the approach to Chiswick House one is struck by the impressive nature of its entrance. With its traditional Palladian architecture and twin staircases, the look is imposing in all its magnificence. Tall double doors sit in the centre of a covered portico, lined by beautiful columns. The centre point of the venue, here is a good location for musicians to accompany the arrival of guests or, alternatively, for couples to stand and greet them. With natural light offering a stunning backdrop to the central dome, it is truly a spectacular sight that is only heightened by the approach of nightfall when the house can be floodlit.

Entering inside, guests are met by a grand octagonal space named the Domed Salon; the only room in the venue licensed for ceremonies. Soaring walls housing magnificent framed portraits meet a high white ceiling, while the floor has a silver star design to denote the centre of the room. Sitting below a glass chandelier, couples will pass over this star to exchange vows.

FOR A FABULOUS CEREMONY AND RECEPTION

In the Domed Salon, soaring walls house magnificent framed portraits meet a high white ceiling

With elaborate arched double doors on the far-side of the room, the Domed Salon opens into the Lord Burlington Gallery, where couples may choose to hold their reception. Three inter-connected rooms linked by small arches, the gallery houses a number of large statues and ornate vases as well as a glorious painted ceiling, copied from the Doge's Palace in Venice.

Also leading on from the Domed Salon are the Red and Green Velvet Rooms. Named as such for their lavish décor decked in a prominent colour they are smaller in size and well suited to intimate wedding breakfasts with a combined capacity of 48.

Boasting a large Venetian window which looks out towards the venue's extensive grounds, The Red Velvet Room is resplendent in ruby and gold with mosaic-print carpet and a beautifully ornate nine-panelled ceiling. In the Green Velvet Room, a similar colour scheme prevails; red replaced by a deep forest green that offsets gilded gold picture frames perfectly. Fabulous locations for a dinner, specific dining requirements – from choosing from a list of accredited caterers to choosing the style of dining – are left up to the couple. Tablecloths can cover small, circular tables for those wanting a more intimate occasion or a long rectangular table for a grand banquet.

During the ceremony couples move through the Red Velvet Room to the Blue Velvet Room, once used by Lord Burlington as his study, where they sign the register at an eighteenth-century desk.

With its traditional Palladian architecture and twin staircases, the look is imposing in all its magnificence

Down the stairs on the ground floor of Chiswick House lies the the Octagonal Hall and adjoining Library. More simply decorated, these rooms make a perfect setting for more informal celebrations, and floor-lights and comfortable seating can be added to enhance the informal ambience. The space is also ideal for dancing and themed decoration is welcome here as the stone-flagged flooring and white, curvaceous ceiling invite individual design innovation. The simplicity is offset by classical figureheads mounted on columns throughout the room, which lend the room its warm, open feel.

From the Octagonal Room, doors lead directly out into a sheltered Courtyard and Baroque gardens beyond. Filled with mature trees and sweeping lawns, they also house unique touches such as classical urns and stone sphinxes. Not only an ideal site for summer drinks receptions, marquees capable of holding up to 150 diners can also be erected here in the Courtyard. They may be equipped with drapes and French style doors. With the addition of beautiful lighting, couples can arrange seating to their liking and use flower arrangements to adorn doorframes and tables.

FOR A FABULOUS CEREMONY AND RECEPTION

Venue Details

Chiswick House
Burlington Lane
Chiswick
London
W4 2RP
t 020 7973 3292
e hospitality@english-heritage.org.uk
w www.english-heritage.org.uk/hospitality/chiswick_house

Licence authority:
Hounslow Register Office
Clovelly House
88 Lampton Road
Hounslow
TW3 4DW
t 020 8583 2090
e denise.corke@hounslow.gov.uk
w www.hounslow.gov.uk

Licensed for ceremony: Domed Salon (100)

Function rooms available: Domed Salon (reception 48, evening 80) Domed Salon with Velvet Rooms (reception 96, evening 150), Red Velvet Room (reception 24), Green Velvet Room (reception 24), Courtyard – marquee site (reception 150, evening 185), Octagonal Hall and Library (dancing 96)

Outside space: Courtyard

Option of a marquee: ✓

Rooms available for overnight accommodation: ✗

Complimentary dressing room for bride available: ✓

SPECIAL NOTES

Licensing hours: Until 11pm (late licence available on application)

Corkage charge: Dependent on caterer

Catering: Recommended caterers

Complimentary menu tasting: ✓

Car parking spaces: Approximately 25

Sound/noise restrictions: Maximum of six-piece band in the marquee and some noise restriction on the dance floor

Fireworks: ✗

Confetti: ✓ (fresh flower petals permitted outside only)

Candles: ✗

PA system: ✓ (supplier recommended)

Helicopter landing permission: ✗

Wedding options

Couples choosing to marry at Chiswick House have exclusive use of the whole venue. The venue's series of rooms on two levels as well as outdoor space means that no two wedding days are the same at this venue.

Ceremonies may only be held from 4pm on Saturday afternoons once the house has closed to the public, but drinks receptions and dinners may take place on any evening, from 6.30pm. The majority of weddings take place on Saturdays so that couples can exchange their vows in the stunning Domed Salon, the only room licensed within the house.

Ceremonies are usually followed by celebration drinks – either amid the exquisite first floor rooms, or outside in the courtyard in fine weather if a marquee is not being used.

Parties with up to 80 guests can dine inside the house, surrounded by artistic treasures and wonderful furniture and furnishings. Those with up to 150 guests usually prefer to opt for a marquee in the courtyard.

The simple white walls of the ground floor of Chiswick House offer a blank canvas which many couples choose to put their personal stamp on. Themed by dramatic lighting, flowers, furniture or special props, this space can be transformed into a romantic, funky or chic area for dining, relaxing dancing or watching entertainers.

Outside, the Baroque Gardens which feature classical busts and statuary, tree-lined walks and a lake, look equally wonderful by day or by night (when lit so that guests can pick their way across the lawns to the lake beyond).

English Heritage provides the services of its professional hospitality team on site to ensure that everything runs smoothly, as well as a list of carefully chosen suppliers, so that couples can rely on top levels of service.

Courthouse Hotel Kempinski

Fabulous because...

This former London courthouse has seen many famous names in history pass through its doors and has been transformed into a wonderfully quirky hotel, retaining many of its distinguishing features

Location: **Soho**

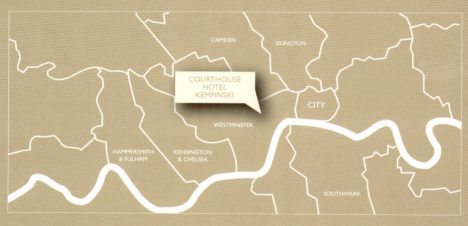

Capacity: **Ceremony 100; Wedding breakfast 120; Evening reception 250**

Minimum number of guests: **30**

Guide Price
Per guest (including venue hire): **£80 – £160**
Venue hire only: **Not available**

When to get married here: **All year round**

Once the largest and oldest Magistrates' Court in England and set in the heart of London's bustling shopping and theatre district, the Courthouse Hotel Kempinski offers a luxurious haven for those wishing to hold their wedding amidst elegance and intriguing history. Remaining in its juridical role until the early 1980s, the Grade II listed building abounds in history and retains a number of quirky, original features. During its years as a courthouse, the building has seen many famous names through its doors, from Napoleon and Oscar Wilde to Mick Jaggar and the artist Francis Bacon. Now, as a celebrated five star hotel, it offers couples a range of rooms to hold their ceremony and reception in inimitable style.

The Great Marlborough Street Magistrates' Court was the venue for numerous famous cases over the years, which were either heard there or taken to full trial at Crown Courts such as the Old Bailey. In 1835, Charles Dickens worked at the courthouse as a reporter for the *Morning Chronicle*, and in 1847, Napoleon appeared as a witness in a fraud case. John Lennon's sensational court case regarding the sale of sexually explicit lithograph drawings was thrown out on a technicality in 1970, and Mick Jagger spent time here defending his name when it was alleged he was caught in possession of cannabis.

From the moment guests step in to the Courthouse, the modern elegance and intriguing design is proudly merged with remnants from the building's recent past. Many remaining features have been incorporated into the building's current scheme. Original Robert Adam fireplaces are features of some of the suites, and elsewhere in the hotel, glimpses of former use can be seen – such as the iron bars that separate the lobby lounge from the bar.

The hotel's impressive, traditional outer façade is softened when guests enter the lobby, dressed in warm colours and void of rigid lines. Guests are then led through original wrought iron prison gates to the hotel's bar for a drinks reception.

FOR A FABULOUS CEREMONY AND RECEPTION

Originally the old Number One court, Silk is covered by a huge vaulted glass ceiling and is framed by original English Oak panelling

The bar at first glance has a very arresting impression with architectural pointers to its historical uses. It successfully fuses the hotel's historic influences with fresh and innovative designs. The original holding cells are still in place, creating three smaller sections to the bar area. Modern touches are added such as low leather cream and black sofas, floors with black Indian mica slate and a long cocktail bar with splashes of crimson. A cool and unusual setting to hold a drinks reception for up to 120 guests, it can be used before or after the wedding ceremony, held in one of the four rooms licensed to hold ceremonies at the Courthouse. In this public space, an area can reseved for up to 30 people.

The Courthouse boasts one of the largest private screening rooms in a London hotel, named 'Release'. Seating 94 people in comfort and style, couples are able to hold their cermony in this impressive space. With its rich aubergine carpet, suede walls and apple green leather seating, this is an unusual and memorable setting in which to be married.

The restaurant and architectural focal point of the ground floor of the hotel, Silk, also holds a ceremony licence, seating 50 people. Originally the old Number One court, the room is covered by a huge vaulted glass ceiling and is framed by original English oak panelling. The Judge's bench, dock and

witness stand have been kept in their original setting and greatly compliment the style of the restaurant. An atmospheric venue for the ceremony, this room is also perfect to hold the couple's wedding breakfast, seating 40 comfortably.

With its distinctively oriental ornaments and plethora of oak, the room beautifully recounts the legacy of the Silk Road, a series of routes that crisscrossed Eurasia over land and sea encouraging trade from the first millennium. The most memorable objects traded were the eighth-century Shosoin collection of objects, which originally belonged to a Japanese emperor and is the single most important group of Silk Road-related luxury items still in existence. This collection reflects the arts of the Mediterranean world, Persia, India, Central Asia, China, Korea and Japan. These are the areas that have influenced the Silk menu with the emphasis on their local dishes, spices and herbs.

On the lower ground floor, The Chambers are found. A series of five interconnecting rooms, which were used by the barristers to prepare, The Chambers are now

used as a contemporary, flexible events space, with its own reception area. Several chambers can be used in conjunction with each other, ensuring these rooms meet requirements for any number of guests, seating 10 to 120 for a wedding breakfast and holding up to 250 for an evening reception. The rooms have fresh walls, wooden finishes and some have the added feature of natural light, through barred windows. Providing a neutral space for both ceremony and reception, the use of these rooms can be coupled with other spaces the hotel offers to provide a different style of room for each part of the wedding.

The Waiting Room was originally used as the waiting area for defendants answering to minor offences, and can now hold a ceremony or a wedding breakfast for 60 at the Courthouse. The room has a colonial feel with Venetian terrazzo flooring and natural light pouring in from the vaulted glass ceiling. The arch of the roof is highlighted by the sky-blue painted wall at one end of the room.

With such an array of rooms to choose from to hold a ceremony, or wedding breakfast, couples are spoilt for choice. Yet hidden at the top of the building is a surprising space, a true pearl in the capital. The Courthouse's Roof Terrace is a large paved area with views over central London. Seating up to 60 for alfresco dining, couples may take a chance and use this venue for their wedding breakfast, or to hold their evening reception for up to 100 guests. There is a sectioned off decked area, where tables and seating can be located at a standing canapé reception. Some couples choose to erect a small canopy, so that the space can still be used in the temperamental English weather.

With 112 contemporary and design led bedrooms, there is ample room for guests of the wedding to continue their stay at the Courthouse. This hotel is also one of the only London hotels to offer a number of Honeymoon suites, for example the Lalique Penthouse Suite, a grandiose apartment named after its original founder and creator Rene Jules Lalique, is the perfect place to begin a honeymoon. Guests at the hotel also have the opportunity to use the Sanook Spa, home to a swimming pool, gym, treatment area and special glass cased treatment room suspended over the pool.

Venue Details

Courthouse Hotel Kempinski
19–21 Great Marlborough Street
London
W1F 7HL
t 020 7297 5555
e conference@courthouse-hotel.com
w www.courthouse-hotel.com

Licence authority:
Westminster Register Office
Westminster Council House
Marylebone Road
London
NW1 5PT
t 020 7641 1161
e registeroffice@westminster.gov.uk
w www.westminster.gov.uk

Licensed for ceremony: Silk (50), The Waiting Room (80), The Chambers (100), Release (94)

Function rooms available: Silk (reception 40, evening 60), The Waiting Room (reception 60, evening 100), The Chambers (reception 120, evening 250), Roof Terrace (reception 60, evening 100), Bar (evening 120)

Outside space: Roof terrace

Option of a marquee: ✗

Rooms available for overnight accommodation: 112 (60 rooms available to wedding guests at a discount of 15%)

Room rates: From £185

Complimentary dressing room for bride available: ✓

SPECIAL NOTES

Licensing hours: Until 1am

Corkage charge: From £15

Catering: In-house

Complimentary menu tasting: ✓

Car parking spaces: NCP in Poland Street (five minute's walk)

Sound/noise restrictions: No music after 11pm on the roof terrace

Fireworks: ✗

Confetti: ✗

Candles: ✓ (permitted in the dining room)

PA system: ✓

Helicopter landing permission: ✗

Wedding options

Couples choosing to marry at the Courthouse Hotel Kempinski benefit from the venue's personal approach to organising a wedding: every wedding is bespoke and individually put together.

The events team promise to provide a 'complete' service, from guidance on flowers to invitations and photography to wedding favours. Wedding packages can range from £80–£160 per person. This can include a champagne reception on arrival, canapés, wedding breakfast, with up to four courses, floral centerpieces, name cards, a table plan, wines and champagne.

Having formed a chef brigade with experience from some of the most renowned hotels and restaurants, the Courthouse's philosophy is to tempt guests visually, aromatically and finally with the satisfying taste. Carefully selected fresh ingredients form part of the tailor-made menus they offer to suit every palate. The executive pastry chef perfectly compliments the dining experience by liaising with the couple to create a classic, traditional or contemporary style wedding cake.

The Courthouse Hotel Kempinski the only hotel in the world with a Lalique Perthouse Honeymoon Suite. It offers luxury and style as its name suggests: beautiful Rene Jules Lalique pieces of furniture and art, it compromises of two bedrooms, both with en suite bathrooms, a living room, dining room and kitchenette. Unwind after the excitement and hire the Sanook Spa exclusively for pampering in the glass therapy room suspended over the pool.

Eltham Palace

Fabulous because...

Mixing medieval and art deco styles, the modern Palace sits on what was once the childhood home of Henry VIII. It retains many original features as well as exuding 1930s glamour

Location: **Eltham, Greenwich**

Capacity: **Ceremony 200; Wedding breakfast 200; Evening reception 300**

Minimum number of guests: **None**

Guide Price
Per guest (not including venue hire): **From £70**
Venue hire only: **From £6,815**

When to get married here: **All year round**

Situated in a prime location in south-east London, Eltham Palace is a spectacular fifteenth-century property that mixes medieval and art deco styles to create a unique and stylish wedding venue. Once the childhood home of King Henry VIII, original ruined walls give way to the wonderfully intact Great Hall and are surrounded by 1930s glamour. With couples marrying here granted exclusive use of the venue, original features such as the ancient oak 'hammerbeam' roof of the Great Hall contrast wonderfully with the modern mirrored ceilings of the art deco mansion and guests will delight in the venue's fascinating history.

Initially a moated manor house, Eltham Palace was gloriously extended in the 1470s under Edward IV and later became the childhood home of one of England's most famous Kings. After years of lavish entertaining, it found itself partially destroyed by the arc of time and only the magnificent Great Hall remains to this day; a fact which makes anyone bearing witness to its splendour all the more awestruck. After years of partial abandonment, in the 1930s, film and textile millionaires Stephen and Virginia Courtauld chose this sumptuous setting to build a stylish mansion that incorporated the Great Hall into a home decked in state-of-the-art mod cons and luxurious furnishings. Now in the care of English Heritage, its legacy has remained. With a blend of original features, detailed re-creations and stunning art-deco designs, the building itself is a work of art.

Creating an excellent first impression, couples arriving at Eltham Palace for either ceremonies or receptions can make an impressive entrance by driving over the ancient stone bridge spanning the moat and circling the drive before pulling up close to the mansion's front entrance. An imposing building, couples view the Great Hall's ancient stone exterior and tall arched windows reminiscent of traditional Church architecture while a stylish array of circular and rectangular windows peek out of the sandy-coloured stone of the adjoining house.

After passing under a beautiful H Carlton Attwood sculpture entitled 'Hospitality' at the main entrance, guests

The grounds include a sunken rose garden, manicured lawns, Japanese rock garden and water features; all of which make a wonderful location for photographs

enter into a small covered porch area. A perfect spot for couples greeting guests and musicians can, if required, provide a warm welcome to wedding parties here. They may also fanfare the bride as this area leads into the most popular ceremonial room; the Entrance Hall.

Moving through glazed double doors, guests enter into the main domed Entrance Hall; a light and airy space with a circular layout that creates an intimate atmosphere for ceremonies with around 100 guests. Dominated by an arched ceiling designed to bathe the room in natural light, this room has a stunning centrepiece of extraordinary proportions. Natural light

floods down from the dome to the circular coffee and cream-coloured carpet that is an exact replica of the Marion Dorn original now housed in the Victoria and Albert Museum.

This carpet gives way to a gleaming floor where rows of chairs can be placed. Complemented by rich wooden walls of Australian blackbean veneer, guests will also note the inlaid marquetry of a Roman soldier and Viking, with scenes from Italy and Scandinavia. Ocean-liner inspired styling includes portholes in two staircases which may be used by the bride to make a grand entrance. French doors lead onto a charming wisteria covered terrace

With a blend of original features, detailed re-creations and stunning art-deco designs, the building itself is a work of art and will delight guests with its fascinating history

above the moat, with views across the water to the trees beyond. Couples holding their ceremony here can emerge outside, where guests can throw rose petal confetti.

From the domed Entrance Hall, guests are invited to pass into the Drawing Room where there is a piano that can be used for background music. A room rich in warm orange hues and elaborate design, it is perfect for drinks receptions or for dining for up to 60 guests. Intricate decoration on overhanging redwood beams imitates Hungarian folk art and pays tribute to Virginia's European ancestry while enormous mosaic-print carpets in black, red and orange bring out the natural tones of the room's yellow walls wreathed in daylight or low-lit lamps. A painting in gold-gilded frame

hangs above a white fireplace while delicately illustrated ivory coloured walls border French doors which open out onto Eltham Palace's large and exclusive terrace. Featuring an attractive pergola covered by mauve wisteria in early summer, this is an enjoyable location for pre-dinner drinks, allowing guests to spill out onto the landscaped gardens beyond. Here, the grounds of Eltham Palace offer a range of delights including a sunken rose garden, manicured lawns, Japanese rock garden and water features; all of which make a wonderful photographic location.

Also accessible from the Domed Hall is the Dining Room. Suitable for drinks receptions this room is a lesson in timeless chic, its shimmering aluminium leaf ceiling with concealed lighting is offset by caramel coloured walls. Greek-style urns sit atop

Eltham Palace was gloriously extended in the 1470s under Edward IV and later became the childhood home of one of England's most famous Kings, Henry VIII

unusually designed black and silver side tables while the centre space is occupied by a dining table, which may be laid with champagne and canapés. The room's black and silver doors are a highlight of the house. They are decorated with Greek key patterns and images of animals and birds, including the Courtauld's pet ring-tailed lemur. The room also contains pink leather chairs – in the 1930s considered to be the colour which set off ladies' evening dresses to the best advantage!

The magnificent Great Hall is the final room available to couples marrying at Eltham Palace and is truly fit for royalty. Originally the Palace Banqueting Hall, it is ideal for lavish dinners and ceremonies alike, able to seat up to 200 guests on tables laid out to the couple's preference. A 21ft long sixteenth-century oak refectory table which sits on a raised dias makes an impressive top table – as it would have done in medieval times.

With fifteenth-century hammerbeam oak roof atop soaring stone walls, crimson coloured drapes, arched windows and high-walled lights this room has an overwhelming ambience of grandeur.

The unique combination of design styles, the regal Banqueting Hall and the stunning landscaped grounds, make this a very special wedding venue.

FOR A FABULOUS CEREMONY AND RECEPTION

Eltham Palace
Court Yard
Off Court Road
London
SE9 5QE
t 020 8294 2577
e nicola.pottage@english-heritage.org.uk
e katharine.parker@english-heritage.org.uk
w www.english-heritage.org.uk/hospitality/eltham_palace

Licence authority:
Greenwich Register Office
Town Hall
Wellington Street
Woolwich
London
SE18 6PW
t 020 8921 5015
e registrar@greenwich.gov.uk
w www.greenwich.gov.uk

Licensed for ceremony: Entrance Hall (100),
Great Hall (200)

Function rooms available: Great Hall (reception 200,
evening 300), Italian Drawing Room (reception 60,
evening 100), Entrance Hall (evening 100),
Dining Room (reception 10)

Outside space: Nine acres of private landscaped gardens

Option of a marquee: ✗

Rooms available for overnight accommodation: ✗

Complimentary dressing room for bride available: ✓

SPECIAL NOTES

Licensing hours: Until 11.30pm

Corkage charge: Dependent on caterer

Catering: Recommended caterers

Complimentary menu tasting: Dependent on caterer

Car parking spaces: Approximately 100

Sound/noise restrictions: ✓ (due to proximity
of neighbours)

Fireworks: ✗

Confetti: ✓ (real rose petals outside only)

Candles: ✗

PA system: ✗

Helicopter landing permission: ✓ (on application)

Wedding options

As with all English Heritage venues, Eltham Palace provides couples with the services of a member of its professional hospitality team to help them plan their day to perfection. They can choose catering, flowers and other services from a range of carefully selected suppliers. Couples hiring Eltham Palace have exclusive use of the art deco mansion and Great Hall.

Ceremonies and receptions can be held from 3pm to midnight on Fridays and Saturdays. Drinks receptions and dinners can take place from 6.30pm to midnight on Sundays to Thursdays.

After a ceremony in the Domed Hall, the terrace is an ideal place for celebration drinks in good weather. As an alternative, doors also connect from this central hall to the dramatic Dining Room and Italian Drawing Room, where drinks receptions may also be held. A piano in the Italian Drawing Room may be used to provide background music.

After drinks, the wedding party can move straight through to the Great Hall for dining – on round or long tables. A minstrel's gallery is often used as it would have been in medieval times for musicians to entertain guests over dinner and the addition of atmospheric lighting brings magic to the ancient hall.

A dance floor can be set up within the hall and doors lead directly onto the lovely south lawn so that guests can enjoy views over the 1930s-style gardens, including the rose garden, Japanese rock gardens, flower borders, cascades, fountains and pools.

Elegant 1930s theming works wonderfully with weddings at Eltham Palace – many brides choose the bias cut simplicity of the chic gowns of the era – and medieval entertainment such as minstrels, jesters and jugglers can add a fun dimension to receptions in the Great Hall.

The Gore Hotel

Fabulous because...

This boutique hotel radiates traditional luxury with its plush interiors adorned with antiques, and is found in the exclusive area of Kensington

Location: **Kensington**

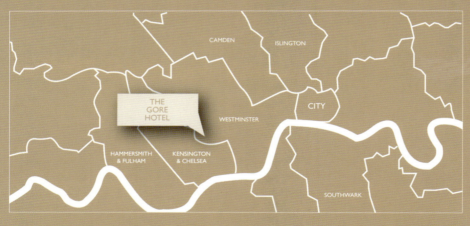

Capacity: **Ceremony 60; Wedding breakfast 60; Evening reception 120**

Minimum number of guests: **None**

Guide Price
Per guest (not including venue hire): **£60**
Venue hire only: **£693**

When to get married here: **Autumn/Winter**

Stepping into The Gore Hotel transports you back to an era full of opulent delights, luxurious fabrics and scattered antiques. On a corner of tree-lined Queen's Gate, less than 100m from Hyde Park, sits two beautifully restored Victorian townhouses providing old-fashioned comfort and modern services. The Gore encapsulates Victorian craftsmanship, while discreetly providing state-of-the-art technology through the hotel. It is filled with wine red carpets, soft, comfy sofas, and a quirky selection of art throughout the building.

The Gore's atmospheric surroundings offer couples the perfect setting for an autumnal or winter wedding, providing inviting, warm spaces framed with style. This is a hotel of sumptuous décor, oozing romance and decadence, and you can just imagine Victorian ladies sashaying down the stairwell surrounded by rich hues and opulent designs. The Gore's events team can enhance this already romantic hotel; candles light the stairways, fresh foliage is strewn around the rooms, and the bedrooms exude decadence.

Founded by two spinster sisters: Miss Ada and Miss Fanny Cooke, the hotel opened its doors in 1892. Its location and charm swiftly made it one of London's most alluring places to stay. One of the two new owners of The Gore reveals how he was personally enchanted by this venue, as he bought the hotel in October and married in it himself two months later.

Benefiting from its position in the heart of Kensington, couples could make use of the nearby Royal Albert Hall and Hyde Park to provide an impressive milieu for wedding photography. Used frequently for professional photo shoots, the hotel's architecture and interior provide many sumptuous and appealing backgrounds.

Guests are welcomed at reception by sweeping curtains and a quaint lobby with 150 pieces of artwork on the ochre walls. They are led into The Gore's bar, (the popular 'Bar 190') which holds none of the cold ambience of some hotel bars but resonates with comfort and warmth; with a long mahogany bar, wood panelled flooring, red and brown leather chairs and candlelit corners. Couples have the option of holding drinks receptions in this inviting space before or after their ceremony and it is through the bar that the Tapestry Room is entered.

Down a sweeping candlelit staircase and behind thick crimson curtains, guests enter the Tapestry Room. This room is enchanting, with its mellow green panelled walls hung with gilded mirrors and French Verdure tapestries. Though full of its own character, the room also has ways in which couples can incorporate their own tastes. Additionally, two grand Portland stone fireplaces are superb features and can be lit to enhance the ambience. This is The Gore's licensed venue and is a truly romantic setting, seating up to 60 guests with space for a band at the far end.

After the vows have been made, or to begin celebrations for couples that have married somewhere else, couples can greet their guests and host a champagne reception in one of the unique spaces throughout the Gore. The Mulberry Room and The Green Room, perfect for drinks receptions, are also available to host smaller wedding breakfasts for the more intimate occasion while the bar provides a space to mingle in a cosy setting.

The Mulberry Room is adjacent to the Tapestry Room and shares its sumptuous décor, with plush sofas placed in front of long sash windows framed by deep mulberry-coloured curtains. This elegant room provides a theatrical setting for intimate candle-lit dinner parties for up to 22 people and is an ideal space to usher guests into after a ceremony.

The name The Green Room is misleading – it actually has warm red walls, and contains a large fireplace, period portraits and a huge book-shelf stacked with old books. Situated on the ground floor of the hotel, at the end of the lobby, this provides an exclusive space for an atmospheric drinks reception. Alternatively, it can accommodate private dinners for up to 22 people.

While both rooms are available for intimate wedding breakfasts as well as receptions, The Tapestry Room provides a larger space for this occasion.

Descending the stairs, couples have the option of making use of the room's large mahogany table to host an exclusive dinner party for a chosen few, or hosting as many as 60 people for dinner on round tables, bedecked with flowing floral arrangements, tall silver candlesticks and fine linens. At one end of this large room, there is space for a a dancing floor adjacent to the band. Since it is in the basement of the hotel, there are no noise restrictions so evening receptions can continue into the night and the room can hold up to 120 people for a cocktail reception, to allow couples to invite additional guests to the evening celebrations.

With a long mahogany bar, wood panelled flooring, red and brown leather chairs and candlelit corners, couples have the option of holding drinks receptions in this inviting bar

After the revelries are over, The Gore's delicacies continue upstairs to their 50 charming rooms available for wedding guests at a 30% discounted rate. The bride and groom can retire up the wrought iron staircase, to one of The Gore's 12 unique suites. Each encapsulating a different style, the most opulent is the Tudor Room, with its dark wood four-poster bed, open fireplace, mock Tudor ceiling and stained-glass windows.

The Dame Nellie Bedroom, named after the Australian opera diva who frequented The Gore in years gone by, follows its founder's theatrical nature, with its bed set into a tented recess and lined with pleated beige silk. There are also French chaise-longues, and a mirror-walled bathroom with two bronze statues – one of David, the other of Venus – at either end of the double-ended bath. Following this theatrical theme, guests can also sleep in Judy Garland's bed in the decadent Venus Room and enjoy the hand painted frescos in its marble bathroom. In addition, there is the Miss Ada suite, with its magnificent oak four-poster bed, wooden panelled bathroom and picturesque views of peaceful, tree-lined Queens Gate.

The events team at The Gore aim to provide a personal and bespoke service to each couple. They will help tailor every aspect of a wedding to suit your demands, from choosing the ideal honeymoon suite to perfecting the menu.

FOR A FABULOUS CEREMONY AND RECEPTION

Venue Details

The Gore Hotel
190 Queen's Gate
London
SW7 5EX
t   020 7584 6601
e   reservations@gorehotel.com
w www.gorehotel.com

Licence authority:
Westminster Register Office
Westminster Council House
Marylebone Road
London
NW1 5PT
t   020 7641 1161
e   registeroffice@westminister.gov.uk
w www.westminster.gov.uk

Licensed for ceremony: The Tapestry Room (60)

Function rooms available: The Mulberry Room
(reception 24, evening 40), The Tapestry Room
(reception 60, evening 120), The Green Room
(reception 22, evening 50)

Outside space: ✗

Option of a marquee: ✗

Rooms available for overnight accommodation: 50

Room rates: From £223 double

Complimentary dressing room for bride available: ✓

SPECIAL NOTES

Licensing hours: Until 2am

Corkage charge: Corkage not permitted

Catering: In-house

Complimentary menu tasting: ✓

Car parking spaces: Metered parking, free on Sunday, NCP nearby

Sound/noise restrictions: ✗

Fireworks: ✗

Confetti: ✓

Candles: ✓

PA system: ✓ (supplier recommended)

Helicopter landing permission: ✗

Wedding options

Every wedding at The Gore is a unique occasion, and couples have the use of its experienced events team to help plan and organise the details of the day. The Gore was host to a traditional evening wedding celebration for 60 guests, but with an Irish twist and bottles of guineas were ordered specially for the day.

As guests arrived, they were ushered into The Gore's bar, exclusively reserved for the wedding party, where they enjoyed pre-ceremony drinks.

The ceremony itself was held downstairs in The Tapestry Room, before guests ascended into the bar again while the room was turned around for the wedding breakfast. Guests then stayed in the Tapestry Room for a three-course dinner, personalised exactly to the couple's liking.

After dinner, more guests joined the celebrations. A DJ set up and guests danced throughout the evening. Later on canapés were served.

The Tapestry Room itself was decorated with candles, candelabras and flower arrangements with a colour scheme in keeping with the rich colours of the room's décor.

'The Gore always looks beautiful and stylish but when dressed for a wedding it becomes magical. We have received many compliments since our wedding from our guests but the one thing that everyone said to us was that, apart from their own, it was the best wedding they had ever been to! Whilst we would like to bask in the glory of such a successful event, we are fully aware that its success was largely due to the magnificent Gore and its fabulous staff.'

Great Fosters

Fabulous because...

This beautiful Elizabethan manor house, with a myriad of gardens and Tithe Barn dating from 1390, provides a historic and idyllic wedding location on the outskirts of London

Location: **Egham, Surrey**

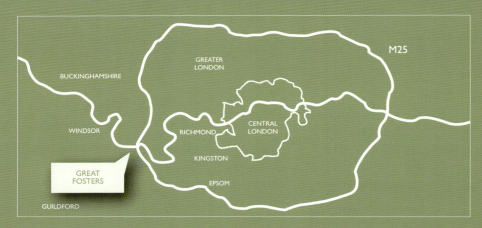

Capacity: **Ceremony 240; Wedding breakfast 180; Evening reception 220**

Minimum number of guests: **Monday to Thursday 50, Friday to Sunday 120 (Tithe Barn)**

Guide Price
Per guest (not including venue hire): **£100**
Venue hire only: **Monday to Thursday and Sunday £4,000, Friday and Saturday £7,500 (Tithe Barn and Orangery)**

When to get married here: **All year round**

A vast lake and a grand lawn leading to an avenue of lime trees create the perfect backdrops for photographs

Built as a royal hunting lodge in 1550, Great Fosters is a magnificent Elizabethan manor house situated in what was once the Royal Windsor Forest of Surrey. Its status as a Grade I listed building and Scheduled Historic Monument ensures the preservation of this venue's historic past. Immediately impressive, the grandiose façade prepares guests for the richness of the interior and the approach is glorified with a private drive.

From its inception as a hotel in 1930, the house has been graced by royalty, film stars, emperors and literary icons. Sympathetically restored, Elizabethan architecture is complemented with modern facilities making this manor house ideal for wedding ceremonies and receptions. Encased on three sides by a Saxon moat, one could hardly find a more idyllic setting only a short distance from London: with excellent access to main routes and within easy travelling distance from Heathrow airport, Great Fosters achieves precedence in the heart of Surrey.

The interior of Great Fosters is as remarkable as the outer façade. With original features such as Jacobean fireplaces, seventeenth-century staircases and acclaimed works of art, each room is brimming with grandeur. Much of it decked in rich oak panelling, Great Fosters marries history and comfort with excellent cuisine and superb wines.

Designed to reflect the intricate beauty of a Persian rug, surrounding the house is a maze of formal topiary gardens, and within them, the Drake sundial, which belongs to the immediate family of Sir Francis Drake and is believed to date back to 1585. Fifty acres of idyllic gardens including a lily pond with a wisteria clad Japanese bridge overlooking a circular sunken rose garden; a vast lake and a grand lawn leading to an avenue of lime trees create the perfect backdrops for photographs.

Couples may hold both their ceremony and reception at Great Fosters, with various options available to them. The hotel offers superb catering facilities, with a highly acclaimed chef's selection of seasonally varied menus for your wedding breakfast, complemented by the hotel's vintage wine list.

Wedding ceremonies are held in The Orangery, bathed in natural light by its tall eighteenth-century arched windows

Ceremonies are held in The Orangery, bathed in natural light overlooking the South Terrace and gardens

over looking the South Terrace and gardens. It accommodates up to 160 guests for a civil ceremony, with an additional 40 guests in the adjacent Conservatory, if required. This spacious room can also be used for a wedding breakfast for up to 100 guests and Great Fosters recommends a drinks reception outside during the summer months on the Magnolia Lawn or on the Terrace. If rain pursues, drinks may be held in the adjacent Painted Hall, with its own private bar.

The remarkable Tithe Barn, which dates from 1390, was painstakingly dismantled from its original site within Surrey and re-built at Great Fosters in the 1930s. It provides an unusual and atmospheric setting for a wedding reception with exposed vaulted English oak beams and a charming Minstrels' Gallery. Ideal for larger numbers with the option of round tables or one oval table, the barn can be adapted to accommodate dancing for receptions extending into the evening.

As an alternative to the Tithe Barn, Great Fosters offers the Anne Boleyn room for more intimate wedding breakfasts. Seating 30 it has the option of a real log fire with

triple aspect views of the gardens and holds a civil ceremony licence for a smaller gathering of up to 45 guests. The Tudor Room, decorated in rich, inviting colours, accommodates 40 guests for a ceremony or 18 for a wedding breakfast.

Great Fosters offers complimentary four-poster bedrooms for the bride and groom on their wedding night – the Queen Anne Suite when couples reserve the Tithe Barn or Panel II if they choose The Orangery. Rooms at Great Fosters are individually decorated, some with four-poster beds, Persian rugs, gilt furnishings and damask walls, many with tapestries, antiques and artefacts dating back hundreds of years. Great Fosters also offers a number of rooms at a discounted price for guests attending a wedding.

Tailored to the individual, Great Fosters boasts a personalised approach to weddings, ensuring the couple really benefit from this beautiful venue. The exquisite gardens and fusing together of historical splendour with modern style make Great Fosters the perfect setting for a wedding of any size, regardless of the time of year.

Venue Details

Great Fosters
Stroude Road
Egham, Surrey
TW20 9UR
t 01784 480402
e weddings@greatfosters.co.uk
w www.greatfosters.co.uk

Licence authority:
North Surrey Register Office
Rylston, 81 Oatlands Drive
Weybridge, Surrey
KT13 9LN
t 01932 794700
e registration.weybridge@surreycc.gov.uk
w www.surreycc.gov.uk

Licensed for ceremony: Tithe Barn (240), The Orangery (160 plus 40 guests in the Conservatory), Anne Boleyn Room (45), Tudor Room (40)

Function rooms available: Tithe Barn (reception 180, evening 220), The Orangery (reception 100, evening 110), Tudor Room (reception 18), Anne Boleyn Room (reception 30)

Outside space: 50-acre estate

Option of a marquee: ✗

Rooms available for overnight accommodation: Receptions: 11 allocated bedrooms available with a 10% discount. Ceremony and Receptions: 20 allocated bedrooms at discounted rate

Room rates: From £135 including full English breakfast

Complimentary dressing room for bride available: ✗

SPECIAL NOTES

Licensing hours: Until midnight

Corkage charge: Wine £16, sparking wine £20, champagne £25

Catering: In-house

Complimentary menu tasting: ✓

Car parking spaces: 160

Sound/noise restrictions: No more than five members in the band in the Tithe Barn. No live music after 6pm in the Orangery, although a disco is allowed

Fireworks: ✗

Confetti: ✓ (biodegradable)

Candles: ✓

PA system: ✓

Helicopter landing permission: ✓

Wedding options

Great Fosters provides an idyllic setting for a wedding all year round. A summer wedding made use of the venue's beautiful grounds.

On arrival at Great Fosters guests were led across the courtyard to The Orangery for the ceremony. Here, a red carpet was scattered with rose petals and flowers were on tall perspex pillars in the corners of the room. Guests enjoyed views of the South Terrace and gardens and were entertained by a string quartet playing in the adjoining conservatory.

Following the ceremony, guests moved through to the Painted Hall and terrace for a champagne and Pimm's reception with canapés including baby Yorkshire puddings and garden pea soup with truffle cream served in a shot glass. The bridal party had photographs on the Japanese bridge, in the sunken circular rose garden and by the Saxon moat.

Once dinner was announced, the guests made their way to the Tithe Barn. The tables were set with white linen and decorated with huge contemporary vases with shocking pink gerbera, roses and variegated ivy. The white chair covers with organza bows and an array of candles completed the look.

To start, the guests enjoyed seared black bean tuna with miso dressing followed by roast peppered beef fillet with pommes dauphinoise and baby spring vegetables and to finish, classic lemon tart with crème fraiche and raspberries. Champagne was served during the speeches and coffee served back in the Painted Hall.

The band and a vodka luge were set up in the Tithe Barn unbeknown to the guests in the Painted Hall. Dancing and revelry began and half way through the evening bacon sandwiches and mini cones of fish and chips followed by bite-size ice creams were served.

The celebrations continued well into the night with those guests resident in the hotel making the most of the private bar available to them before retiring to bed. Breakfast the following morning was served in the comfort of a separate room reserved for the wedding party.

The HAC

Fabulous because...

Unexpectedly set in six acres of land while being situated in the City of London, this venue combines wonderful views with stunning interiors, bedecked in original features

Location: **The City**

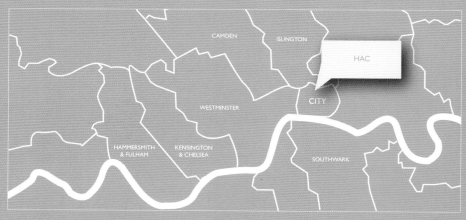

Capacity: **Ceremony 120; Wedding breakfast 450; Evening reception 750**

Minimum number of guests: **40**

Guide Price
Per guest (not including venue hire): **From £48**
Venue hire only: **£2,938**

When to get married here: **All year round**

This classic Georgian building is decorated with Portland stone quoins and a Doric portico

Armoury House, situated in the heart of the City of London, is the home of the HAC (Honourable Artillery Company), the oldest regiment in the British Army. This magnificent Grade II listed building is steeped in history and tradition yet maintains a distinctive glamour that makes the HAC a remarkable venue with a great sense of occasion. History aside, what makes the HAC truly unique is the six acres of immaculately maintained gardens that extend in front of the building.

The HAC have owned the City Road site since 1641 and the existing Armoury House in was built in 1735. The Company was incorporated by Royal Charter in 1537 by King Henry VIII and regiments have fought in both World Wars. Its current Regiment forms part of the Territorial Army and the company is also responsible for providing Guards of Honour for members of the Royal Family and for visiting Heads of State or Commonwealth Prime Ministers.

Moments from Old Street and Moorgate, the HAC is accessed through a secure, military entrance and guests are immediately greeted with the impressive outer façade of Armoury House and its six-acre lawn. This classic Georgian building is decorated with Portland stone quoins, a Doric portico and possesses a striking flag tower. At the forefront, old cannons sit facing the expansive grounds.

Through the pillared entrance, guests enter a magnificent hallway, with dark oak panelling and marine blue walls. The Queen's Room and Ante Room, both licensed to hold ceremonies for up to 60 people, are found off this hall and can also be used to hold intimate dinners. Couples often hold their wedding ceremony, again for up to 60 guests, in one of these rooms before ascending to The Long Room.

On a nice day, sunlight streams through a multicoloured stained glass window that overlooks the staircase and on the landing between floors, the gleaming brass barrels of two old cannons are displayed.

FOR A FABULOUS CEREMONY AND RECEPTION

A valuable portrait of King Henry VIII, acquired from the National Gallery, is exhibited

Either side of the doors into The Long Room treasures from the HAC's collection are displayed; the only known surviving archery mark from the City of London and the bell of the ship that transported members of the HAC to France in 1914. Entering The Long Room, guests never fail to be impressed by this beautiful, oak panelled hall with its lustrous red ceiling. This elegant, spacious room can seat up to 150 guests for lunch or dinner. Around the walls, paintings of past Captains-General are exhibited, the most recent additions being of Queen Elizabeth II and a valuable portrait of King Henry VIII, acquired from the National Gallery. Above the King, a charming minstrels gallery, offers the perfect setting for a trio of musicians to serenade diners. The room's huge picture windows give excellent views over the garden and out to the City beyond. At each end, on the two chimneybreasts, the Royal Coat of Arms and Regimental Coat of Arms are displayed.

As well as being perfect to hold lavish banquets, The Long Room is licensed for ceremonies for up to 120 guests. Couples can therefore, if they wish, take their vows in this dramatic room; enjoy drinks in the downstairs rooms and spill out onto the lawns before moving to The Long Room again for dinner.

Two additional rooms are located off the main landing. In the Court Room the HAC's most precious pieces are displayed – including a relief of King George, a double-faced clock and a silver Elizabethan tilting coat of armour. Across the way, the Medal Room, as the name suggests, displays the many medals

awarded to members of the Company. This room also contains a licensed bar which can be opened for the evening reception. Both rooms have doors which open onto The Long Room, making them perfect additional spaces for guests to sit in, or break from the party. Through another door from The Long Room, the Drum Room is found. This is a charming space that can be used as a sitting area for elderly relatives to escape the noise of the reception.

A wonderful feature of having your celebration at the HAC is undoubtedly the six-acre Artillery Garden at the front of the Armoury House. Making an ideal venue for a champagne reception, the garden is an enviable asset of the HAC. The ground follows the building's historical leanings, as it has been alleged that the first ever game of cricket was played here in 1725 and in summer months today, cricket games are held here as well as games of rugby in the far corner. The Artillery Garden is also where, in 1784, Vincenzo Lunardi launched the first hot air balloon in England, in front of huge crowds. The garden is now lined with trees planted to celebrate the Millennium and the Royal Family have donated seven magnolia trees that are planted in front of Armoury House.

Behind the main building sits the Prince Consort room, a spacious, contemporary venue that was opened by the Queen on 18 May 2007. Formally a large Victorian drill hall, its iron-trussed roof, originally pillar-box red, has been maintained and painted a more fitting gunmetal colour. This venue is one of London's largest entertainment venues, holding up to 450 for a lavish dinner. The space has its own private entrance through a pretty courtyard, but can also be accessed through doors in the entrance hal of Armoury House. This flexibility means couples can use the traditional part of the house for their ceremony, and then move into the Prince Consort room for a spectacular dinner and reception. To marry this contemporary space with the traditional interior of the main house, historical uniforms are exhibited and a display of old rifles and swords mounted on the walls.

The HAC's chosen caterers permanently reside at Armoury House and have over ten years experience catering for events there. They can help with every aspect of the wedding organisation, with a recommended list of established suppliers for flowers and the like.

Venue Details

The HAC
Armoury House
City Road
London
EC1Y 2BQ
t   020 7382 1537
e   hac@hac.org.uk
w   www.hac.org.uk

Licence authority and registrar details:
Islington Town Hall
Upper Street
London
N1 2UD
t   020 7527 6350
e   registrars@islington.gov.uk
w   www.islington.gov.uk

Licensed for ceremony: The Long Room
(120), Queen's Room (60), Ante Room (60),
Prince Consort Room (to be licensed)

Function rooms available: Prince Consort Room
(reception 450, evening 750), The Long Room (reception
150, evening 250), Queen's Room (reception 40,
evening 60), Ante Room (reception 40, evening 60)

Outside space: Six acres of lawn

Option of a marquee: A marquee is erected in
summer and winter, and can hold 200–3,000 guests

Rooms available for overnight accommodation: ✗

Complimentary dressing room for bride available: ✓

SPECIAL NOTES

Licensing hours: Until 11pm (late licence available
on application)

Corkage charge: £10.50 per person

Catering: Requisite caterer

Complimentary menu tasting: ✓

Car parking spaces: Disabled parking available.
NCP at Finsbury Square, two minute's walk away

Sound/noise restrictions: Noise limiters in place
(up to 96 decibels)

Fireworks: ✓

Confetti: ✓

Candles: ✓

PA system: ✓

Helicopter landing permission: ✓

Wedding options

Couples holding a summer wedding at the HAC are able to make full use of the six-acre garden, and are still situated right in the heart of the City of London.

Guests are able to enjoy the magnificent backdrop of Armoury House as they sip a glass of champagne or Pimm's on the lawns. The bride and groom might even make a spectacular entrance in a helicopter.

As guests move into Armoury House for dinner they walk past treasures that are centuries old. They enter the elegant Long Room as a harpist or string quartet play softly in the background and take their places ready to greet the bride and groom.

The Long Room can be dressed with beautifully laid tables with floor length cream linen and organza overlays, chairs covered in matching linen with silver tassel tiebacks, candelabra entwined with ivy and full blown roses, frosted glass and napkins hand tied with the simplest of ivy twists and a single flower.

Highly trained waiting staff enter the room to serve dinner: a timbale of roasted aubergine with onion, red pepper and coriander to start, roast rump of lamb, and individual strawberry and passion fruit pavlovas to finish.

With speeches and toasts safely behind them, the bride and groom cut the cake and take to the floor as guests gather to watch their first dance. As the end of the evening draws near, guests gather outside the entrance with sparklers at the ready to wave off the newly weds in their waiting car. As they do so, a grand finale of spectacular fireworks could light up the City skyline.

Harrow School

Fabulous because...

Founded in 1571 and once home to Winston Churchill, parts of this prestigious, world-renowned school may be hired out for exclusive wedding parties that take advantage of the spectacular views permitted by the 430-acre estate

Location: Harrow on the Hill

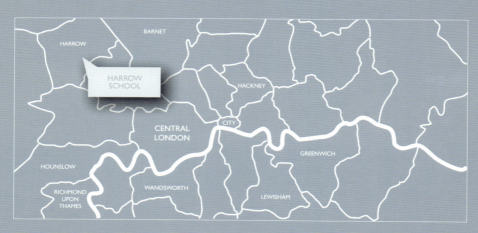

Capacity: Ceremony 120; Wedding breakfast 120; Evening reception 250

Minimum number of guests: 40

Guide Price
Per guest (not including venue hire): £50 – £60
Venue hire only: £375 – £450

When to get married here: School holidays and half terms only

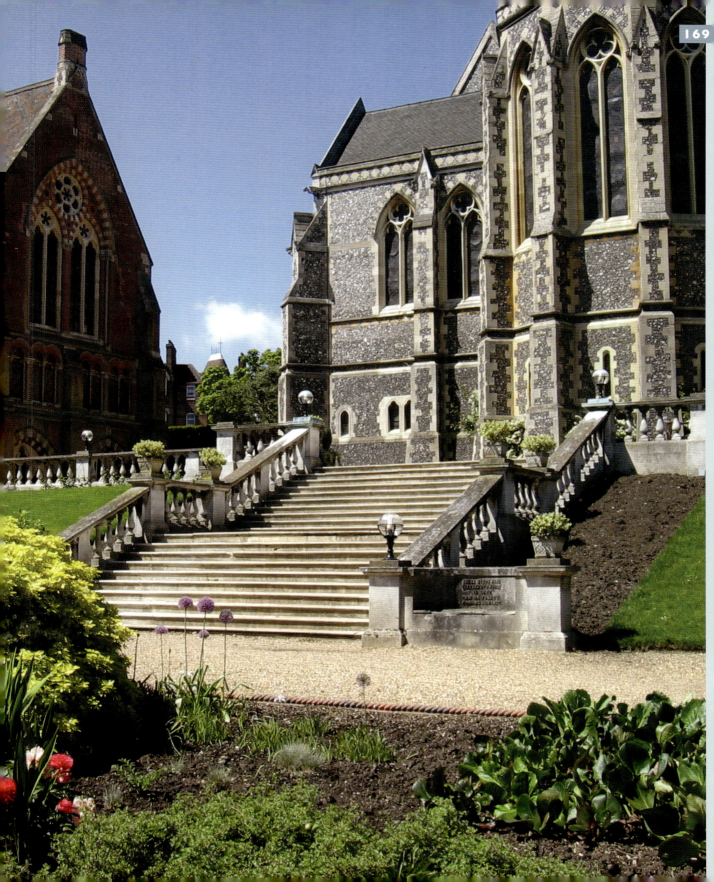

A roofed lawn terrace permits fantastic views across London

Founded in 1571 and set in 430 acres of breathtaking land, Harrow School is a traditional estate that makes a beautiful and historic wedding venue. Dominating the picturesque village of Harrow-on-the-Hill, its buildings are in excellent condition and still stand in their original form, delighting the thousands who pass before them, with their impressive history and architectural brilliance.

Harrow School has educated seven Prime Ministers and was once home to such statesmen and poets as Churchill and Byron. It opened its doors in 1572 after John Lyon, a local farmer, was granted a Royal Charter by Elizabeth I. Still one of Britain's leading independent schools, it is now available as a wedding venue for couples wishing to marry outside term-time, with its extensive grounds making it a perfect rural retreat for those wanting to remain in easy reach of central London.

As well as reception space in all of its three available rooms, Harrow School offers couples a room that is licensed for the exchanging of vows. This is The Old Harrovian Room, a light and spacious area that is able to seat up to 120 guests. Situated opposite the School Chapel, The Old Harrovian Room also lies in close proximity to Old Schools, a building which dates back to the seventeenth century.

The Old Harrovian Room is accessed through the War Memorial Building; a structure that was designed by Sir Herbert Baker and whose foundation stone was laid by the Archbishop of Canterbury — himself an Old Harrovian. Exuding an antiquated feel and air of traditional grandeur, features include polished oak panelling, large, expansive windows and wooden flooring. Its impressive heritage is recalled by portraits of the School's former Headmasters and famous old Harrovians while a grand

Its buildings are in excellent condition and still stand in their original form with their impressive history and architectural brilliance

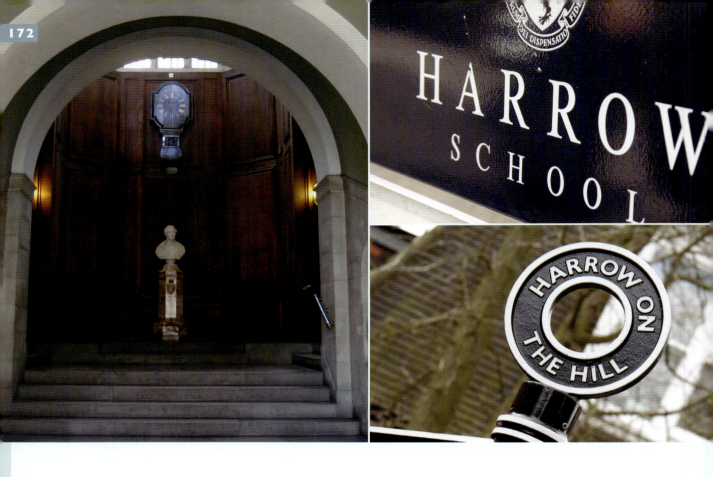

Harrow School has educated seven Prime Ministers and was once home to such statesmen and poets as Churchill and Byron

piano sits at one end of the room. For couples interested in hiring musicians, this is available for use at a small charge and promises couples an elegant entrance.

Following the wedding ceremony, the wedding breakfast is held in the Shepherd Churchill Room, designed by civic trust award winner Dennis Lennon, and which can accommodate up to 120 guests. Providing an elegant and relaxed ambiance, this room benefits from a roofed lawn terrace where fantastic views across London are permitted. A perfect location for exclusive wedding photographs, couples may also enjoy hosting pre-dinner drinks here in its elevated outdoor position while the room itself is set for dinner. Even when the room is set

for dinner a small band or quartet can be positioned in the corner to play either during or after the meal.

Situated immediately below The Shepherd Churchill Room, the larger Shepherd Churchill Hall caters comfortably for up to 250 guests in the evening. Featuring a long balcony with the same fantastic vista as The Shepherd Churchill Room, where guests can again take in breathtaking views of the School's grounds with the city as a backdrop, the Shepherd Churchill Hall has a flexible layout and is suited for musical entertainment or a bar, as well as having space for a dance floor.

FOR A FABULOUS CEREMONY AND RECEPTION

Venue Details

Harrow School
5 High Street
Harrow on the Hill
Middlesex
HA1 3HP
t   020 8872 8381
e   events@harrowschool.org.uk
w www.harrowschoolenterprises.com

Licence authority:
Harrow Register Office
Civic Centre
Station Road
Harrow
HA1 2UX
t   020 8424 1618
e   register.office@harrow.gov.uk
w www.harrow.gov.uk

Licensed for ceremony: The Old Harrovian Room (120)

Function rooms available: The Shepherd Churchill Room (reception 120), The Shepherd Churchill Hall (evening 250)

Outside space: Roof terrace overlooking London

Option of a marquee: ✗

Rooms available for overnight accommodation: ✗

Complimentary dressing room for bride available: ✗

SPECIAL NOTES

Licensing hours: Until 11pm

Corkage charge: Wine £6.50, sparkling wine £8, champagne £10

Catering: In-house

Complimentary menu tasting: ✗

Car parking spaces: 140

Sound/noise restrictions: No music after 11pm

Fireworks: ✗

Confetti: ✗

Candles: ✓ (in The Shepherd Churchill Room only)

PA system: ✓ (in The Shepherd Churchill Hall)

Helicopter landing permission: ✗

Wedding options

A bride recalls her fabulous day at Harrow:

When we were looking for a venue to hold our wedding we wanted something that was going to be really spectacular and relaxed so that our guests would all enjoy themselves yet our day would stick in their mind. We both grew up in Harrow and the school was suggested to us by a friend. When we saw the rooms where we might have our ceremony, wedding breakfast and evening party we were smitten! We had to make sure that the date of our wedding was out of term time, but that was fine as we had our hearts set on the week before Christmas.

The events team at Harrow School were fantastic – they helped us choose the right menu for our guests, dealt with all of the queries we had, liased directly with our florist, pianist, photographer and band and calmly dealt with last minute changes! We were married in front of 100 guests in the historic surroundings of The Old Harrovian Room. We opted to have a small number of large flower arrangements, but the room itself is so grand that it really didn't need to be overly decorated.

We had some fantastic group photographs taken of all of our guests on the steps outside the school and then we all crossed the road to The Shepherd Churchill Room for the wedding breakfast.

The atmosphere was very relaxed and our guests were well looked after while we went out onto the roof terrace to have our photographs taken. The views from the roof terrace were absolutely breathtaking so everyone was happy to wander around outside and take in the London skyline or sit inside and mingle.

The food was beyond our expectations – all our guests commented on how much they enjoyed it. We had a winter theme to our menu and we had our cake served up as a dessert with winter berries and cream.

After the meal, the cutting of the cake and the speeches, we all went downstairs to The Shepherd Churchill Hall to have our evening party. As the hall can accommodate more people we had another 50 friends come along to join us. The bar was reasonably priced for our guests and we had a buffet brought out half way through the evening. The band we had was fantastic.

I have so many wonderful memories of our day which I will cherish forever.

The Hempel

Fabulous because...

This boutique, minimalist hotel is the epitome of contemporary chic. A fusion of modern rooms and antique artefacts creates a haven of design

Location: Bayswater

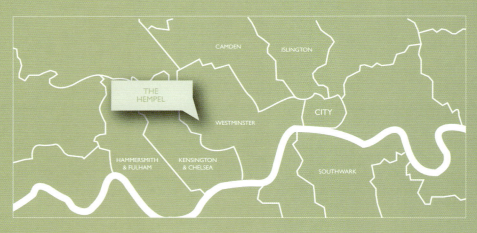

Capacity: Ceremony 100; Wedding breakfast 300; Evening reception 500

Minimum number of guests: None

Guide Price
Per guest (not including venue hire): **£50**
Venue hire only: **£8,225**

When to get married here: All year round

The Hempel's garden, three symmetrical square ponds, is a Zen inspired haven in central London

The boutique Hempel hotel, situated in an exclusive part of Bayswater and moments from the north side of Hyde Park, is an architectural statement in original design and contemporary chic. Now in its 10th year, the five-star hotel has become renowned on the London circuit and as *Tatler* magazine claims, it has hosted 'two of the world's top 10 parties of the year'. It has a variety of intriguing spaces for couples to hold both their ceremony and reception, and with the addition of the Zen Garden, provides the opportunity to invite up to 700 people for the most lavish events.

Acclaimed British designer Anouska Hempel's unobtrusive designs resonate throughout this modish London hotel, which took three years to build, as she aimed to translate the oriental concept of simplicity to the hotel. Identified by the unobtrusive black 'H' on a pillar, The Hempel provides a venue at the height of exclusivity in London. Throughout, simple spaces are contrasted with antique Asian artefacts. These intricate, wood and metal pieces and fresh oriental flower displays complement soothing neutral colours and the simple use of black on white.

The beauty of The Hempel lies in its intricate and highly thoughtout design. The rooms need no decorating, as, by their very nature, they are simplistically beautiful and perfect for the most glamorous of occasions and most visitors choose to leave the spaces in their simplistic form: often all that is required are additions of flowers, or table displays to personalise these extraordinary spaces. Though the hotel is happy for couples to decorate more extensively should they wish. Exclusive use of the hotel is available on rare occasions, and most likely to be possible on weekends.

The hotel is comprised of five Georgian townhouses, yet on entering The Hempel, guests are transported into a synthesis of minimalism and texture. After passing through the Victorian exterior, guests enter the cool simplicity of the hotel lobby, paved throughout with Portland limestone. There are two sunken seating areas around tables constructed from Thai bullock carts with huge cast iron urns at the centre. At each end of the room lie low, elongated fireplaces, while candles flicker in glass goblets throughout the day. In the centre

The rooms need no decorating, as, by their very nature, they are simplistically beautiful

of the room, in front of reception, stands a baby grand piano. Although this first remarkable space is the main entrance to the hotel, with some logistical thought it can be used for a drinks reception almost exclusively, or even as the location for the wedding ceremony itself, since it holds a wedding licence.

Concealed entrances either end of the lobby lead to the H-bar, with its red, high backed chairs and chic, petite bar, and No35, a lounge area which can act as an alternative reception space with its comfortable mustard coloured sofas and dark wood furniture.

Descending the sea-green glass stairs leading from the lobby, guests enter the basement which contains the spectacular monochrome I-Thai restaurant. This oblong venue is ideal for drinks reception parties of over 150 and can accommodate up to 100 guests for a ceremony and 80 for a seated wedding breakfast. The room is separated from the Shadow Bar, a small bar situated outside the restaurant area, by vast suspended glass screens, between which the 'diving board' – a long, metal shelf – protrudes into the restaurant. A permanent feature, built in I-Thai's design, this can be used to hold the wedding cake, or display food.

The I-Thai room itself is minimalist with clean lines throughout. At one end of the room, there is an opening in the wall covered by a honed glass sliding door. The Jade Room can be accessed through this opening and can be used in conjunction with the I-Thai space. Previous brides have made their entrance through this room to enter the ceremony and walk down the aisle of chairs to take contemporary twist on a traditional entrance. A separate entrance to the Jade Room ensures the bride is not seen before she enters. I-Thai also has a private entrance onto street level, so that parties can immediately enter into the entertainment space.

If both the ceremony and reception are to be held in I-Thai, guests can gather for a drinks reception upstairs in No35, or step across the road to No17 and make use of the garden before returning to the restaurant to be seated for the wedding breakfast.

The Hempel's chefs specialise in a Japanese/French/Thai fusion, and can suggest a range of menus or can tailor-make

menus to include the couple's specifically requested dishes.

Across the road from the main hotel building, with a private entrance up stone steps, No17 can be found. This building provides two symmetrically bright rooms, with ceilings over 3m high. The space contains Portland stone floors and honed limestone fireplaces and overlooks the Hempel's Zen-inspired garden square. Above No17, the Hempel's six apartments are found, perfect for guests staying longer in the city to use either side of the event.

Couples can hold both their ceremony and reception at No17, and French doors open along the outer wall onto the garden terrace. A wedding ceremony can be held in either of the two rooms accommodating 40 guests. In fine weather, the numbers can be increased by opening the doors, letting guests join the ceremony

At each end of the room lie low, elongated fireplaces, while candles flicker in glass goblets

from the terrace. Upon entering, a drinks reception could be held among the black bamboo sofas of the first room, before guests are led through the connecting walkway into the far room for the wedding ceremony. Through the venue, antique Chinese chests and cabinets are displayed, complementing the otherwise simple décor.

No17 can host a wedding breakfast for around 30 guests. To accommodate more guests the party could move to the I-Thai restaurant, or a marquee could be erected in the magnificent Zen Garden.

The Hempel's garden, three symmetrical square ponds surrounded by lawn and imported Italian white pebbles, is a Zen inspired haven in central London. The garden features in the film *Notting Hill* as the venue of the leading characters' wedding reception at the end of the film. Exclusively for use by guests of the hotel and residents of Craven Hill Gardens, this space can hold a drinks reception for up to 700 people – under a canopy or marquee. A marquee covers two or three of the garden squares; this space will seat up to 300 people for a banquet, and up to 500

for an evening reception. Amplified music can be played in No17, but non-amplified music, such as a sting quartet, can be situated in the marquee. Due to the residential nature of the area, guests must vacate the garden by 11pm. The celebrations can then continue in the I-Thai restaurant in the basement of the hotel, where there are no noise restrictions.

Guests of the wedding receive special rates on the 41 individually designed bedrooms of which five are suites. The lift and corridors are bathed in bluish light, and rooms are entered from a stark white corridor through floor-to-ceiling hidden doors. These suites include the Lioness' Den, with its sofa area, metal trough-like bath and stairway up to a Japanese-style bed suspended from the ceiling by metal rods, and modern facilities are well hidden behind its minimalist appearance. When couples spend over £15,000 on their wedding in total, The Hempel offers a complimentary room for the bride and groom, which the bride can also use during the day, so to continue enjoying the luxurious surroundings of their wedding day.

Venue Details

The Hempel
31–35 Craven Hill Gardens
London
W2 3EA
t   020 7298 9070
e   Radka.Kisskova@the-hempel.co.uk
w www.the-hempel.co.uk

Licence authority:
Westminster Register Office
Westminster Council House
Marylebone Road
London
NW1 5PT
t   020 7641 1161
e   registeroffice@westminster.gov.uk
w www.westminster.gov.uk

Licensed for ceremony: No17 (40),
I-Thai restaurant (100), The Lobby (60)

Function rooms available: No17 (reception 30,
evening 120), I-Thai restaurant (reception 80, evening
150), Marquee (reception 300, evening 500), garden
(drinks reception 700), Jade Room (reception 16,
evening 20), The Lobby (drinks reception 200)

Outside space: Zen Garden

Option of a marquee: ✓

Rooms available for overnight accommodation: 41

Room rates: Special rate of £259 for wedding guests

Complimentary dressing room for bride available: ✓

SPECIAL NOTES

Licensing hours: Until 11pm (late licence available
on application)

Corkage charge: Wine £15, champagne £25

Catering: In-house

Complimentary menu tasting: ✓

Car parking spaces: Metered parking
or NCP five minute's walk away

Sound/noise restrictions: No restrictions

Fireworks: ✗

Confetti: ✓

Candles: ✓

PA system: ✓

Helicopter landing permission: ✗

Wedding options

**The Hempel offers couples a bespoke service, providing them
with a list of recommended suppliers to help organise the
entertainment, flowers and details.**

Couples usually keep the rooms simple and minimalist in line with
The Hempel style. Candles, rose petals and arrangements of elegant
exotic flowers work well in the already stylish venue rooms.

The hotel's unique fusion of Asian and French influences
makes food at The Hempel unique. Canapés such as pickled
cucumber and wakame salad, served in a miso soup spoon and
tuna carpaccio with celeriac remoulade on crostini can be served
and the sushi chef can also demonstrate sushi preparation before
serving it to guests.

In the past, couples have chosen unique wedding cakes, such
as a cake with feathers made of rice so they were edible or the
unconventional chocolate fountain to replace the traditional food.

The Hempel provides examples of the type of menus and
wedding pacakges that might be created. Prices are based on the
following minimum numbers: Jade Room (12), No17 (24),
I-Thai (60).

Option A

£50 per person, exclusive of room hire

- Carpaccio of langoustine with beluga caviar cream and sweet
  basil emulsion
- Loch Duart salmon and black tiger prawns kastu curry served
  with steamed Thai rice
- Passion fruit crème brulee served with fresh berries

Option B

*£89 per person, inclusive of room hire and a complimentary glass of
wine per person*

- Thai beef salad with fresh lime and fish sauce
- Lime granite
- Slow cooked pork fillet with Thai spices and caramelised
  red cabbage
- Orange and Grand Marnier chocolate pudding

Hendon Hall

Fabulous because...

This cosmopolitan and chic north-west London hotel, abounding in history, can play host to a stylish and intimate wedding in a range of different sized rooms

Location: Hendon

Capacity: Ceremony 130; Wedding breakfast 240; Evening reception 350
___
Minimum number of guests: 30
___
Guide Price
Per guest (including venue hire): £80 – £100
Venue hire only: Not available
___
When to get married here: All year round

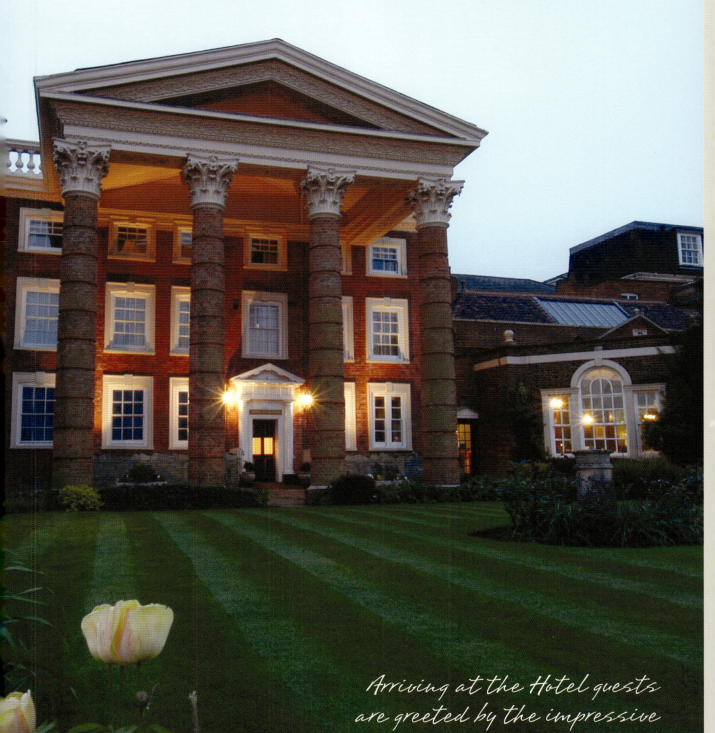

Arriving at the Hotel guests are greeted by the impressive four-pillared Georgian façade

Nestled in a suburban area of north-west London, Hendon Hall provides a historic yet edgy place to be married. Its bold exterior is mirrored inside by the retention of the original style with accentuating modern twists. Having undergone a recent refurbishment, this 230-year-old cosmopolitan mansion house provides a wonderful setting for a modern and stylish wedding.

Originally known as Hendon Manor, the hotel was mentioned in the Doomsday Book. After Henry VII had seized the manor during the English Reformation, his son King Edward VI gave the Manor to the Earl of Pembroke and he, in turn, gave it to his son as a wedding present in 1569. The Pembroke family lost the Manor during the Civil War, maintaining their allegiance with the Crown. Just over a decade later, they regained the Manor at the time of the Restoration of King Charles II.

The memorial title, rights and income of Hendon Manor were sold for £13,000 in the late eighteenth century to David Garrick, the famous actor and manager of the Drury Lane Theatre. Garrick achieved such fame that his head was even engraved on the halfpenny coin. He fervently admired Shakespeare and created a memorial to him in the grounds of Hendon Manor. There is also a memorial to David Garrick, who died as Lord of the Manor of Hendon in 1779, in the front of the grounds.

In 1852, Hendon Hall became a school and in 1911, first opened its doors as a hotel. During the Second World War, it closed to become an RAF convalescent home before returning to its function as a hotel. The history of the hotel continues – in 1966, the victorious England football team stayed at Hendon Hall, using the two smaller events rooms as entertainment spaces. Today, Hendon Hall is an established hotel, proud of its heritage, but also leaping into the twenty-first century.

Arriving at the hotel, guests circle the drive and are greeted by the impressive four-pillared Georgian façade of this red-bricked building. Beneath the entrance, a cobbled area leads into the house. Entering reception, guests are greeted with white marble floors, deep leather sofas and oriental

In 1966, the victorious England football team stayed at Hendon Hall

features. Its sumptuous décor is complemented by period details, retaining the venue's 'foot in the past'.

Hendon Hall has three spaces holding a ceremony licence, all of which can also seat the guests for dinner, as well as an alternative reception space. Varying in size and décor, the venue is sure to meet the bride and groom's requirements.

The Sheridan Room and The Johnson Room are accessed from the lobby. Of similar size, both are licensed to hold civil ceremonies and also make warm venues for smaller dinners. Stepping away from the modern décor found elsewhere, these rooms are decorated in the original manor house style, with plush floral curtains, large oak tables and fireplaces originally from Grade II listed Wandsworth House. The Johnson Room also houses a beautifully restored original wall fresco. Both rooms can seat up to 35 for a ceremony and 30 for dinner.

The Pembroke suite, located in a separate building to the left of the main hotel, is the venue's largest entertaining space. Guests ascend marble steps, laid with a red carpet, into the suite's long bar area. Two entrances into the main ballroom ensure couples can section off this room for the ceremony and open it up for the wedding breakfast. The ballroom, neutrally decorated in muted creams, is an adaptable space. The room can be classically dressed, or adapted to suit a more contemporary feel, with the option of colour washing the walls with lights to give the space a dramatic effect.

Ceremonies conducted here usually take place in half of the room, with the dividers in place and couples can invite up to 130 guests. After the ceremony, guests can adjourn to the bar area or to the gardens behind the main house while the room is opened up and dinner is set. Accommodating up to 240 guests for a wedding breakfast, the ballroom provides a large, but flexible space. A permanent dance floor and moveable stage area also makes this room perfect for evening receptions, accommodating 350 standing. With an adjustable lighting system comprising of four candelabras, spotlights in the ceiling and up lights on the walls, couples are able to choose their lighting to reflect the time of day and mood of the event.

In the main house, through frosted glass doors from the 'Den' bar area, The Lounge and White is found. The two sections to the room – the lounge and the 'white' area – can hold both dinner and evening reception, should couples wish to merge the two. The Lounge's mustard walls contrast with the White's notably neutral area with floor to ceiling windows that let in natural light, and the two are separated by thick curtains which can divide the spaces. Wedding breakfasts for around 30 people can be held in the Lounge area, with couples using the White as an area filled with sofas and chilled out music for a more relaxed affair or to house a dance area.

The ballroom can be classically dressed or adapted to suit a more contemporary feel, with the option of colour washing the walls

Alternatively, the whole of this space can be used to seat 70 for a wedding breakfast. In close proximity to the delightful 'Den' public bar, guests are able to make use of their cocktail range and can spill out into this cosy room, enjoying its plush furnishings decorated with reds, purples and browns.

Hendon Hall's landscaped garden provides a wonderful outside area to enjoy drinks or entertain in. Its terraced area is ideal for a drinks reception after the ceremony, and the lawns and planting provide many an opportune photography spot. In the past, couples have used the garden for entertainment, for

example, one wedding enjoyed fairground themed rides and activities, organised by the events team at the hotel.

The hotel has its own wedding team who are able to fulfil couples' requests and be as involved as is needed. A bespoke menu can be designed for each wedding, with scope from informal British classics to sumptuous gastronomic delights. Hendon Hall assures couples theirs will be the only wedding occurring on any given day.

FOR A FABULOUS CEREMONY AND RECEPTION

Venue Details

Hendon Hall
Ashley Lane
Hendon
London
NW4 1HF
t   020 8203 3341
e   info@hendonhall.com
w   www.hendonhall.com

Licence authority:
Barnet Register Office
182 Burnt Oak Broadway
Edgware Middlesex
HA8 0AU
t   020 8731 1100
e   first.contact@barnet.gov.uk
w   www.barnet.gov.uk

Licensed for ceremony: The Pembroke Suite (130),
The Sheridan Room (35), The Johnson Room (35)

Function rooms available: The Pembroke Suite
(reception 240, evening 350), The Sheridan Room
(reception 30, evening 40), The Johnson Room
(reception 30, evening 35), The Lounge and White
(reception 70)

Outside space: Landscaped garden

Option of a marquee: ✓

Rooms available for overnight accommodation: 57

Room rates: Preferential bedroom rates
offered depending on the time of year

Complimentary dressing room for bride available: ✗

SPECIAL NOTES

Licensing hours: Monday to Friday until midnight,
Sunday until 11.30pm

Corkage charge: Corkage not permitted

Catering: In-house (own caterer permitted
when hiring the Pembroke Suite)

Complimentary menu tasting: ✗

Car parking spaces: 70

Sound/noise restrictions: Music allowed until midnight

Fireworks: ✗

Confetti: ✓ (in the garden)

Candles: ✓

PA system: ✓

Helicopter landing permission: ✗

Wedding options

At Hendon Hall, every wedding is unique, and their team of
experienced wedding coordinators can help in all areas of
organising the important day. The team aim to listen to couples'
ideas and inspirations, their preferences and priorities, and then
work together to create a truly memorable day. Below is a
guide package for those considering the hotel.

From £80 per head

- Red carpet on arrival
- Bucks fizz served on arrival
- Three course menu of your choice
- Half a bottle of wine per person
- Sparking wine for the bridal toast
- A member of the team to act as toastmaster for the day
- Luxury overnight accommodation for the bride and groom on
  the wedding night
- Disco
- Chair covers

From a traditional wedding breakfast with champagne, caviar and
a string quarter to a themed wedding – Thai beach or Highland
fling, the possibilities at Hendon Hall are endless. Each of the
hotel's events spaces are blank canvases, permitting couples to
decorate them as they wish. There is also the option of having a
more simple reception, for example a barbeque, cider cups and
strolling players, seating guests on straw bales around rustic tables
decorated with armfuls of daffodils, then ending the evening with a
traditional barn dance.

HMS Belfast

Fabulous because...

Moored on the River Thames close to Tower Bridge, HMS *Belfast* exists as a living testament to its war history and is an impressive and unusual wedding venue

Location: On the River Thames, Southwark

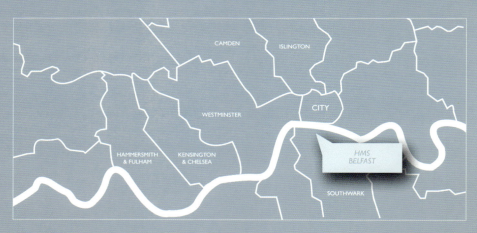

Capacity: Ceremony 110; Wedding breakfast 144; Evening reception 450

Minimum number of guests: 15

Guide Price
Per guest (not including venue hire): **From £26**
Venue hire only: **£588**

When to get married here: **All year round**

*Some couples choose for their guests to arrive by boat
allowing for the full magnificence of the ship
to be taken in on the approach*

Moored in a prime location between London Bridge and Tower Bridge, HMS *Belfast* is the largest surviving example of Britain's twentieth-century naval prowess. Best known for her role in supporting allied troops on D-Day, 6 June 1944, this vast ship is now owned and managed by the Imperial War Museum who have helped preserve the ship as a living time capsule for guests to explore. A powerful and impressive event venue, it is available for private hire and provides an unusual backdrop for couples wishing to marry 'on board' without going to sea. The ceremony can take place in numerous parts of the vessel such as the Admiral's Quarters, Officers Wardroom or the Ship's Company Dining Hall. With optional event enhancements including the hire of 1940s costumed actors who can greet guests and recreate the recruit induction procedure, each wedding on board HMS *Belfast* will be fabulous and memorable.

Commissioned into the Royal Navy on 5 August 1939, HMS *Belfast* has a proud heritage. Serving the nation throughout the Second World War, the ship also played a leading role in the Battle of North Cape and the Normandy Landings. Going on to offer support in The Korean War, she eventually retired from the Royal Navy in 1965, becoming immortalised on the banks of the River Thames in 1971 as the only surviving example of the Navy's great fleets of big-gun armoured warships in the first half of the twentieth century.

For couples wishing to marry on board this historic ship there are more possibilities for a variety of wedding options than one might imagine. A variety of rooms are suited for ceremony, reception and wedding breakfast, and exclusive hire of the whole ship is also available.

In keeping with the venue itself, some couples choose for their guests to arrive by boat allowing for the full magnificence of the ship to be taken in on the approach. Any number of guests can be collected from any pier on the Thames.

An alternative for those arriving by foot is to board by crossing the ship's gangway which leads onto the Quarterdeck where

In the exposed inner structure of the ship, wedding parties can attend an informative exhibition

guests are greeted on a traditional wooden deck in the open air. Parties arriving for a ceremony on board the ship can then make their way down the walkways and enter the interior of the ship and will be guided to the chosen room for the ceremony.

The first of these rooms that are available for ceremony hire are the Ward Room and Ward's Ante Room; originally the Officers' Mess where officers would meet away from the rest of the ship's Company. Swathed in shades of blue and decorated with paintings of the ship and those in the same convoys as HMS *Belfast*, a ceremony can be set up in one room while guests gather in the other, taking in the fine details such as the original booth seating. Able to seat up to 50 guests for the ceremony, these rooms also include access to a bar.

The second room to hold a licence for wedding ceremonies is the Ship's Company Dining Hall where up to 110 are able to witness the exchanging of vows. The dining hall (originally for the ship's hungry sailors) has been largely preserved in its original state, with carpet and air conditioning added for comfort. Decked in white and blue with low-level ceilings giving way to exposed wiring and piping, guests may also note the authentic scuttles which line the walls and permit views from what is a privileged position of the city's historic riverbank.

Wherever couples choose to hold their ceremony, hire of the HMS *Belfast* entitles wedding parties to free access to all of the museum's exhibits. After the ceremony is over, guests can move through the ship towards their reception space taking a trip down to the lower decks if they wish, since these are open until 6.30pm.

*The only surviving example of the Navy's great
fleets of big-gun armoured warships*

There are many areas where guests can see the exposed inner structure of the ship, including original piping, and the free exhibitions available to wedding parties include other original artefacts ranging from photographs to uniforms. An interactive children's area is also open to the guests, children and adults alike.

Once guests have explored these exhibitions, they may wish to ascend a level towards the Boat-Deck where the Gun Room offers reception space for up to 100 people. Similar in style to the Ward Room, it offers a space that is decorated in sophisticated shades of brown and white. Lined once more with scuttles and related paintings, this room can be used as a formal area in conjunction with another smaller space that is located nearby. This small space is actually the museum's café during the day but can be converted into a dancing area for people to use after dinner in the Gun Room. While the café area may be replaced by a bar,

the room's tiled linoleum floor make it ideal for dancing while red piping, white walls and the ship's trademark scuttles add character.

The final area available for hire is the Admiral's Quarters. The smallest of the venue's spaces, it is made up of the Day Cabin, Dining Cabin and Sleeping Quarters, although the Sleeping Quarters are not open to the public. With the scuttles and paintings which adorn so much of the ship's interior, the main room also contains original service hatches. Guests dining in this room alone are privy to use of HMS *Belfast*'s crested crockery which can offset perfectly the flowers and candelabras which decorate the retractable table that is laid for fine dining in the centre of the room.

Whichever room couples decide to hire, marrying on board the HMS *Belfast* will be an exciting and timeless wedding day.

Venue Details

HMS *Belfast*
Morgan's Lane
Tooley Street
London
SE1 2JH
t 020 7403 6246
e hms.belfast@sodexho-uk.com
w www.hmsbelfast.org.uk

Licence authority:
Southwark Register Office
34 Peckham Road
London
SE5 8QA
t 020 7525 7651
e registrars@southwark.gov.uk
w www.southwark.gov.uk

Licensed for ceremony: Ward Room and Ward's Ante Room (50), Ships Company Dining Hall (110)

Function rooms available: Admiral's Quarters (reception 20, evening 35), Ward Room and Ward's Ante Room (reception 50, evening 100), Gun Room (reception 60, evening 100), Ships Company Dining Hall (reception 144, evening 240), Whole ship (evening 450)

Outside space: Quarterdeck and boat deck

Option of a marquee: ✗

Rooms available for overnight accommodation: ✗

Complimentary dressing room for bride available: ✗

SPECIAL NOTES

Licensing hours: Until 1am

Corkage charge: Wine £14, champagne £28

Catering: In-house

Complimentary menu tasting: ✗

Car parking spaces: Car park 10 minute's walk away

Sound/noise restrictions: No amplified music on the deck

Fireworks: ✗ (but can have a barge in the river)

Confetti: ✗

Candles: ✗

PA system: ✓ (to hire)

Helicopter landing permission: ✗

Wedding options

Offering a bespoke wedding service that is catered to each individual wedding, HMS *Belfast* also offer a number of guide wedding packages for couples considering a wedding on board this illustrious cruiser.

A basic wedding package could be priced at £99 per head. This would include:

- Room hire
- Sparkling wine or bucks fizz reception
- Three course meal
- Glass of sparkling wine for the toast
- Half a bottle of house wine
- Half a bottle of mineral water
- Music during ceremony or use of CD player
- Fresh flower table centres
- Fresh flower spray for top table
- Fine table linen
- Use of wedding cake stand and knife
- Production of table plans
- Personalised wedding menus
- Place cards
- On-site event manager

With a number of event enhancements available to those wanting a distinct and distinguished day, couples may choose from a list of wedding extras. These include a fabulous wedding greeting where guests are piped on board in traditional naval style as well as talks from war veterans who sailed on board HMS *Belfast*. The use of 1940s actors who will meet and greet guests is also popular as the lieutenant then bellows out orders to sailors in a re-enactment of the induction procedure.

Themed weddings which include specialised meals are also welcomed and options range from a Brazilian themed two-course finger buffet to a BBQ freshly cooked on the boat deck!

Horniman Museum

Fabulous because...

This Grade II listed Victorian conservatory is set in attractive gardens and is one of the most original Art Nouveau buildings anywhere in Britain

Location: Forest Hill, Lewisham

Capacity: Ceremony 100; Wedding breakfast 100; Evening reception 100

Minimum number of guests: None

Guide Price
Per guest (not including venue hire): **Not available**
Venue hire only: **£987 – £3,208**

When to get married here: **April to October**

One of London's gems in its treasure-trove of museums, the internationally acclaimed Horniman Museum provides couples with a spectacular location for their wedding. Combining its wonderful history and unusual exhibits with majestic surroundings, the Museum offers exclusive hire of the Grade II listed Victorian Conservatory where up to 100 guests can attend ceremony and reception alike. Surrounded by 16.5 acres of award-winning Gardens, its location appears surprisingly rural and has been compared to 'a Home Counties country estate in the middle of London'. Fabulously rich in ornate detail and benefiting from its own private terrace, the Conservatory is an inspiring and idyllic venue for a special occasion.

The Horniman Museum was founded by the Victorian tea trader, MP and philanthropist Frederick John Horniman who began collecting artefacts and specimens from around the world in the 1860s. Opened to the public in 1901, the Museum was dedicated with the surrounding land, and original collection, as a gift to the people of London. Designed by Charles Harrison Townsend who also designed the Whitechapel Art Gallery in London, it has been recognised in the 'Building of England' series as 'one of the most original Art Nouveau buildings anywhere in Britain'. The original collection comprised of natural history specimens, cultural exhibits and musical instruments and although the original artefacts make up only 10% of the current collection they form the foundation of the museum's exhibits today. These include three main collections; anthropology, which features the third most significant ethnographic collection in the UK, the natural history collection, and a world renowned collection of musical instruments. The museum's aquarium is also notable. Reopened in 2006, it displays a variety of live species including jellyfish and seahorses.

A graceful new centenary development was added in 2002 and this provided a link to the gardens and Victorian Conservatory where couples marrying at the museum will

A number of original characteristic features including a roof formed of glazed fish scales make it a timeless architectural feat

spend the majority of their time. The Conservatory itself did not begin life in its current location and was originally built in 1894 for the Horniman family home, Coombe Cliff, in Croydon. The Conservatory was moved to the museum site in 1988 and now stands as an important example of Victorian engineering and design in its own right. Originating from Macfarlane's Foundry in Glasgow, it is a tall building with an imposing white structure adorned with glass. Still with a number of its original characteristic features including a roof formed of glazed fish scales, it is a timeless architectural feat that offers couples a flexile space in which to plan celebrations.

Drawing inspiration from the magnificent Crystal Palace which was sited only a stone's throw away, the Conservatory has large glass panels offset by delicate detail on the building's exterior. With minimal in-built decoration, it is a bright and airy space where light ricochets off the ceiling and onto the tiled ceramic floor. A great photographic location, it looks as good illuminated by candlelight as it does glinting in the sunshine and can easily be set for dinner and dancing. A popular ceremony venue, for those couples who hire the venue for both a ceremony and reception a marquee will be required which can be used to hold an additional 20 guests. This can be erected on one of several sites on

The gardens provide a versatile backdrop for wedding photographs and include an exotic African garden and rose garden

the Conservatory's adjourning private terrace area, and helps safeguard against unpredictable weather as well as offering a greater expanse of space for larger reception parties.

For couples marrying at the museum, another complimentary feature of the venue is its beautiful gardens, which can be seen from the Conservatory. The gardens provide a versatile backdrop for wedding photographs and include an exotic African garden and a rose garden. This latter area features flowers and blooms in an array of vivid colours with square paving leading to a beautiful rectangular centerpiece. Providing access to the Conservatory, a historic avenue lined with horse chestnut trees can leave

a memorable first impression and reveals a breathtaking view of the Victorian Conservatory on its approach.

Whatever concerns a couple may have, with a designated team on hand to facilitate all their needs, the Horniman Museum endeavours to provide a complete service that includes lists of accredited suppliers and the venue's sole accredited caterer who can suit any style or budget.

With wedding hire available from April to October, from 3pm to 11pm, it is a venue that is a true fairy-tale spot, its history and heritage adding a further dimension to its appeal.

FOR A FABULOUS CEREMONY AND RECEPTION

Venue Details

Horniman Museum & Gardens
100 London Rd
Forest Hill
London
SE23 3PQ
t   020 8693 1476 (contact details for Suzanne James)
e   hornimanconservatory@suzannejames.co.uk
w www.horniman.ac.uk

Licence authority:
Lewisham Register Office
368 Lewisham High Street
Lewisham
London
SE13
t   020 8690 2128
e   register.office@lewisham.gov.uk
w www.lewisham.gov.uk

Licensed for ceremony: The Conservatory (100)

Function rooms available: The Conservatory
(reception 100, evening 100), additional
guest marquee (reception 20)

Outside space: Terrace and 16.5 acres of garden

Option of a marquee: ✓

Rooms available for overnight accommodation: ✗

Complimentary dressing room for bride available: ✗

SPECIAL NOTES

Licensing hours: Until 11pm

Corkage charge: No charge

Catering: Requisite caterer

Complimentary menu tasting: ✓

Car parking spaces: Ample parking
available on nearby streets

Sound/noise restrictions: Music permitted until 10.45pm

Fireworks: ✗

Confetti: ✗

Candles: ✓ (restrictions apply)

PA system: ✓ (supplier recommended)

Helicopter landing permission: ✗

Wedding options

All events at the Horniman Conservatory are run by Suzanne James Ltd and are tailored to suit their client's specific requirements.

For a civil ceremony in the Conservatory guests would arrive to find the stunning room set up with theatre style seating. After the ceremony the wedding party could meander into the exquisite award-winning gardens for photographs. This would be followed by champagne or Pimm's and canapés enjoyed in the marquee or al fresco on the terrace area, while Suzanne James sets up the Conservatory for dinner. The Conservatory has a wonderfully enchanting ambience on balmy summer evenings.

An example menu at the Horinman might include:

- Caramelised fig, roasted pancetta and seared haloumi salad with rocket leaves and balsamic syrup
- Rack of lemon peppered Welsh spring lamb with rosemary dauphenoise, sauteed ratatouille, lamb & madeira jus
- Vanilla panna cotta with kissel and fairy floss

The Conservatory looks stunning when illuminated only by candlelight and with simple decoration. After dinner, music and dancing can take place in the Conservatory, with the removal of several tables.

Kew Gardens

Fabulous because...

World-renowned Kew Gardens provides a plethora of wonderful buildings in a green and luscious setting amongst palm trees and exotic flowers and is a venue that cares for the environment

Location: **Kew, Surrey**

Capacity: **Ceremony 80; Wedding breakfast 400; Evening reception 600**

Minimum number of guests: **None**

Guide Price
Per guest (including venue hire): **Not available**
Venue hire only: **£3,500 – £12,000**

When to get married here: **All year round**

The Royal Botanic Gardens, Kew is world-renowned for its beautiful flora, iconic buildings and conservation work and was officially inscribed as a Unesco World Heritage Site in 2003. Kew is a prestigious venue, and has played host to royalty and film stars alike in its 350 acres of greenery. Open to the public year round, the Gardens provide a plethora of venue choices for ceremonies and celebrations and each one promises to make a memorable setting for the couple's important occasion. From marrying in a former royal residence to dining amidst a tropical rainforest, the Garden's extensive landscape is unrivalled throughout the capital.

Kew Garden's history is extensive; owned by the royal family until the early twentieth century, it was given to the state in 1840. In 1751 Queen Augusta began a small nine-acre botanic garden and had several garden buildings built, including the present Orangery, Pagoda and Ruined Arch. Under George III, botanical collectors began collating specimens across the globe and began a centre of botanical research. After his death, the Gardens were neglected and in 1840 the royal family donated this, and some surrounding land, to the state, bringing the total area of the Gardens up to 200 acres. Kew benefited from further donations of land and reached its current size of 300 acres in 1902.

Marking Kew Gardens apart from many wedding venues is their concern for the environment. A 'green wedding' in every sense, not only are couples surrounded by lawns and plants, but the funds generated from venue hire are a vital source of income for Kew, and contribute to the funding of Kew's plant conservation and research work. For this reason also, Kew encourages guests to use the excellent public transport routes to reach the Gardens. Kew is the perfect option for environmentally conscious couples to enjoy their wedding in a spectacular venue, whilst contributing to the surroundings.

It is worth noting that for weddings held at Kew, all guests have access to the Gardens free of charge before

A Grade I listed building, The Orangery is one of Kew's most magnificent glasshouses

To banquet in the Temperate House is to dine in a tropical rainforest, surrounded by over 1,700 species of plants from the sub-tropical regions of the world

the event they are attending. If previously requested, the Kew events team will inform gate staff of the wedding party name and a guest list is not required.

There are four main parts of the Gardens that can be used to host wedding celebrations. The most popular venue, holding the Garden's only civil wedding licence is Cambridge Cottage. Named after the Duke of Cambridge, Cambridge Cottage facilitates a leisurely setting where couples can hold both their ceremony and reception in a Grade II listed building. Approaching Cambridge Cottage through it's own private entrance off Kew Green, guests are greeted with a Portland stone façade and enter into the Edwardian entrance hall. The

adjoining Drawing Room and Gallery open out onto the secluded Duke's Garden and their neutral décor lends itself well for colour themes in accordance with individual taste.

Ceremonies take place in the Georgian drawing room, providing space for up to 80 guests as couples take their vows overlooking the Duke's Garden. On its wall are paintings from Kew's historic collections and the room harks back to its former proprietor, with the bust of King George III on display. The neighbouring Gallery houses intricate paintings and sketches of orchids and the room's neutral colours allow for subtle themes should couples wish. All of the guests who attended the ceremony can

FOR A FABULOUS CEREMONY AND RECEPTION

be accommodated for a wedding breakfast, and couples have the option of inviting an additional 70 guests for an evening reception. Unlike many royal abodes, Cambridge Cottage allows music, dancing and even red wine.

The Meeting Room, used by the registrar, can also be used as a dressing room if desired. A corridor, which links the entrance hall to the drawing room, is filled with early twentieth-century London Underground posters displaying how to get to Kew Gardens.

Nearby, The Princess of Wales Conservatory contains rare orchids and 10 climate zones including a tropical area, an arid area and a lily pond. It can be used in conjunction with Cambridge Cottage as for an evening drinks reception and give guests a real taste of Kew.

Separate from Cambridge Cottage are the alternative settings of The Orangery and The Temperate House, two extraordinary venues available for dinners and receptions. Only available in the evenings, when the Gardens are closed to the public, guests can enjoy the terrace and spectacular vistas.

The Orangery was designed by Sir William Chambers in 1761, and as a Grade I listed Orangery is one of Kew's most magnificent glasshouses. A restaurant in the day, the space is cleared to create a blank canvas for exclusive evening dining starting at 7pm. The venue is only a short walk from the Main Gate, and in the evenings both the route and Orangery are lit.

White walls, Portland stone floors and a scattering of citrus trees create a simplistic interior to which detail can be easily added. High arched windows overlook the terrace where couples can hold drinks receptions in fine weather. The terrace leads on to a superbly manicured lawn with views of the sweeping vistas of Kew and night-lit trees.

The Temperate House was designed by the famous architect Decimus Burton and built in 1860. It is the largest surviving Victorian glasshouse in the world, covering an area of 4,880 square meters. The House, as its name implies, retains a constant temperature, unaffected by that outside. To banquet in the Temperate House is to dine in a tropical rainforest, surrounded by over 1,700

The Princess of Wales Conservatory contains rare orchids and ten climate zones

species of plants from the sub-tropical regions of the world. Available in the evenings only, the plants and foliage are illuminated by discreet spotlights producing one of the most exotic and exceptional venues in London.

Receptions can be held in the North or South Octagons before dining in the Central House amongst a collection of 45 different palm trees. Two wide pathways spanning from north to south and from east to west accommodate round tables and create space for a top table as they cross in the middle of the House.

For the most impressive dining of up to 200 people, the whole House can be utilised. Dancing can easily be accommodated in the entrance spaces.

Finally, the fourth and largest venue within the gardens suitable for hosting celebrations is The Palace Pavilion. Situated in a secluded corner of the Gardens the Pavilion enjoys picturesque views of Kew Palace. This purpose-built temporary structure provides complete flexibility

for daytime and evening events and is run by an events team. It can hold wedding receptions for up to 400 people. Couples can create their own theme in the Pavilion, with scope for lavish of parties or impressive formal banquet.

Although this is a temporary structure, open from 1 May to 30 September, the Pavilion does not compromise on quality and includes fully integrated lighting and sound systems, air-conditioning and bar areas. A fenced private garden area overlooks a lake and is an ideal setting for outdoor receptions.

With an array of choice in its inimitable grounds, Kew Gardens is a unique London venue and one that ensures an unforgettable occasion.

Venue Details

Royal Botanic Gardens, Kew
Richmond
Surrey
TW9 3AB
t 0870 141 3061
e weddings@kew.org
w www.kew.org/venues

Licence authority:
Richmond Register Office
1 Spring Terrace
Richmond
Surrey
TW9 1LW
t 020 8940 2853 or 020 8940 2651
e registeroffice@richmond.gov.uk
w www.richmond.gov.uk

Licensed for ceremony: Cambridge Cottage (80)

Function rooms available: Cambridge Cottage (reception 80, evening 150), The Orangery (reception 200, evening 400), Temperate House (reception 200, evening 400), Palace Pavilion Marquee (reception 400, evening 600)

Outside space: All venues have private garden or terrace space plus access to Kew Gardens

Option of a marquee: ✓ (Palace Pavilion temporary structure)

Rooms available for overnight accommodation: ✗

Complimentary dressing room for bride available: ✓

SPECIAL NOTES

Licensing hours: Until midnight

Corkage charge: Dependent on caterer

Catering: Recommended caterers

Complimentary menu tasting: Dependent on caterer

Car parking spaces: Free parking available on Kew Green

Sound/noise restrictions: Sound limiters in place, DJ permitted until midnight

Fireworks: ✗

Confetti: ✗

Candles: ✓ (tea lights only)

PA system: ✓ (supplier recommended)

Helicopter landing permission: ✗

Wedding options

Kew's selection of venues can be used in conjunction with each other to create a truly unique wedding for the most fabulous of celebrations. **By varying the locations for the ceremony, wedding breakfast, and even a drinks reception, couples will experience Kew in all its glory and host a spectacular and memorable event.**

Suggested paring: Cambridge Cottage and The Orangery
Guests enter the Gardens through the private entrance on Kew Green. A late afternoon, intimate ceremony with 80 guests is held in the Drawing Room at Cambridge Cottage, followed by champagne and canapés on the lawn. Guests then take a five-minute walk through the gardens to the illuminated Orangery, where other guests join the party for a larger evening reception for up to 200 people. (Approximate total fee £30,000 including catering)

Suggested paring: Cambridge Cottage, The Prince of Wales Conservatory and the Temperate House
After a marriage ceremony at Cambridge Cottage, a drinks reception is held at The Princess of Wales Conservatory, amongst rare orchids. From here, guests either take a short 15-minute walk through the gardens, or journey on the Kew Explorer (seats 70) to the magnificent Temperate House to dine amongst exotic plants. On arrival, a champagne reception is held in the South Octagon before proceeding into dinner. The House itself can be lit by coloured spotlights to suit a colour theme and cast shadows on the exotic plants. up to 200 guests are seated along the walkways, and a head table is set up at the centre of the House. A band and dance space can be set up in the North Octagon. (Approximate total fee £50,000 including catering)

Before each wedding, guests are invited to visit Kew, free of charge.

The Law Society's Hall

Fabulous because...

Swathed in history, this nineteenth-century building provides elegant and grandiose rooms in an enviable central location, moments from Fleet Street

Location: **Holborn**

Capacity: Ceremony 150; Wedding breakfast 200; Evening reception 350

Minimum number of guests: **55**

Guide Price
Per guest (not including room hire): **£106**
(catering minimum spend £4,500)
Venue hire only: From **£3,525**

When to get married here: **All year round**

*Features including crystal chandeliers,
and sweeping staircases create a sumptuous
and opulent setting*

Steeped in history, The Law Society's Hall is an impressive building, positioned close to Fleet Street and only a short stroll from the River Thames. From its outer façade, the venue breathes magnificence, as guests are greeted with Palladian style pillars and Portland stone. Inside, the wonder continues, with features including marble pillars, crystal chandeliers, and sweeping staircases, creating a sumptuous and opulent setting in which to hold the wedding ceremony and reception.

The Law Society was founded on 2 June 1825, after several prominent attorneys decided to raise the reputation of the legal profession by setting standards and ensuring good practice. The Society acquired its first royal charter in 1831, and opened a new building in Chancery Lane in 1832, where it has remained ever since. The organisation became known colloquially as the Law Society although its first formal title was 'The Society of Attorneys, Solicitors, Proctors and others not being Barristers, practising in the Courts of Law and Equity of the United Kingdom'. In 1903 the Society changed its official name to the more pronounceable 'The Law Society'. Today, The Law Society represents solicitors in Britain and abroad, and regularly publishes reports on trends in the solicitors' profession.

Available for exclusive hire at weekends, The Law Society's Hall is comprised of a number of rooms

Rich mahogany panelling, peacock-tiled fireplaces and marble pillars fill the room with sophistication

perfect to hold a whole day of celebrations. Able to accommodate dinners for up to150 guests, and receptions for 350, there is a great deal of flexibility in which to organise a perfect day, whatever the size of the party, without compromising on atmosphere or elegance. The elegant function rooms contain stunning nineteenth-century features, such as wrought iron balconies, and dramatic seventeenth-century stained glass windows.

Couples are invited to hold their wedding ceremony in the impressive Reading Room, beneath its 12m high glass ceiling and surrounded by a colour scheme of classic blues and creams. This galleried room can comfortably seat up to 150 guests for a wedding ceremony and is an atmospheric place to take the significant vows. The room can also be used for evening receptions and banquets.

The Law Society's largest room, The Common Room, is reached via a sweeping marble staircase, between symmetrical arches. Seating up to 200 guests for a banquet, this grand room boasts many striking features; chandeliers hang throughout the room, rich mahogany paneling adorns the walls and peacock-tiled fireplaces and marble pillars fill the room with sophistication. The Common Room itself can accommodate up to 300 people for an evening reception, in addition to which the adjoining rooms, the Strand, Fleet and Bell Suite, can be opened and combined with The Common Room to

The Reading Room's high glass ceiling and classic colour scheme make an apt ceremony venue

host 350 for a larger drinks reception. A space in the middle of the room can be left to act as a dance area for evening receptions, while not disturbing the party's flow.

For more intimate receptions, The Law Society's Hall offers the Old Council Chamber and Dining Room, which can accommodate up to 55 guests for a formal banquet. This smaller room is full of beautiful pieces, and richly decorated mahogany panelling is set off with gold walls. The double-height windows provide streaming natural light and an ornate fireplace creates an old world charm in this room.

The Law Society's internal caterer liaises with a Michelin starred chef to create a sumptuous, individual menu for each event. The team bring a creative approach sourcing

the finest and freshest ingredients. Couples have the option of appointing their own caterer for an additional price.

The Law Society team are seasoned in wedding planning and can assist couples in every aspect of organising their wedding. Owing to the venue's heritage and daily usage, practicing solicitors receive a 15% discount on venue hire. Guests attending events at the venue receive a discount at the Renaissance Chancery Court Hotel.

The Hall's location and grandeur create the setting for an impressive wedding celebration.

Venue Details

The Law Society
113 Chancery Lane
London
WC2A 1PL
t 020 7320 9555
e events@lawsociety.org.uk
w www.lawsociety.org.uk

Licence authority:
Westminster Register Office
Westminster Council House
Marylebone Road
London
NW1 5PT
t 020 7641 1161
e registeroffice@westminster.gov.uk
w www.westminster.gov.uk

Licensed for ceremony: Reading Room (120)

Function rooms available: The Reading Room (drinks reception 210), The Common Room (reception 200, evening 350), Old Council Chamber and Dining Room (reception 55, evening 130)

Outside space: ✗

Rooms available for overnight accommodation: ✗

Complimentary dressing room for bride available: ✓

SPECIAL NOTES

Licensing hours: Until 11pm (late licence available on application)

Corkage charge: From £10.50

Catering: Requisite caterer; own caterer permitted for a fee

Complimentary menu tasting: ✓

Car parking spaces: Metered parking around venue, free after 6.30pm and 1.30pm on Saturday

Sound/noise restrictions: No restrictions

Fireworks: ✗

Confetti: ✓

Candles: ✓

PA system: ✓

Helicopter landing permission: ✗

Wedding options

The Law Society plays host to weddings year round, and provides delectable seasonal food from their requisite caterers, Charlton House.

Adorned with pink and white flowers, candles and gold accessories, The Law Society can be transformed into a relaxed spring wedding venue, and hold a ceremony and banquet for 120 guests:

The Reading Room is set up with gold high-backed chairs and hurricane lanterns down the side of the aisle; pea lights are entwined in the balcony. For the ceremony, a harpist plays during the bride's entrance, signing of the register and while guests depart the room. Following the ceremony, guests are directed into the bar where champagne and a selection of canapés are served including honey roast fig, marjoram and lemon marinated mozzarella wrapped in prosciutto and roast red pepper and rosary ash goat's cheese puff. The wedding party has photographs on the grand staircase, which is lined with lanterns.

Dinner is announced by the master of ceremonies, and is held in The Common Room. The tables are decorated with white linen, gold napkins, tall glass vases with pink and white bouquets of calla lilies. The wedding breakfast menu consists of smoked salmon, lemon and caper tartare, dill pickled cucumber, horseradish cream and crispy pancetta, roast rack of spring lamb with wild garlic, wilted watercress, spring onion buttered new potatoes, sorrel jus and to finish, baked vanilla cheesecake with mixed berry compote.

After dinner, speeches are held, followed by the cutting of the cake – a three-tiered round fruitcake with pink and white flower detail. Flowing into the evening reception, a Beatles tribute band entertains guests. A buffet is served with cheeseboards and Mediterranean platters.

London Zoo

Fabulous because...

The world's oldest scientific zoo offers animal lovers a choice of event from holding a reception in an animal house to witnessing a bear feed, and all profits are fed back into conservation projects

Location: Regent's Park

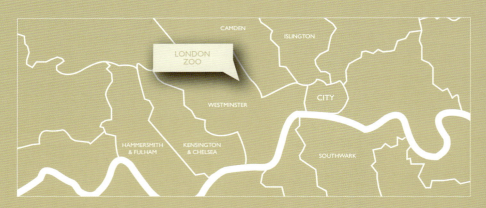

Capacity: Ceremony 210; Wedding breakfast 210; Evening reception 300

Minimum number of guests: 40 (Mappin Pavilion), 100 (Prince Albert Suite)

Guide Price
Per guest (not including venue hire): From £46
Venue hire only: £2,056 – £3,525

When to get married here: All year round

ZSL London Zoo is the world's first scientific zoo. Situated in the beautiful London oasis of Regent's Park it is home to more than 650 different species of animals. A truly exotic wedding venue, it is a one-off location for marrying couples, offering animal-lovers the chance to host their celebrations among creatures great and small.

Located in the grounds of Regent's Park, ZSL London Zoo covers a magnificent 36 acres of grounds and is positioned in the beauteous Regent's Park. Founded in 1826, it is the dwelling place for reptiles, amphibians, mammals and birds alike and plays a leading role in the breeding of endangered animals. Now home to 112 threatened species, carefully recreated environments have been built to house and protect such animals and are a fascinating learning experience for everyone.

ZSL (Zoological Society of London) is a charity, and by holding a wedding at the zoo couples are able to turn their personal celebration into a worthy financial contribution to a cause they believe in. With ZSL running a number of different projects around the globe which assist the preservation of ecosystems, habitats and endangered species, funds can be channelled into conservation projects in a practical and effective way.

ZSL London Zoo offers a bespoke and flexible wedding service, understanding that couples holding their weddings at the zoo have different requirements. Something all couples choose to include in their day is a trip to see the animals themselves. A series of memorable experiences are on offer here from watching hippos getting their teeth brushed to meeting the giraffes close up and feeding them. Visits to wedding suites can also be arranged for some of the more easily transferable animals such as Max the Eagle Owl, Honey the Kinkajou and Pepe the Skunk!

With beautifully landscaped surroundings and an array of animal enclosures and suites, the zoo has many opportunities for those once-in-a-lifetime wedding photographs. With

FOR A FABULOUS CEREMONY AND RECEPTION

A series of memorable experiences are on offer here from watching hippos getting their teeth brushed to meeting the giraffes close up

many suites available for both ceremonies and receptions, the zoo's on-site team will establish which is best suited to a particular wedding while couples are encouraged to tour the zoo when in the planning stages to see the options that are available to them and soak up the vibrant atmosphere.

Although a number of rooms can be made available for reception parties, only a few are suited for the purposes of tying the knot. The first of the venues suitable for the ceremony is the beautiful and versatile Mappin Pavilion; a light and open room that can seat up to 80 guests. A Grade II listed Orangery-style room, it sits in the centre of the zoo and means guests will have to pass through

the zoo's grounds to reach it. Built with several connected full-length French windows, couples are treated to views of the venue's surrounding grass areas as well as the Sloth Bears and Komodo Dragon House that it overlooks. With natural light spilling generously in, spirals are cast across the original 1920s parquet flooring while the rear side permits humbling views of the sun setting in the evening.

If couples time it right, a ceremony here can pre-empt the closure of the zoo. If this is the case, after the ceremony the wedding party can filter out onto the terrace or move into the Komodo Dragon House. Taking advantage of the attractive surroundings for photographs,

Through French windows, couples are treated to views of the Sloth Bears and Komodo Dragon House

the zoo can arrange for guests to view a bear feed while the room is re-set for the wedding breakfast.

The other room available for ceremony hire is the Prince Albert Suite which can seat up to 210 people. This suite can also be used for evening reception celebrations. Classically decorated, it is the first-floor room of a 1930s art deco styled building and backs onto the Members Terrace and Lawn where champagne and canapés are typically served. Illuminated by fairy lights at night, it boasts a sprung wooden dance floor and fixed bar. Decked in funky animal-style prints and with large windows, its licence lasts until midnight but can be extended until 2am for the real party animals.

Another option for a swinging reception is the Raffles Suite. A contemporary location for a wedding breakfast, it is centred in the heart of the zoo's grounds. It has a private courtyard and separate bar area that can provide dining space for up to 80 guests and can be hired from 5pm, making it a great location for evening celebrations with a good area for dancing. Its contemporary design and colours creates a wonderful and fun party venue.

For couples who really want to take advantage of their surroundings, a pre-dinner drinks reception can be held in one of the zoo's animal houses, alongside the creatures' enclosures. There are an array of different exhibits to choose from including the magnificent Gorilla Kingdom, Reptile House and the zoo's tropical exhibit; the Clore Rainforest Lookout. These are only available in the evening once the zoo has closed, and provide a fitting backdrop for a reception like no other.

Venue Details

ZSL London Zoo
Outer Circle
Regent's Park
London NW1 4RY
t 020 7449 6562
e functions@zsl.org
w www.zsl.org

Licence authority:
Westminster Register Office
Westminster Council House
Marylebone Road, London
NW1 5PT
t 020 7641 1161
e registeroffice@westminster.gov.uk
w www.westminster.gov.uk

Licensed for ceremony: Mappin Pavilion
(80), Prince Albert Suite (210)

Function rooms available: Mappin Pavilion (reception 80, evening 150),
Prince Albert Suite (reception 210, evening 300), Raffles Suite (reception 80, evening 160),
Member's Terrace and Lawn (drinks reception 300), Barclay Court (drinks reception 300),
Lion Terraces (drinks reception 300), Reptile House (drinks reception 300), B.U.G.S
(drinks reception 300), Komodo Dragon House (drinks reception 100), Gorilla
Kingdom (drinks reception 120), Clore Rainforest Lookout (drinks reception 100)

Outside space: The zoo grounds include
numerous terraces and lawns

Option of a marquee: ✓

Rooms available for overnight accommodation: ✗

Complimentary dressing room for bride available: ✗

SPECIAL NOTES

Licensing hours: Until midnight (late licence available on
application for Prince Albert Suite and Raffles Suite)

Corkage charge: Wines and champagne only.
Please enquire for prices

Catering: In-house with exceptions for specialist menus

Complimentary menu tasting: ✓

Car parking spaces: Main car park 250 (fee applicable)

Sound/noise restrictions: No amplified music outside for
the protection of the animals. The zoo reserves the right to
ask for volumes to be lowered if they feel they are too loud

Fireworks: ✗

Confetti: ✓ (biodegradable only, no fresh petals)

Candles: ✓ (restrictions apply)

PA system: In Prince Albert Suite and Raffles Suite,
not in Mappin Pavilion

Helicopter landing permission: ✗

Wedding options

ZSL London Zoo offers a venue that is as wild or as tame as the couple. The zoo's dedicated team will guide couples through every stage of the planning process, first establishing which is the best suite for each individual occasion. All weddings are planned on a bespoke basis with a wedding planner on hand.

The team will show couples the numerous options available to them to find the right combination. A tour around the zoo doesn't just involve looking at suites, couples may also catch the animals being fed – not a usual wedding venue! Once the choice of suite is established, the team will assist in planning the timings for the day, including guests' Animal Encounter.

In addition to this encounter, after a late afternoon ceremony at either the Mappin Pavilion or the Prince Albert Suite, couples can hold a drinks reception in one of the animal areas, including the Lion Terraces, Gorilla Kingdom, the Reptile House, B.U.G.S, Clore Rainforest Lookout and Komodo Dragon House. These are only available one hour after zoo closing (from 6.30pm) and have restricted options for catering. The Lion Terraces, Clore Rainforest Lookout and Gorilla Kingdom can be hired out in the summer only.

The events team can assist in choosing the right menu and wines to match, created by their internal caterer. They can also offer advice on coordinating the theme, flowers and entertainment.

ZSL London Zoo is owned by the charity ZSL. Holding your wedding at the zoo ensures a vitally important contribution to conserving the planet's wildlife.

LSO St Luke's

Fabulous because...

Owned by the London Symphony Orchestra, this converted church is home to an elegant and surprisingly modern interior, whilst retaining some of its original features

Location: The City

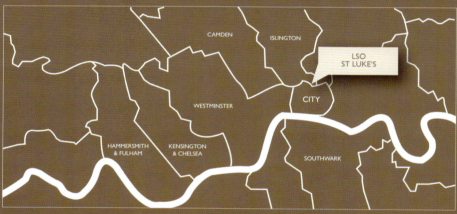

Capacity: **Civil partnership ceremony 360;**
Wedding breakfast 250; Evening reception 360

Minimum number of guests: **None**

Guide Price
Per guest (including venue hire): **Not available**
Venue hire only: **£4,994 – £7,346**

When to get married here: **All year round**

LSO St Luke's is an award winning conversion of an eighteenth-century Hawksmoor church situated off Old Street in the City of London and has been the home of London Symphony Orchestra's educational programme since 2003. The Grade I listed church's impressive traditional outer façade is married with an elegant modern interior, surprising guests as they step into a contemporary and distinctive space. This well-appointed venue can offer couples a flexible space to hold a lavish wedding breakfast, in a setting that has been decorated to their tastes. Music lovers will appreciate the scope of performers gracing LSO St Luke's, ranging from Elton John, Sting and Bruce Springsteen to the London Sinfonietta, Asian Music Circuit and Aled Jones.

Consecrated in 1733, St Luke's was one of the last churches to be constructed in the City of London due to the Churches Act of 1711. The following centuries saw St Luke's endure severe subsidence and structural unrest so that by 1959, the building was declared unsafe. The church was gutted and only the spire remained, leaving the interior exposed to the elements. In the mid-1990s the LSO raised the idea of rebuilding the disused Hawksmoor church of St Luke's close to the Orchestra's home at the Barbican as a base for the LSO Discovery music education programme, and an £18 million renovation ensued.

The result is a glorious contemporary interior, warmed by many eighteenth-century details. The new structure and galleries are a defiantly modern intervention, so the building's architecture reflects the layers of its unique history. The church clock has been renovated and the flaming golden dragon restored to the top of the spire. The heart of the building, the Jerwood Hall, is now an adaptable entertaining space, with lofty ceilings and steel columns. Keeping the rough texture of the original brickwork brings warmth to this minimalist room, and lighting can be cast upon it to create myriad atmospheres around the room. A balcony surrounds the higher level of the hall with two stylish spiral staircases that lead you down to the hall's wooden floor.

FOR A FABULOUS CEREMONY AND RECEPTION

The Grade I listed church's impressive traditional outer façade is married with an elegant modern interior

Its lofty ceilings are an additional space for creativity – in the past, giant butterflies, chandeliers and even aerialists have all been suspended from the beams. Huge glazed windows surround the hall and provide an abundance of natural light. These can be dramatically lit at dusk, while electronic blinds provide the opportunity to block out the light for atmospheric events. They also ensure that the space is soundproofed so music can be enjoyed fully.

This distinctive space can host dinners for up to 250 guests, and standing receptions for 360 and hosts many formal receptions. The adaptability of the space also means smaller dinners are not swamped by the vastness: the space can be divided by plants or screens to create a drinks reception area, a stage for musicians and a dance floor. Dinners of 80 can enjoy the hall's atmosphere, while more guests are able to join the celebrations for a larger evening reception, or a standing canapé reception.

The lower level of LSO St Luke's houses a cafe which provides a flexible space to hold a drinks reception for up to 150 people before commencing dinner. This area can also be used to hold children's entertainment during speeches in the main Hall. The Green Room, a valuable accompanying room, provides a place for the bride and groom to use throughout the day, with its own en-suite facility.

Outside, the charming churchyard area is perfect for wedding photography as the church's eighteenth-

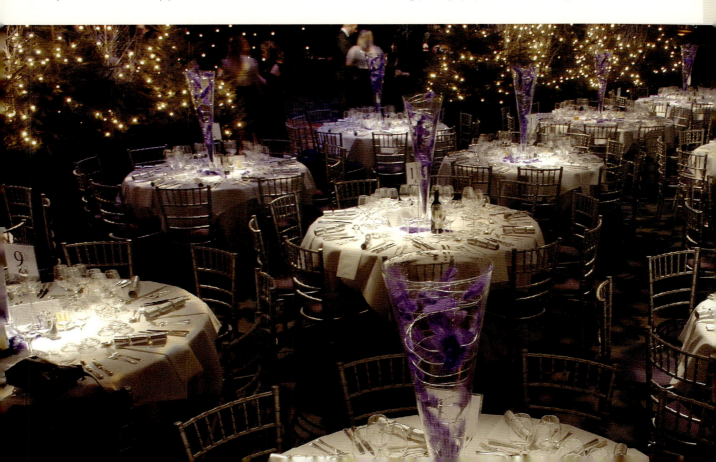

The exterior is lit up at night, highlighting the magnificent architecutre and welcoming winter guests

century architecture stands as the backdrop. The exterior is also lit up at night, highlighting the magnificent architecture and welcoming guests in the winter.

Having been a function venue since its renovation it is only recently that LSO St Luke's has acquired a civil partnership licence.

As LSO St Luke's works as a musical performance space, they offer extensive PA equipment and a technical team experienced in assuring quality sound and lighting for events is always on hand. Their engineers can adapt the lighting of the venue to complement the time of day and mood of the event. This accommodating space also includes a Steinway

D Concert Grand Piano, specially selected for the Jerwood Hall and maintained by Steinway & Sons.

LSO St Luke's recommended caterers are practised in all aspects of creating the perfect day, and can provide flower arrangements, decorations, additional seating and those all-important details that are essential when creating a unique and memorable event.

The distinctive Jerwood Hall is a very unique space for couples to personalise, and will surprise guests, being found inside this beautiful church.

Venue Details

LSO St Luke's
UBS and LSO Music Education Centre
161 Old Street
London
EC1V 9NG
t 020 7490 3939
e lsostlukes@lso.co.uk
w www.lso.co.uk

Licence authority:
Islington Town Hall
Upper Street
London
N1 2UD
t 020 7527 6350
e registrars@islington.gov.uk
w www.islington.gov.uk

Licensed spaces: Jerwood Hall (360, civil partnerships only)
Function rooms available: Jerwood Hall (reception 250, evening 360), Crypt Café (drinks reception 120)
Outside space: Churchyard
Option of a marquee: ✗
Rooms available for overnight accommodation: ✗
Complimentary dressing room for bride available: ✓

SPECIAL NOTES

Licensing hours: Until midnight (late licence available on application)
Corkage charge: Dependent on caterer
Catering: Recommended companies
Complimentary menu tasting: Dependent on caterer
Car parking spaces: Barbican NCP nearby
Sound/noise restrictions: Music permitted until 11pm
Fireworks: ✗
Confetti: ✗
Candles: ✓ (restrictions apply)
PA system: ✓
Helicopter landing permission: ✗

Wedding options

LSO St Luke's is a venue full of potential and its spaces can be adapted for weddings held in any season:

For a summer wedding reception for 80 guests, Jerwood Hall can be transformed into a floral themed banqueting room, with palm trees dividing the hall into drinks reception and dining spaces. The hall's lighting will change throughout the evening depending on the areas used and time of day.

Following a ceremony elsewhere or a civil partnership ceremony at LSO St Luke's, the couple have photographs taken in the churchyard area. Meanwhile guests enter through the south entrance, either side of tall flower arrangements to be greeted by a champagne and canapé reception in the area coined off by palm trees, as a string quartet plays.

Guests take their seats at round tables and the top table is situated under the east window, framed by flowers. A four-course dinner followed by coffee and petit fours is prepared and served by one of the venue's accredited caterers. During dinner, the band sets up on stage in the reception area and a bar area and evening buffet are also set up in reception area, before more guests arrive after speeches for the evening.

A winter wedding at LSO St Luke's can make use of the Crypt Café, providing a cosy drinks reception venue, before entering the hall for a banquet seating up to 150 people.

Once again guests would enter through the South entrance where flambeaux flank the door. Guests are directed down to drinks reception in Crypt Café which is set up with flowers and additional lighting, in keeping with the theme of the event. Post-drinks reception, the couple could bring in children's entertainer in the Crypt Café space. Guests make their way up to Jerwood Hall, where a group photograph is taken (using dramatic structure of balconies) before being seated for dinner. During the three-course wedding breakfast, a pianist plays the Steinway Grand and a small band sets up in dance area at the back of the hall.

Mandarin Oriental Hyde Park London

Fabulous because...

Situated in the heart of Knightsbridge adjacent to Hyde Park, this acclaimed hotel mixes contemporary Western opulence with distinctive Asian service

Location: Knightsbridge

Capacity: Ceremony 250; Wedding breakfast 250; Evening reception 400

Minimum number of guests: None

Guide Price
Per guest (not including venue hire): From £60
Venue hire guide price: From £1,000

When to get married here: All year round

Standing tall in the heart of cosmopolitan Knightsbridge, Mandarin Oriental Hyde Park London also backs onto Hyde Park and lies in a serene and rural location. Over 100 years old, its exterior is spectacular; an imposing building that is fully lit at night and whose entrance faces out towards some of London's most feted stores, including Harvey Nichols. A bastion of luxury, the hotel has a unique design and has long been a haven for the rich, the famous and the royals.

An ideal venue for couples wanting to experience splendour with an Oriental flavour, the interior of the building displays a multiplicity of colour and fabric which merges traditional Victorian design with modern opulence. Having played host to the legendary Balaclava Ball in 1948 it is a venue which knows how to celebrate in style; mixing tranquil views accross peaceful gardens with an array of historic interiors.

Well versed in good service, weddings taking place here benefit from an experienced events team which will look after every aspect of the wedding from conception to finish. Offering unique extras such as the Wedding Belles programme which offers brides-to-be a three-part spa package in advance of their big day, Mandarin Oriental Hyde Park is well equipped to deal with all the specifics of a wedding.

On arrival at the hotel, couples wishing to make a grand entrance into the venue will not be disappointed. Having long since had an association with the Household Cavalry, the events team can arrange for couples to arrive in a horse-drawn carriage from anywhere within a two mile radius! Offering a number of different suites suitable for both ceremony and reception, Mandarin Oriental Hyde Park London can provide for parties of different sizes with each room offering a distinct twist on the hotel's general style of décor.

Particularly spectacular, the Ballroom is a licensed space that can seat up to 250, doubling as a fantastic reception space. The main venue for Baroness Thatcher's 80th birthday celebrations, it passed into legend when Her Majesty and the late Princess Margaret first learned to dance on what is now one of London's only sprung dance floors.

FOR A FABULOUS CEREMONY AND RECEPTION

The Ballroom's 24-carat gilding shimmers
in the natural daylight which pours in

Passing into the Ballroom is a sight to behold. With a gleaming chequered marble floor that leads up a staircase to the bright red-carpeted reception room, parties will pass under glittering circular chandeliers before emerging before the stunning main room. Having recently undergone a £1 million restoration programme, the room is most notable for the newly woven carpet which was inspired by the powder blue of the London sky and the lush green of Hyde Park's gardens and foliage. Suitably positioned to overlook the Park, the carpet's colours are beautifully offset by white walls and glass windows which grant the room a sunny and airy feel. A wash of 24-carat gold gilding shimmers in the natural daylight while table settings sparkle in the sunshine which pours in.

Further down the hall is The Loggia, a favourite room for more intimate weddings. Famed for its royal entrance, it is said that as a private 'Gentleman's Club' the original entrance was through The Loggia; however, when the building re-opened as the Hyde Park Hotel in 1902, the postal address changed from Albert Gate to 66 Knightsbridge. Tradition has it that as the Queen would not allow any form of advertising in the park itself, she insisted the main entrance be moved from the park side to Knightsbridge, preserving the original opening for royal use alone.

Following the extension of this privilege during the coronation of George VI in 1937, parties can now take part in this grand tradition by requesting permission from the Royal Parks for use of the entrance for weddings.

For couples marrying in the Loggia, Mandarin Oriental Hyde Park London's events team will go all out to make good use of the room's location. While guests can be seated in rows facing the immaculate royal entrance, couples may pass through a trim walkway that takes in the park's stunning landscape before entering

From the building's cupola with a modern black and white design and gilded top the beautiful sights of the Park can be viewed stretching beyond the treetops

the cool and circular room gorgeously decorated in a shade of green. Wooden floors and plush, sweeping curtains complete this look while a gilded chandelier draws attention to the centre point of the room that falls perfectly in line with the makeshift walkthrough.

With two other suites available for both ceremony and reception, Mandarin Oriental Hyde Park offers couples much choice, with each wedding party organised on a bespoke basis. Other rooms available include The Carlyle Suite and The Rosebery Room which have a unique decorative scheme that incorporates vast windows, chandeliers and exotic print carpets with classic prime-colour design.

Whichever room couples decide to use, they can also take advantage of Mandarin Oriental Hyde Park's beauteous surroundings after their ceremony. Permission from Royal Parks along with a donation will enable the wedding pictures to be taken with a stunning country backdrop while in the very heart of London. In addition to this the venue itself houses many exotic gems and from the building's cupola, with a modern black and white design and gilded top, the beautiful sights of the Park can be viewed stretching beyond the treetops.

To finish the day, the bride and groom retire to an opulent complimentary suite for their first night. This haven is richly furnished with spectacular views and can be prepared with scented candle-lit baths. The hotel offers a further 197 rooms for guests to also retire to bed in style.

FOR A FABULOUS CEREMONY AND RECEPTION

Venue Details

Mandarin Oriental Hyde Park London
66 Knightsbridge
London SW1X 7LA
t 020 7235 2000
e molon-events@mohg.com
w www.mandarinoriental.com

Licence authority:
Westminster Register Office
Westminster Council House
Marylebone Road
London
NW1 5PT
t 020 7641 1161
e registeroffice@westminster.gov.uk
w www.westminster.gov.uk

Licensed for ceremony: The Ballroom (250), The Carlyle
Suite (60), The Rosebery Room (60), The Loggia (40)

Function rooms available: The Ballroom (reception 250,
evening 400), The Carlyle Suite (reception 150,
evening 250), The Rosebery Room (reception 60,
evening 150), The Asquith Room (reception 30,
evening 70), The Loggia (reception 30, evening 70),
The Balfour Room (reception 30, evening 70)

Outside space: ✗

Option of a marquee: ✗

Rooms available for overnight accommodation: 198

Room rates: From £525

Complimentary dressing room for bride available: ✓

SPECIAL NOTES

Licensing hours: Until 1am

Corkage charge: Corkage not permitted

Catering: In-house

Complimentary menu tasting: ✓

Car parking spaces: Nearby NCP car park

Sound/noise restrictions: Amplified live music permitted
until midnight. Soft background music between midnight
and 1am permitted

Fireworks: ✗

Confetti: ✓

Candles: ✓

PA system: ✓ (can be arranged)

Helicopter landing permission: ✗

Wedding options

**Every wedding at Mandarin Oriental Hyde Park
is tailored to the individual.**

Personal event specialists are on hand to discuss everything from banqueting rooms to flower arrangements to menus over afternoon tea, at a time convenient for the couple. Floral requirements can be discussed with the hotel's master florist, and elegantly printed menu cards are supplied for each guest. The team will also discuss couples' precise entertainment needs and assist in the selection process as required.

On the day itself, guests arrive through The Ballroom Entrance on Knightsbridge while the bridal party can choose to arrive via the Royal Entrance to The Loggia. Traditional doormen would be stationed at The Ballroom Entrance to offer guests a warm welcome.

When the day draws to a close, Mandarin Oriental Hyde Park invites the bride and groom to spend the first night of their honeymoon in a complimentary overnight room, with an upgrade to the best available accommodation.

Wedding Belles

The award-winning spa at Mandarin Oriental offers a three-step luxurious Wedding Belles package. Ideal for brides-to-be, the programme consists of three treatments spread over a two-month pre-wedding period to ensure a radiant wedding day glow. Detoxification begins with a Purifying Programme to cleanse and re-energise, followed two weeks before the wedding by an Oriental Ritual to revitalise and re-hydrate the skin. Two days before the wedding, the ultimate in relaxation completes the programme. Oriental Harmony is a thoroughly relaxing massage with two therapists who massage the body in synchrony to uplift the mind, energise the body and leave skin exotically fragrant. As a gift for the honeymoon, wedding belles will float home with a bath and body oil from the spa's Signature Product range.

Mint Leaf

Fabulous because...

This Asian inspired restaurant is acclaimed for its gutsy modern Indian cuisine in a flamboyant, distinctively designed post-modern space

Location: **Haymarket**

CAMDEN
ISLINGTON
MINT LEAF
CITY
WESTMINSTER
HAMMERSMITH & FULHAM
KENSINGTON & CHELSEA
SOUTHWARK

Capacity: **Ceremony 80; Wedding breakfast 220; Evening reception 450**

Minimum number of guests: **20**

Guide Price
Per guest (not including venue hire): **Not available**
Venue hire only: **Minimum spend £2,000**

When to get married here: **Autumn/Winter**

The restaurant is decked throughout in dark mahogany panels and angular features which are lit by innovative fibre optic lighting

Mint Leaf has been hailed as one of London's most stylish and contemporary restaurants and offers a completely unique experience for couples wishing to hold their wedding ceremony, civil partnership or reception in a distinctively different venue. Located in the heart of the West End, just off the Haymarket, Mint Leaf is an underground oasis of tranquillity, surrounding guests with sleek surfaces and luxurious designs.

Famous for its exceptional modern Indian cuisine, the distinctly stylish décor of the interior contrasts with the culinary spices. The restaurant, formerly a bank vault, comprises a bar area, large dining room, and, hidden at the back of the venue, the Jaipur Room, a private events space. Couples can have exclusive use of the whole of this atmospheric venue throughout the day, from the ceremony through to an Indian inspired banquet, or they can opt to use the Jaipur Room for a smaller event. The venue is decked throughout in dark mahogany panels, black and brown furnishings and angular features which are

lit by discreet and innovative fibre optic lighting: down lighting illuminates seemingly dark areas, to create a mystic ambience.

From Suffolk Place, guests enter through black doors, set against the white Portland stone of the outer façade. Down stairs and through a minimalist, smart reception area, they enter the striking lounge that stretches down the side of the restaurant, with its 20m bar and over 500 illuminated bottles of spirits. Holding a cocktail reception here is fabulous – couples can make the most of more than 1,000 cocktail options from Mint Leaf's experienced team of mixologists. Uruguayan grey slate walls and the amalgamation of metal and wood creates an impressive space to receive guests and gather before moving through to a ceremony or wedding breakfast.

Through the restaurant, the Jaipur Room is situated. This space is licensed for wedding ceremonies and can accommodate up to 80 people in a theatre style. Continuing the dark wood theme, the space appears larger due to mirror panels along the back wall. The dark décor contrasts with the bright splashes of pinks and purples in the mounted artwork, and exotic flower pieces work wonderfully to decorate the

FOR A FABULOUS CEREMONY AND RECEPTION

Exotic flower pieces work wonderfully to decorate the space, in keeping with its edgy style

space, in-keeping with its edgy style. This room can also be used to hold a drinks reception for up to 100 guests before entering dinner in the main restaurant, or alternatively, can be transformed to hold a wedding breakfast for 60 while guests adjourn to the bar area.

The restaurant itself is a spacious room divided into three intimate and extravagant areas by dark-wood slates that resemble giant Venetian blinds. Tables can be arranged to fit any capacity from 20 up to 220 diners. The dark wood tables themselves need no decorating necessarily, but couples are welcome to add their own touches to the restaurant's décor, with linens, floral arrangements and table decorations. Hailed for its fine Indian cuisine, the head chef takes much inspiration from the northern regions of India. Delicate flavours, light textures and stunning presentation blend to ensure wedding parties enjoy a contemporary and unusual wedding breakfast menu.

The atmosphere and flexibility of the restaurant make it an ideal evening reception venue. The central section of the restaurant can be cleared to house a band, with space for dancing, while other guests can enjoy the entertainment from their seats. Alternatively, a DJ could set up in the Jaipur Room to create a 'mini nightclub' area within the restaurant.

Mint Leaf provides an experienced in-house team to meet couples' requirements and can provide a bespoke package to suit any mood. They will organise the hiring of entertainment, arrange for fresh flower displays, and erect a dance floor and a PA system if required.

Described in *Tatler* for being 'as remarkable for its flamboyant, post modern Indian design as for its gutsy, evolved cooking', Mint Leaf was recently named the Best London Restaurant at the British Curry Awards 2007.

Venue Details

Mint Leaf
Suffolk Place
Haymarket
London
SW1Y 4HX
t 020 7930 9020
e reservations@mintleafrestaurant.com
w www.mintleafrestaurant.com

Licence authority:
Westminster Register Office
Westminster Council House
Marylebone Road
London
NW1 5PT
t 020 7641 1161
e registeroffice@westminster.gov.uk
w www.westminster.gov.uk

Licensed for ceremony: Jaipur Room (80)

Function rooms available: Exclusive hire (reception 220, evening 450), Jaipur Room (reception 60, evening 100)

Outside space: ✗

Rooms available for overnight accommodation: ✗

Complimentary dressing room for bride available: ✗

SPECIAL NOTES

Licensing hours: Monday to Wednesday until midnight, Thursday to Saturday until 1am (late licence available on application)

Corkage charge: Wine £15, champagne £25

Catering: In-house

Complimentary menu tasting: ✓

Car parking spaces: ✗

Sound/noise restrictions: No restrictions

Fireworks: ✗

Confetti: ✓

Candles: ✓

PA system: ✓

Helicopter landing permission: ✗

Wedding options

This atmospheric restaurant can be hired exclusively, or couples can solely hire the Jaipur Room for a dinner for 60 guests.

A typical wedding at the restaurant might be decorated with lilies and dark green foliage, and candles placed throughout. Cocktails such as a Very Berry and an Apple Mojito are served whilst guests await the arrival of the bride and groom. Guests then move through to the Jaipur Room for the ceremony.

After, photographs are taken in the lounge bar, and champagne and cocktails are served while the Jaipur Room is prepared for dinner and the DJ sets up. Guests can choose from a variety of freshly made cocktails available.

The banqueting manager announces dinner, the party moves to the Jaipur Room which has dark mahogany tables with red rose petals and floating candles. Menus are printed on gold tinted paper rolled up and tied with red ribbon.

Example menu:

- Grilled lobster spiced with Bengali mustard
- Whole wild catch jumbo prawns in garlic chilli sauce
- Tandoor roasted rack of lamb marinated in spicy yoghurt with Indian cottage cheese with assorted pimentos, chicken biryani, naan
- Rose flavoured white chocolate mousse with mixed berries

Guests return to the bar while the room is transformed into an evening venue. A Proctor screen in the back of the function room plays a DVD of photographs of bride and groom as a backdrop as more reception guests arrive.

Platters containing various canapés and small bites are offered to guests along with the wedding cake served canapé style. Confetti is thrown over the bride and groom as they leave the reception.

Northbrook Park

Fabulous because...

This beautiful eighteenth-century country house is set in 120 acres of parkland and charming grounds providing a wonderful rural haven on the doorstep of the capital

Location: Farnham, Surrey

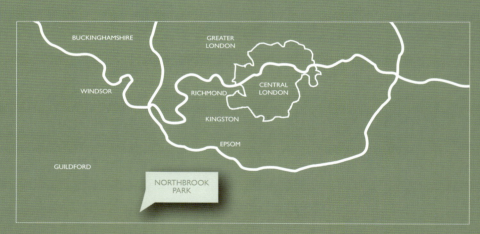

Capacity: Ceremony 200; Wedding breakfast 250; Evening reception 300

Minimum number of guests: **None**

Guide Price
Per guest (not including venue hire): **Catering from £55**
Venue hire only: **£4,500 – £9,000**

When to get married here: **All year round**

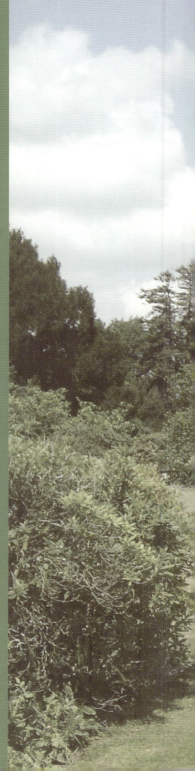

Bordering Surrey and Hampshire, Northbrook Park is a spacious delight found outside of London, set in 120 acres of parkland. This Grade II listed eighteenth-century manor house is privately owned and can be hired exclusively for wedding celebrations. The peaceful property is an idyllic setting for Londoners to make the most of the countryside on their doorstep: peacocks roam the grounds while guests meander through charming walled gardens adorned with climbing roses.

Northbrook Park is fitting for both the ceremony and reception and couples have exclusive use of the rooms and gardens for their wedding, the only distraction coming from the wildlife and white doves in the gardens. The site boasts a standing marquee that facilitates larger parties, and the use of the enchanting Vine Room, with its tall windows and views of the grounds. Its two walled gardens not only provide an exquisite backdrop to wedding photography but are a wonderful setting for guests to enjoy a country garden and its romantic ambience. Northbrook's charming gardens are kept by a full time gardener who maintains the grounds' pristine condition throughout the year.

Guests approach the house from a grand drive, lined with clusters of daffodils in the spring, and are given an impressive first glimpse of the grand country house. The drive circles a flagpole, which can be raised on arrival with the couple's chosen flag.

The entrance opens into the Vine Room, the perfect space for an elegant ceremony, holding up to 200 guests. Polished white marble floors and whitewashed walls with delicate vine-leafed engravings create a classic room, detailed with a stone fireplace and two crystal chandeliers. French windows, all of which can be opened in the summer, let in an abundance of light, and the room enjoys triple-aspect views over the terrace and grounds. Underfloor heating, open fireplace and delicate up-lighting make the Vine Room very enticing for a winter wedding. There is also a delightful terrace for guests to gather and take in the views over Northbrook's landscaped grounds.

Peacocks roam the grounds while guests meander through charming walled gardens adorned with climbing roses

French doors at the end of the Vine Room open onto the Nun's Garden. This is a delightful walled garden with two water features and a large magnolia tree providing welcome shade in the summertime, making it an idyllic space to hold a drinks reception while the Vine Room is being prepared for dinner. Wisteria and mature climbing roses scale the reclaimed brick walls; in spring shrubs burst through the soil and in the summer, the garden is in full bloom. Northbrook has thoughtfully provided the Garden Room, a permanent structure found through a door in the Nun's Garden, lest bad weather ensues. While the Nun's Garden is available for those choosing to hold their reception in the Vine Room, through a wooden door, another garden is discovered.

The Secret Garden is reminiscent of the children's book's delights, with its sunken central lawn, mature fruit trees and multitude of scents. A herbaceous bed borders the lawn, including rosemary, lavender and bay leaf trees, producing a pleasing aroma all year round. Mistletoe entwines apple and plum trees' branches, and discreet lighting illuminates the foliage, while overhead spotlights make evening use of the garden possible. A small paved area provides the ideal space for musicians to serenade a drinks reception, with the use of an electric point. In the past, various blessings have occurred in the sunken garden, after the civil ceremony takes place in the Vine Room. Couples can use this as an enchanting additional space in conjunction with the Vine Room, and this is included when couples use the marquee.

*The bride and groom can be chauffeured through the grounds,
up a private track, to a secluded wooden chalet*

Through a garden door at the end of the Secret Garden, the marquee is found. It has wooden and carpeted floors, and can accommodate individual tastes to suit any theme. The marquee can hold a dinner for up to 250 guests and includes a dance floor. Couples hiring the marquee have use of all areas, from the Vine Room through to the Secret Garden.

Northbrook Park has chosen their recommended caterer, who has over 20 years of culinary experience, and will ensure the menu is perfect for your occasion. They can provide champagne and wine, but also do not charge corkage so couples can supply their own drinks. If couples choose to use an alternative caterer, an additional charge of 15% of the venue hire is required.

The venue also has a secreted chalet ideal for a perfect first night together. Whisked away from the party, the bride and groom can be chauffeured through the grounds, up a private track, to a secluded wooden chalet. Here, they can spend their first night in comfort, and wake the next morning to stunning views over a lake and Surrey hillsides. Northbrook Park also enquires into the newlyweds' preferred breakfast preferences to makes sure the lodge is supplied with delicious choices for breakfast.

In the main house there are rooms for the bride and her bridesmaids to get ready, accessible from 10am on the morning of the wedding. The large en-suite double bedroom and twin room, as well as a sitting room, all have impressive views of the grounds and traditional furnishings. From here, the bride is able to go straight down into the Vine Room for the ceremony and has access to these rooms all day.

FOR A FABULOUS CEREMONY AND RECEPTION

Venue Details

Northbrook Park
Farnham nr Bentley
Surrey
GU10 5EU
t 01420 525 084
e info@northbrookpark.co.uk
w www.northbrookpark.co.uk

Licence authority:
Alton Register Office
4 Queens Road
Alton
GU34 1HU
t 01420 85410
e alton.registrars@hants.gov.uk
w www.hants.gov.uk

Licensed for ceremony: The Vine Room (200)

Function rooms available: Vine Room (reception 120, evening 180), Marquee (reception 250, evening 300)

Outside space: Terrace and walled gardens

Option of a marquee: ✓

Rooms available for overnight accommodation: Chalet

Room rates: £250

Complimentary dressing room for bride available: ✓

SPECIAL NOTES

Licensing hours: Until 11.30pm

Corkage charge: No charge

Catering: Requisite caterer, own caterer permitted for a fee

Complimentary menu tasting: ✓

Car parking spaces: 100

Sound/noise restrictions: Music permitted until 11pm at 92 decibels

Fireworks: ✗

Confetti: ✓

Candles: ✓

PA system: ✗

Helicopter landing permission: ✓

Wedding options

Northbrook Park ensures that couples have the use of the venue exclusively. Beside the stylish architecture and beautiful gardens, the venue can accommodate any style of wedding imagined. The venue's caterer, Occasional Cuisine, can accommodate all styles of celebration.

Last summer, Northbrook Park played host to the most spectacular brown and turquoise themed wedding in their marquee, with everything from coloured glassware and linen on the tables, a luxurious bar area and a fabulous circular sofa with a stunning palm tree in the centre.

This year, the venue began their wedding season with an Indian themed wedding. The bride and groom choose to hold a christening blessing for their three-month-old son, after the civil ceremony, with a harpist playing in the gardens.

A delicious menu of Indian food and fine champagnes followed. The couple organised a 'fairyland' for the children, with a magician, balloon modelling and a chocolate fountain on display in the gardens. Meanwhile, their parents enjoyed a sumptuous banquet in the specially illuminated marquee. Thereafter, all the guests were entertained by Malaysian dancers – a truly tropical experience.

The newly-weds stayed over night in the secluded chalet where they watched their very own special video diary, filmed throughout the wedding day with friends seated on a scarlet sofa in the shape of a pair of lips!

Old Royal Naval College

Fabulous because...

Standing prominently on the banks of the River Thames, this architecturally magnificent myriad of buildings abounds with history and artistic wonder

Location: Greenwich

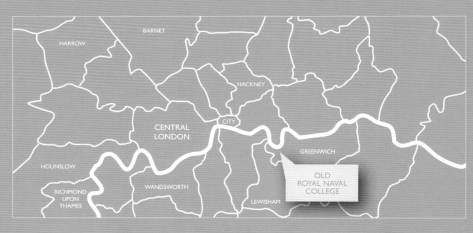

Capacity: Ceremony 200; Wedding breakfast 480; Evening reception 480

Minimum number of guests: 20

Guide Price
Per guest (not including venue hire): From £65
Venue hire only: £1,175 – £5,288

When to get married here: All year round

Set upon the banks of the River Thames at Greenwich, the Old Royal Naval College is a sight to behold. Classic Baroque architecture, coupled with the precision of the lawns and courtyards makes this venue not only spectacular, but also inherently regal. Its expanse of rooms provides couples with a very flexible venue, steeped in history and grandeur. Symmetrically designed around the broad vista from the river to the Queen's House, the Old Royal Naval College is a spectacular architectural myriad of buildings and rooms, looking out onto the Thames and the City beyond and intentionally built backing onto Greenwich Park.

Next to the Cutty Sark and sitting below the Royal Observatory, the site that the Old Royal Naval College now stands upon has a rich history even before its creation in the seventeenth century. In Tudor times, Henry VIII's favourite palace, Greenwich Palace, lay here, his birthplace as well as that of his daughters Mary and Elizabeth.

Following heavy casualties at the Battle of La Hogue in 1692, Queen Mary II hoped to commission the building of a hospital for naval pensioners. After her sudden death, her husband realised this desire on her behalf and commissioned Sir Christopher Wren and diarist and former naval officer John Evelyn to action the planning. Begun in the 1690s, the Royal Hospital for Seamen (commonly known as the Greenwich Hospital) was completed in 1752 and served as a hospital for retired and injured sailors. Over the years, some of Britain's finest architects, such as Nicholas Hawksmoor, Inigo Jones and John Yenn have contributed to the construction to ensure Wren's original design was realised.

As the nineteenth century wore on, with peace established, numbers of naval pensioners declined and the Hospital finally closed in 1869. Soon after this the Royal Naval College moved in heralding a new beginning for the site as a naval training centre for officers from around the world. In 1998 the Royal Navy departed for its new base at Shrivenham and responsibility for the College passed to the newly established Greenwich Foundation, a charitable organisation. The Greenwich Foundation began a £34 million renovation project, and welcomed its first tenants, the University of

Classic Baroque architecture, coupled with the precision of the lawns and courtyards, make this venue inherently regal

Greenwich and subsequently Trinity College of Music. The buildings now stand proud as one of the most extensive groups of public buildings in the Baroque style in Britain and are the only ones built for charitable public purposes, rather than to glorify personal status.

For couples choosing this location for their special day, both a ceremony and reception can be held in either the grand Painted Hall or the more intimate Admiral's House – the College is able to accommodate parties from as few as 20 to as many as 200 guests for a ceremony and 480 for a spectacular reception. The flexibility of the venue is clear, as there are also numerous other spaces perfect for an evening reception, and plentiful outside space for photography

Arriving at one of the two grand entrances, or even by boat, guests are greeted by the College's immaculate grounds; passing through the beautiful lawns, courtyards and colonnades, below the domed tops of the two central buildings which overlook the grounds.

Sir James Thornhill's masterpiece, the Painted Hall, is a breathtaking work of art. The artist was commissioned in 1708 to paint this vast space, and finally completed it in 1727. The result was spectacular: two halls, the larger Lower Hall and the raised Upper Hall, both with ceiling frescoes. The Lower Hall abounds in light, with high arched windows on both sides surrounded by tromp l'oeil painting, and a ceiling themed with images of the triumph of Peace and Liberty over Tyranny and tributes to King William III and his wife Queen Mary II and British maritime power. An archway, bedecked in gold, leads through into the Upper Hall where

The Lower Hall abounds in light, with high arched windows on both sides surrounded by tromp l'oeil painting

walls are filled with glorified images of Queen Anne, surveying the continents of the world and her successor, George I.

Couples can hold both their ceremony and wedding breakfast in these spectacular surroundings. Large, oak tables are situated at diagonals down two sides of the Lower Hall and in the Upper Hall. These beautiful, robust tables and their sturdy benches are very heavy and not often moved. The tables are adorned with hefty, silver candelabras, needing no tablecloth and little decoration, contrasting beautifully with the magnificence of the ceiling above. The black and white chequered floor contrasts with the original ceiling frescos. At full capacity, the Hall can sit up to 480 guests, the Upper Hall seating 128 while the Lower Hall seats 350.

It is common for couples to hold their ceremony in the Lower Hall, standing on the steps under the archway with their guests seated in a semi-circular theatre style. Afterwards they may enjoy a drinks reception either in the colonnades outside or in the Lower Hall in autumn and winter months. Then, returning to the Upper Hall for the wedding breakfast, the top table will be positioned along the back wall. For parties of around 100, this makes use of the Painted Hall's spaces, without it feeling too large for the occasion. Ceremonies can only be held in the Painted Hall after 4.30pm since it is open for visitors before this time.

Using the Lower Hall for the wedding breakfast, an additional 80 guests can be seated on round tables down the centre of the room. Another option is the venue's caterers' creation, The Chef's Table. This is served on round tables placed down the Lower Hall, each table with a different course containing platters of food, including a carvery table, seafood selection, salads and desserts.

FOR A FABULOUS CEREMONY AND RECEPTION

The buildings now stand proud as one of the most extensive groups of public buildings in the Baroque style in Britain

There is ample space for musicians to play during the ceremony and wedding breakfast, and they could be positioned on the steps between Lower and Upper Halls. Dancing is not allowed in the Painted Hall due to its historic nature, so couples have the option of descending below the hall into the King William Restaurant, or down through the chalk walk to the newly refurbished Queen Mary Undercroft (hire of an additional room is included in the Painted Hall hire price).

In a separate part of the College, on the river front, the Admiral's House is found. This is a self contained series of rooms forming part of the King Charles building. This venue is ideal for up to 50 guests for both the ceremony and wedding breakfast. Entering into a quaint entrance hall, pannelled with oak and the same chequered flooring as the Painted Hall, guests are led into the Webb Room, with its oak pannelled floors, delicate cornincing, royal purple curtains and views of the river. Mounted on the walls are portraits of former Governors of Greenwich Hospital and Sir James Thornhill.

After a ceremony, guests can move across to the colonnades for a drinks reception, or outside by the river. Ascending the robust oak stairs, guests enter the Wren Room where the wedding breakfast is held. This light room, decorated in creams and mustards, provides an intimate venue for a select dinner. Like the Painted Hall, dancing is not allowed in the Admiral's House, but use of the King William Restaurant is included in the hire fee. Therefore, it is possible for the guests to move the party to the restaurant and invite more guests to attend an evening reception.

The King William Restaurant is situated under the Painted Hall with its own entrance from outside. It can seat 120 guests for a wedding breakfast and the same number for an evening reception with dancing. The whitewashed room has

a dance floor in its centre and with emerald green carpets and a vaulted ceiling, it provides a welcome venue to house a reception after a ceremony at the Admiral's House.

The final reception space at the Old Royal Naval College is the Queen Mary Undercroft, located at the end of the 'chalk walk', a long, white corridor leading underground from the Painted Hall and King William Restaurant. The room has been refurbished and transformed into a bright and airy space. While it is possible to hold wedding breakfasts for up to 200 in this room, the room perfectly suits acting as an evening reception venue after banqueting in the Painted Hall, or over at the Admiral's House. Accommodating up to 250 people, couples using the Admiral's House are then able to invite more guests to their evening event.

The room itself, lined with the original stone pillars, has a wood pannelled walkway and a ready-made dance floor. Vaulted ceilings and large windows high up make this a charming, light space. Blinds can be drawn for evening receptions and uplights cast light on the columns throughout the room.

A long bar with green marble top is already in place, facilitating this room's use. Under the College and near the Queen Mary Undercroft lies the Skittle Alley. A working game, guests can take part during the evening reception, and the alley, with its vaulted ceilings, also doubles as another break-out space.

The College's Chapel of St Peter and St Paul, in the building facing the Painted Hall, is a beautiful example of 'Greek revival', neoclassical style, after the original Baroque interior was gutted following a fire in 1779. An active church, members of the diocese can also hold their ceremony here if they wish, before crossing the courtyard to the Painted Hall.

One of London's architectural wonders, providing both magnificent and intimate settings, the Old Royal Naval College is a delightful wedding venue.

FOR A FABULOUS CEREMONY AND RECEPTION

Venue Details

Old Royal Naval College
2 Cutty Sark Gardens
Greenwich
SE10 9LW
t 020 8269 2131
e leiths.greenwich@compass-group.co.uk
w www.oldroyalnavalcollege.org

Licence authority:
Greenwich Register Office
Town Hall
Wellington Street
Woolwich
London
SE18 6PW
t 020 8921 5015
e registrar@greenwich.gov.uk
w www.greenwich.gov.uk

Licensed for ceremony: Painted Hall (200), Admiral's House (50)

Function rooms available: Painted Hall (reception 480, evening 400), Admiral's House (reception 50, evening 50), Queen Mary Undercroft (reception 200, evening 480), King William Restaurant (reception 120, evening 150)

Outside space: Grassed areas, colonnades and pathways

Option of a marquee: ✗

Rooms available for overnight accommodation: ✗

Complimentary dressing room for bride available: ✓(in the Admiral's House only)

SPECIAL NOTES

Licensing hours: Until 11pm (late licence available on application)

Corkage charge: Wine £12, champagne £18

Catering: Requisite caterer

Complimentary menu tasting: ✓

Car parking spaces: 50 (subject to availability)

Sound/noise restrictions: No restrictions

Fireworks: ✗ (option of hiring a barge to set fireworks off from the river)

Confetti: ✗

Candles: ✗

PA system: ✓

Helicopter landing permission: ✓ (restrictions apply)

Wedding options

Leith's, the Old Royal Naval College's caterer and events organiser can arrange every aspect of the wedding day; from lending their expertise when choosing the menu, to the entertainment, photographer and florist.

A wedding held at the College in May saw 130 guests enjoy a summer wedding in the Painted Hall and colonnades.

The bride arrived by boat, while guests entered through the east gate. As members of the congregation, the bride and groom wed in the magnificent chapel at a mid-afternoon service. Afterwards, pink champagne was served in the colonnades.

Just before 5pm, the party made their way across the courtyard to the Lower Hall in the Painted Hall, where guests took their seats on the long oak tables for the wedding breakfast.

To start, guests enjoyed a warm tart of roasted asparagus on crisp cabbage and a puy lentil dressing, followed by roasted rump of lamb with a minted crust and a redcurrant sauce. To finish, guests were served the chocolate wedding cake, with mixed berry coulis. During the speeches, champagne was served and a whisky tray brought round.

For the evening reception, guests made their way along the chalk walk to the Queen Mary Undercroft, as 50 more guests arrived. These guests were presented with champagne on arrival and entered through the Queen's Entrance.

A cheese board was served during the evening, accompanied by port, and the bar was open throughout. Around the room, tables were placed for seating and the centre of the room left for dancing. The couple chose a swing band, which played until 1.30am.

One Whitehall Place

Fabulous because...

This majestic Grade I listed building is situated in the heart of Westminster on the River Thames, and its grand marble staircase is reputed to be the largest of its kind in Europe

Location: Whitehall

Capacity: Ceremony 240; Wedding breakfast 228; Evening reception 350

Minimum number of guests: 50

Guide Price
Per guest (including venue hire): **£95**
Venue hire only: **Price on application**

When to get married here: **All year round**

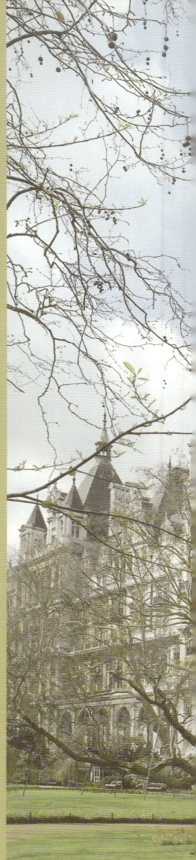

Situated in the heart of Westminster just a short walk from St James Park, One Whitehall Place is a grand Grade I listed building that exudes glamour. Originally designed by Alfred Waterhouse for the National Liberal Club, One Whitehall Place is often considered to be one of the architectural landmarks of London; with a spectacular winding staircase and classically themed pillars lying at the heart of a beautiful building. An architectural gem, the building is an idyllic location for weddings all year round, with the high ceilings and large windows creating a romantic setting that is bright and airy.

Proud of its enviable heritage, One Whitehall Place was built in the 1880s with the first stone laid by William Gladstone. Indeed, this foundation stone still has pride of place in the venue's cellars, where, legend has it, there was once a secret passage leading to the Ministry of Defence. Since its initial function as part of the National Liberal Club, One Whitehall Place has been incorporated into the Royal Horseguards Hotel.

The venue can host events for parties of up to 228 and offers overnight luxury accommodation for 280 guests.

Whether couples choose to arrive after church or to take their vows within one of the stunning suites licensed for ceremonies, One Whitehall Place promises a majestic welcome from the moment of their arrival. After entering in through the wide doors at the hotel's entrance, guests are transported into a world of breathtaking luxury. The grand marble staircase cut from solid Sicilian marble is reputed to be the largest of its kind in Europe with the design based on a smaller cantilevered staircase in the Berberini Palace, Rome. This wonderful staircase is a picturesque position for some of the wedding photographs.

The venue also boasts a private terrace area which leads into Whitehall Gardens. Here guests can enjoy champagne and canapés in the sunshine while photographs are taken in the gardens.

Couples choosing to hold either just their reception or their ceremony here are spoilt for choice. After a drinks

FOR A FABULOUS CEREMONY AND RECEPTION

Tall pillars accentuate the height of the Reading and Writing Room, drawing your eye to the Victorian chandeliers

reception in a suite or on the terrace, there are a number of private suites available for hire. Amongst these are the historic Gladstone Library and adjoining Reading and Writing Room.

The largest of these suits is the Gladstone Library; magnificently sized and complete with an intricately designed ceiling and tiled pillars. With high ceilings and mahogany tipped gantry, the room is grand and infused with a sense of history. The library was once home to 30,000 books, however the orginals are now kept in trust at Bristol University, and have been painstakingly replaced with wooden fascias in the exact location of the original book. This room is an ideal banqueting venue with impeccable table settings including candelabras and

mirror centrepieces, fine china and traditional silver service. It is here that the bride and groom will sample the menu prior to the wedding as part of the venue's flexible wedding package.

The Reading and Writing Room is attached to the library and is ideal for a welcome drinks reception. Tall pillars accentuate the height of this splendid room, drawing your eye to the Victorian chandeliers. Guests can take advantage of the natural daylight afforded by the large windows, since this room was once used to retire to for the leisure of reading the books. These windows also permit spectacular night-time views of the City. A wooden dance floor, normally hidden under the carpet, is available in this room.

With high ceilings and mahogany tipped gantry, the Gladstone Library is infused with a sense of history

Adjacent to the Reading and Writing room, The River Room was previously used as the Ladies' Lounge. As a smaller room, it provides for a more intimate gathering. With a magnificent backdrop of the River Thames and the London Eye, mahogany panelling, wonderful framed portraits and stunning chandeliers this room can host a wedding party of of 40 to 70 guests.

Once the smoking room and billiard room, the Whitehall Suite was also formally for gentlemen's use only. Now open to all, it is a wonderful setting for a ceremony of greater proportions with a layout reminiscent of a great dining hall. The room contains many of the venue's original features including the faience tiling and high pillars, with another example of Waterhouse's elaborately decorated ceiling. Vast windows beneath heavy, sweeping curtains complete the magnificence

of this room. With space to host up to 220 guests, dancing and celebrations can also be held here as a beautiful mosaic dance floor can be revealed from underneath the carpet.

After the celebrations have drawn to a close, One Whitehall Place is happy to accommodate guests in its beautiful bedrooms. Stylish in tone, these rooms have a classic feel with a white and cream design and each room offers unique furnishings with an individual touch. Overnight accommodation for the bride and groom is included in the venue's wedding package and it is here that couples can revel in the finishing touches such as champagne and chocolates left in the bedroom.

This is a spectacular setting in a historical building set against the backdrop of the River Thames.

FOR A FABULOUS CEREMONY AND RECEPTION

Venue Details

The Royal Horseguards
2 Whitehall Court
Whitehall, London
SW1A 2EJ
t 020 7839 3344
e onewhitehallplace@thistle.co.uk
w www.theroyalhorseguards.co.uk

Licence authority:
Westminster Register Office
Westminster Council House
Marylebone Road
London
NW1 5PT
t 020 7641 1161
e registeroffice@westminster.gov.uk
w www.westminster.gov.uk

Licensed for ceremony: The Gladstone Library (240),
Reading and Writing Room (144), The River Room (64),
The Whitehall Suite (240)

Function rooms available: The Gladstone Library
(reception 228, evening 350),
Reading and Writing Room (reception 150, evening 250),
The River Room (reception 70, evening 70),
The Whitehall Suite (reception 200, evening 250)

Outside space: Terrace, leading to public gardens

Option of a marquee: ✗

Rooms available for overnight accommodation: 280

Room rates: Reduced wedding package rate,
subject to availability

Complimentary dressing room for bride available: ✓

SPECIAL NOTES

Licensing hours: Saturdays until 1am,
Fridays and Sundays until midnight

Corkage charge: Corkage not permitted

Catering: In-house with exceptions for specialist menus

Complimentary menu tasting: ✓

Car parking spaces: ✗

Sound/noise restrictions: No restrictions

Fireworks: ✗

Confetti: ✓

Candles: ✓

PA system: ✓

Helicopter landing permission: ✗

Wedding options

One Whitehall Place offers couples a flexible wedding package that can be tailored to meet individual requirements. This provides the opportunity to personalise the rooms and table decorations with chosen flower arrangements, place settings and musicians.

A rate of £95.00 per person would include:

- Complimentary hire of the reception rooms
- Drinks reception (two glasses of house wine)
- Three-course wedding menu
- Half a bottle of house wine
- Half a bottle of mineral water
- One glass of champagne for the toast
- Candelabras, mirror centrepieces
- Use of cake stand and knife
- Personalised menus and table plan
- Overnight accommodation for the bride and groom
- Champagne and chocolates in their bedroom
- Menu tasting for the bride and groom
- Fully staffed cloakroom
- Dance floor

Couples can also enjoy a first year anniversary dinner at One Whitehall Place, the price of which is included in the wedding package.

The Royal Horseguards Hotel has 280 rooms and suites, many with views of the River Thames and all stylishly furnished, blending period features with the latest communication systems. The eclectically designed signature suites include The Tower, The Library, The Egyptian and The Apartment, all dramatically different in character and ambiance.

Parkstead House

Fabulous because...

Offering spectacular views of neighbouring Richmond Park, this Georgian Villa is a rural haven just five miles from the centre of London

Location: **Roehampton**

Capacity: **Ceremony 120; Wedding breakfast 150; Evening reception 200**

Minimum number of guests: **None**

Guide Price
Per guest (including venue hire): **£118**
Venue hire only: **£2,174**

When to get married here: **All year round**

Initial impressions of Parkstead House are marked by the home's entrance, dominated by large columns and grand, twinned staircases

A Grade I listed building, Parkstead House is an elaborate Georgian Villa that is situated in a 14-acre estate within a conservation area. Just five miles from the centre of London, the venue's spectacular views of neighbouring Richmond Park gives a rural feel to the location and provides breathtaking scenery. High up on the romantic balcony of Parkstead House, guests will enjoy the distant free-roaming deer for which the park is known while enjoying the home's own sophisticated heritage; designed by Sir William Chambers for the second Earl of Bessborough, Parkstead House is more than 200 years old.

A lasting homage to the sophisticated Palladian designs so prevalent at the time, initial impressions of Parkstead House are marked by the home's entrance, dominated by large columns and grand, twinned staircases. Parkstead House was designed by the same architect who designed Somerset House and the Pagoda at Kew Gardens and is the first in a series of Palladian Villas. It plays an important role in the history of English architecture with some of the original designs still preserved in the lustrous Victoria and Albert Museum.

Originally used by the Earl as a place for lavish entertainment and a base for hunting expeditions in Richmond Park, Parkstead House has, in recent years, been used for a variety of purposes. Having featured in pop videos, adverts and television dramas including the Brontës' Documentary, it is now in the hands of Whitelands college and has been fully restored to it's original glory with renovation advice from English Heritage.

A romantic setting for a wedding, couples entering the mansion's main entrance are met by an airy hallway. With cream walls and an open design, an attractive staircase with gleaming oak handrail leads the way upstairs towards a number of function rooms that are available to couples for ceremony hire.

The first of these is the Richmond Room; a beautiful and simple space in the heart of the house that can seat up to 90 guests for the ceremony. One of a number of different rooms that are decorated in a similar style, it features ivory and cream wall panelling that stretches to meet a high ceiling topped with a pale green border. Offset by ceiling detail that

FOR A FABULOUS CEREMONY AND RECEPTION

Gorgeous ivory coloured walls meet in elaborate arches while a globed ceiling with gilded decoration and delicate panelling inspire awe in those standing beneath

includes a central design and a gilded chandelier, it is a seductive space whose neutral colour scheme welcomes sophisticated decorative arrangements. A marble fireplace built into the near-wall serves as the central position for couple's taking their vows.

There are a number of other rooms similarly styled, including the Bessborough Room, Ponsonby Room, Ruskin Room and Hopkins Room. Collectively referred to as The Chambers Suite, they are suited not only to ceremonies but also make an elaborate reception space. Featuring decorative fireplaces and ornamental ceilings, the rooms are marvellously interconnected and able to accommodate up to 200 guests for a standing drinks reception.

Adjoining to the main Villa lies an alternative ceremony location, the Manresa Hall. Boasting a unique history, the Manresa Hall began life as a chapel when the site on which it sits was acquired by the Society of the Jesuits in the 1860's. Surrounded by a number of Victorian buildings which create an enclosed courtyard space, it was deconsecrated in 1961 and, retaining all the beauty of a church building, can now be used for civil ceremonies.

The Manresa Hall is a tall building with a stunning interior that belies description. As couples enter along a stone white pillared corridor, they may be showered with confetti before stopping to

High up on the romantic balcony of Parkstead House, guests will enjoy the distant free-roaming deer while enjoying the home's sophisticated heritage

face the expanse of space that opens up before them. Gorgeous ivory coloured walls meet in elaborate arches while a globed ceiling with gilded decoration and delicate panelling inspire awe in those standing beneath. The ceilings are the crowning feature of this room with panels painted in powder blue alongside Latin inscriptions.

After a ceremony in the Manresa Hall, guests can spill out onto the lawns for photographs, making sure to take full advantage of the spectacular views across to Richmond Park. The Hall can then be re-arranged for the wedding breakfast for parties of around 150, and the Loyola Room can be used in conjunction with the Hall, providing 80 extra seats.

The venue also contains Bar Code, a modern area with a stylish pure-white bar. This room can also be used as an informal dancing area when receptions are held in the Manresa Hall. Leading on to another balcony and with outside decking, it is just one option of many and demonstrates well the versatility of the House.

The outside lawns can also be used as a marquee site to host all or part of the reception celebrations. Licensed for ceremonies and able to hold in excess of 150 diners, the marquee is perfect for summer weddings when guests can take in the full panoramic sights of Richmond Park before a backdrop of the main Villa. Guests can still have use of the House for drinks and the bride and groom can make a grand entrance out onto the balcony of the house before descending the staircase towards the marquee. Flexibly sized, the marquee itself can accommodate a large number of guests.

Venue Details

Parkstead House
Holybourne Avenue
Roehampton
London
SW15 4JD
t 020 8392 3505
e info@parksteadhouse.co.uk
w www.parksteadhouse.co.uk

Licence authority:
Wandsworth Council
Wandsworth Town Hall
Wandsworth High Street
SW18 2PU
t 020 8871 6108
e registeroffice@wandsworth.gov.uk
w www.wandsworth.gov.uk

Licensed for ceremony: Ruskin Room (30), Richmond Room (90), Manresa Hall (120)

Function rooms available: Ruskin Room (reception 30), Richmond Room (reception 50, evening 100), Manresa Hall (reception 150, evening 200), Marquee (reception 120+, evening 200+)

Outside space: Seven acres of ground and two courtyards

Option of a marquee: ✓

Rooms available for overnight accommodation: 250 from June to September

Room rates: From £39

Complimentary dressing room for bride available: ✓

SPECIAL NOTES

Licensing hours: Until midnight (late licence available on application)

Corkage charge: £9

Catering: Recommended caterers

Complimentary menu tasting: ✓

Car parking spaces: Approximately 100 spaces

Sound/noise restrictions: Limitations for marquee events

Fireworks: ✓

Confetti: ✓

Candles: ✓ (restrictions apply)

PA system: ✓ (for an additional fee)

Helicopter landing permission: ✓

Wedding options

Every wedding at Parkstead House is a tailor-made experience and the venue's wedding coordinators are dedicated to provide personal attention to each wedding. They can assist couples every step of the way, from choosing a menu, to entertainment and are there on the day to ensure everything runs smoothly. There is an approved list of quality suppliers to provide catering, flowers, atmospheric lighting and entertainment.

Inside Parkstead House there is a choice of five different rooms for civil ceremonies or partnerships. Three of these rooms have views over looking Richmond Park with one leading out onto the House balcony. After a ceremony in the Manresa Hall, guests can be ushered into Parkstead House for a drinks reception, so that the hall can be transformed into the evening wedding reception room.

For evening receptions there is a choice of having a formal seated three-course dinner, a buffet or a more informal drinks reception with canapés. Again there is choice of using the rooms inside Parkstead House, the Manresa Hall or a marquee on the lawns. Weather permitting, drinks receptions are often moved onto the lawns of Parkstead House or into the large courtyard.

The venue's room hire charge includes the following:
- Exclusive use of all rooms booked
- An events manager
- Events stewards to greet guests on arrival and help direct guests around the site
- A staffed cloakroom
- Toilet attendant
- Easel and boards for table plans

30 Pavilion Road

Fabulous because...

This Georgian town house, situated in the heart of Knightsbridge, presents a luxurious venue for intimate celebrations, and is available for exclusive hire

Location: **Knightsbridge**

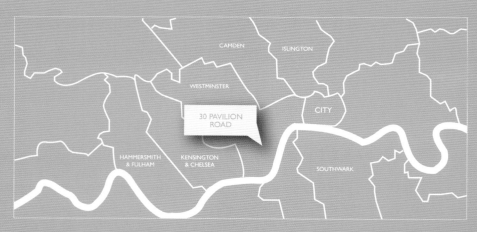

Capacity: Ceremony 100; Wedding breakfast 120; Evening reception 240

Minimum number of guests: None

Guide Price
Per guest (including venue hire): **£190**
Venue hire only: **£3,114 exclusive hire**

When to get married here: All year round

I n the heart of Knightsbridge, a stone's throw from Harrods, 30 Pavilion Road provides a haven of luxury and an intimate venue for wedding celebrations. With the exclusive use of the Georgian town house couples can relax and enjoy a private day with their family and friends. Originally a water pumping station, the building has been transformed into a luxurious contemporary town house, still retaining the charm of its heritage. The house stands prominently on a corner, in the prestigious area of Kensington and Chelsea.

30 Pavilion Road lends itself perfectly to all aspects of wedding celebrations, with an array of suitable rooms, and attentive, unobtrusive staff on hand to create a memorable day. Natural daylight pours into the beautifully designed hallways and striking ballroom, providing light and airy spaces to receive guests. With exclusive use of the house, the location for ceremonies and receptions are flexible, yet 30 Pavilion Road can suggest rooms that work particularly well as ceremony and reception venues.

Upon entering the house guests enter the Stone Hall, an intimate setting for a ceremony of 80 guests, but it also has the option of including an additional 40 guests seated in the adjoining Dining Room. White stone floors with black detailing and a large, traditional fireplace create a wonderfully majestic atmosphere for a wedding ceremony. The fireplace brings warmth and provides a focal point to the hall, as its mantelpiece can be adorned with seasonal floral displays; in front of which the couple exchanges their vows. If couples choose to hold the ceremony elsewhere, these two rooms can be used to hold champagne receptions, or smaller, more intimate dinners.

A wrought iron staircase which can be lit with tea lights leads from the Stone Hall up to a luxurious landing, with a seating area and period pieces.

Upstairs, the antique-panelled Library provides an unusual backdrop for wedding photograhs as guests make their way to the adjoining Ballroom for the wedding breakfast. This ornately decorated room is brimming with character, with its mustard coloured walls, mounted candelabra, gilted mirrors and chandeliers, yet it allows for personal touches to be added. Linen tablecloths, elegant flower centre pieces and intricate name places are just some of the touches the house is able to provide to a couple's individual specifications. To continue

A wrought iron staircase leads from the
Stone Hall up to a luxurious landing

celebrations into the evening, the Ballroom is also ideal for dancing, with oak parquet floors and an extended licence until 1am. Guests can be invited downstairs into the Stone Hall to enjoy coffee and the cutting of the cake, and ascend once again to the Ballroom, set up for dancing with space for a live band. This space can accommodate additional guests, and the whole house can host an evening reception for up to 240 guests.

With the facility of a lift, the house ensures good wheelchair access is maintained throughout.

30 Pavilion Road prides itself on the bespoke approach the wedding team take to each event. The experienced team can offer suggestions and support couples through every important decision down to the smallest of details. Using the finest seasonal ingredients, the house's family-run private caterers can produce individually tailored menus and complimentary taste testing. On the day itself, the staff deliver discreet service, ensuring every guest's individual needs are attended to.

Hidden away at the top of the house is a marvellous addition to this venue: Roof Garden Bedrooms, a guesthouse with 10 distinctive suites and access to a rooftop garden, where guests can enjoy breakfast in good weather, a fine feature so centrally located. These exclusive rooms have a separate entrance at street level and offer a unique alternative to large hotel chains. A complimentary room is offered to the bride and groom, accessible all day to dress and change in. If the couple choose, the room can be available the night before the wedding instead of the wedding night, providing a luxurious setting for the bride to get ready for her special day in the height of comfort.

Venue Details

30 Pavilion Road
Knightsbridge
London
SW1X 0HJ
t 020 7823 9212
e 30pr@searcys.co.uk
w www.30pavilionroad.co.uk

Licence authority:
Kensington and Chelsea Register Office
Chelsea Old Town Hall
Kings Road
London
SW3 5EE
t 020 7361 4100
e chelsea.registeroffice@rbkc.gov.uk
w www.rbkc.gov.uk

Licensed for ceremony: Stone Hall (100)

Function rooms available: Ballroom (reception 120, evening 120), Stone Hall (reception 48, evening 120), Dining Room (reception 16), Whole House (evening 240)

Outside space: ✗

Rooms available for overnight accommodation: 10

Room rates: £160 including breakfast

Complimentary dressing room for bride available: ✓

SPECIAL NOTES

Licensing hours: Until 1am

Corkage charge: Wine £14, sparkling wine £18, champagne £24

Catering: In-house

Complimentary menu tasting: ✓

Car parking spaces: NCP across the road

Sound/noise restrictions: Maximum 85 decibels

Fireworks: ✗

Confetti: ✓

Candles: ✓

PA system: ✓ (in the Ballroom)

Helicopter landing permission: ✗

Wedding options

In December, 30 Pavilion Road held a wedding ceremony, reception and sit-down dinner for 119 people, catered for by the venue's requisite caterer, Leith's.

The day began with a reception in the Stone Hall, with a selection of drinks including Searcys Brut NV, Kir Royale and Cranberry Juice and a selection of hot and cold canapés. A pianist and soloist played and a guest book was displayed for guests to write their messages to the couple.

The newly weds then made their way to the Library to have their wedding photographs taken, as guests ascended the stairs to the Ballroom.

The Ballroom was arranged with a top table and round tables for the guests for a three-course banquet, which included Scottish smoked salmon, three bone rack of lamb with wilted spinach, fondant potato, glazed cocotte carrots, redcurrant jus and raspberry brûlée with tuille biscuit.

After the speeches, guests descended into the Stone Hall for the cutting of the cake. The round chocolate cake was decorated with flowers and rose petals were scattered around the cake table. The cake was served canapé style with coffee while the Ballroom was prepared for the evening reception.

A full bar was set up on the staircase landing and a five-piece band and DJ played during the evening. A cheese platter was later served in the Library.

At 1am, guests gathered in the Stone Hall to see off the bride and groom, and the ladies were handed baskets of confetti to throw. The roses in the table centrepieces were wrapped separately and given by the bride's mother to guests on departure.

Plaisterers' Hall

Fabulous because...

One of the largest Livery Halls in London, the history of this building dates back to the sixteenth century. Recently renovated, it now boasts a wonderful mix of contemporary and classical styles

Location: **The City**

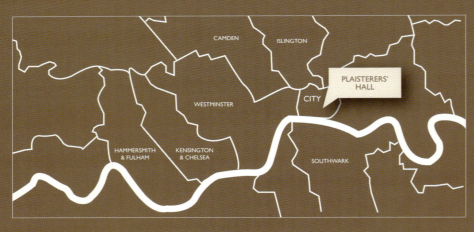

Capacity: **Ceremony 120; Wedding breakfast 350; Evening reception 600**

Minimum number of guests: **20**

Guide Price
Per guest (not including venue hire): **£45 – £75**
Venue hire only: **£6,000**

When to get married here: **All year round**

One of the largest Livery Halls in London, Plaisterers' Hall is a building loaded with history and is now a fine backdrop for a grand wedding party. Situated close to St Paul's Cathedral it has undergone a major refurbishment and offers a spacious haven for ceremony and reception alike.

An important part of the Livery Companies of London, The Plaisterers' Company was one of the first trade organisations; formed in 1501 to support the development of the plastering profession.

The first Plaisterers' Hall was bequeathed to the Plaisterers' Company in 1556. Situated in a central location, it was destroyed by The Great Fire of London in 1666 and replaced just three years later by a building designed by Sir Christopher Wren. Also ruined by fire in 1882, the present hall is its second replacement and opened in 1972, re-opening in 2004 after it was renovated. Offering an innovative mix of classical and contemporary styles, it is perfectly suited to hosting private events.

At it's maximum capacity Plaisterers' Hall can host a reception event for 600 guests, though it can also cater for a wedding breakfast for a party of as few as 20. The building is comprised of The Great Hall, which gives way to the adjourning Mott Room and Livery Hall, which in turn leads into the Humber Room. Couples can hire the whole venue, and although the décor throughout is that of the neo-classical style created by Adam in the eighteenth century, each room exudes grandeur in its own distinct way.

Close to the Livery church at St Brides, couples can hold their ceremony elsewhere and arrive at the Hall for the reception. For couple's wishing to marry at Plaisterers' Hall itself, the venue's licensed space is the Livery Hall. This Hall can seat 120 guests for a ceremony, and is a long room marked by a distinctive deep red carpet with circular design. Offset by a panelled ceiling with unusual rounded lighting in a chandelier style, its walls are punctured by a series of double-doors that lead into the adjourning Humber Room and The Great Hall.

*Glittering chandeliers hang from
a delicately enamelled ceiling
with a spectacular print*

With two windows allowing natural light to filter in among the ornate fixtures, the room is coloured in muted shades making it a warm and wonderful setting for a ceremony.

After the ceremony is over and couples have taken advantage of the neo-classical décor for unusual photographs, they may wish to take the opportunity for further photographs in the venue's garden. History at every turn, a distinctive feature of the garden is the original Roman London Wall.

The wedding party can then filter into the chosen function room. While some couples choose to re-enter the Livery Hall for the reception, others prefer to hold their wedding breakfast in one of the other rooms. In addition to these rooms there is ample private space for use by the bride to prepare or for the presents to be stored.

The first function room available is The Great Hall, a fantastic space that can seat up to 300, or host 600 for a standing reception. A dramatic backdrop for receptions and formal meals, glittering chandeliers hang from a delicately enamelled ceiling with a spectacular print, while the red carpet that featured in the Livery Hall continues in through into here. Upon camel coloured walls modestly sized paintings hang beneath arched wall panelling and with three high windows situated at the end of the hall, it is a bright and airy space with a sophisticated ambience.

For couples requiring a smaller space for their celebration, the Humber Room leads on directly to the Livery Hall, and can seat around 20 guests. A smaller room, the Mott Room is discreetly positioned just off the Great Hall and can seat 10 guests for a small wedding breakfast before a more grand reception party. It is an immaculately designed room with a warm white and red colour scheme. White panelled walls give way to a gold-gilded white border round the room's double doors and a chandelier hangs above the table. For this purpose, and all other dining experiences, the venue's in-house caterers will provide a menu that caters to all palettes and tastes.

FOR A FABULOUS CEREMONY AND RECEPTION

Venue Details

Plaisterers' Hall
One London Wall
London
EC2Y 5JU
t 0870 111 2302
e events@plaistrershall.com
w www.plaistrershall.com

Licence authority:
Islington and London City
Islington Town Hall
Upper Street
London
N1 2UD
t 020 7527 6350
e registrars@islington.gov.uk
w www.islington.gov.uk

Licensed for ceremony: Livery Hall (120)

Function rooms available: The Great Hall (reception 400, evening 600), Livery Hall (reception 80, evening 220), Humber Room (reception 20), Mott Room (reception 10)

Outside space: Small garden with original Roman London Wall

Option of a marquee: ✗

Rooms available for overnight accommodation: ✗

Complimentary dressing room for bride available: ✓

SPECIAL NOTES

Licensing hours: Until midnight

Corkage charge: £4.50 per person

Catering: In-house

Complimentary menu tasting: ✓

Car parking spaces: One space available on the premisis, further parking available at the NCP half a mile away

Sound/noise restrictions: No restrictions

Fireworks: ✗

Confetti: ✗

Candles: ✓ (smokeless)

PA system: ✓

Helicopter landing permission: ✗

Wedding options

In-house caterer Create Food and Party Design have a mantra that they use in their work for every event that is '*design, detail, delicious*'. They will provide an in-house designer to work with couples' own ideas and colour schemes and a party creator to look after every aspect of the event.

On arrival bridal parties and their guests walk through the contemporary steel and glass entrance hall, down the broad staircase and arrive in the beautifully appointed Robert Adam interior of the reception area.

Through to the Livery Hall, smartly attired waiting staff await guests with oak trays offering flutes of champagne and non-alcoholic cocktails such as raspberry and fresh orange or pink ginger and elderflower.

While the bride and groom have photographs taken in one of the other rooms or by the original Roman London Wall in the garden, guests mingle, and are served beautifully presented canapés including cocktail sized tuna sashimi, crayfish and asparagus with dipping sauces and hot little beignets of crisp seasonal vegetables in light batter.

The toastmaster announces dinner and the doors to The Great Hall are opened to reveal its chandeliers, colour washed ceiling and crisp linen clothed tables lain with silver and crystal. The bride and groom will have selected their favourite dishes with Create which could include Mediterranean dishes or sturdy British dishes: it is the couple who decides the exact menu.

Create Food and Party Design pride themselves on their attention to detail, delicious food, impeccable service and a sense of occasion that can be created at Plaisterers' Hall.

The Ritz London

Fabulous because...

Weddings at this iconic and prestigious London hotel are held in the recently opened William Kent House which makes for an opulent occasion

Location: **Green Park**

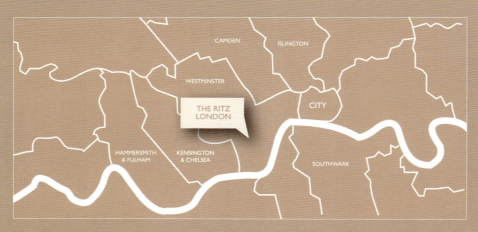

Capacity: **Ceremony 60; Wedding breakfast 60; Evening reception 120**

Minimum number of guests: **None**

Guide Price
Per guest (including room hire): **From £100**
Venue hire only: **From £1,500**

When to get married here: **All year round**

The Ritz delights those who choose to visit for its prestigious afternoon tea

Situated in the heart of Piccadilly, the esteemed work of the 'hotelier to Kings and king of hoteliers' César Ritz needs little introduction. An iconic landmark that is an institution in itself, The Ritz London is a sensational building whose far-reaching reputation for exceptional service and breathtaking luxury has found world acclaim.

Carefully crafted under the watchful eye of Ritz, The Ritz is a spectacular Grade II star listed building of virtually unequalled proportions. Displaying the influence of Parisian architectural traditions, its interior is bedecked in a dazzling display of ornate furnishings and rich fabric. Delighting the many guests who choose to visit the hotel for the venue's prestigious afternoon tea, its sumptuous settings make it the perfect place to host a wedding year round. Displaying Edwardian splendour, The Ritz skilfully combines a subtle use of the most sophisticated technology available. With licensing hours until midnight, its selection of 112 guest rooms and 24 suites further mean that after the celebrations are over, guests may extend their stay by relaxing in bedrooms of unparalleled luxury.

Created by the successful partnership of Charles Mewes and Arthur Davis in 1904, The Ritz London was designed following the success of the Hotel Ritz in Paris and the Carlton Hotel in London's Haymarket. Sharp and innovative, César Ritz led the way in many quintessential

Glittering chandeliers hang from a delicately enamelled ceiling in a spectacular print

hotel designs such as an en suite bathroom in each guestroom and upon its opening the hotel was praised for 'its brilliant refinement of detail and architecture'.

Since opening to great acclaim in 1906, The Ritz has enjoyed a constant stream of the famous and fabulous through its doors, including King Edward VIII, Churchill, Eisenhower and the American actress, Tallulah Bankhead. Now itself a byword for luxury, its reputation has never wavered in its 100-year history and The Ritz promises a rich and healthy future; after beginning a meticulous and ongoing £25 million refurbishment in 1995, November 2006 saw the opening of the William Kent House, an eighteenth-century mansion house next door to the hotel.

The house is named after its original architect and it is this building that is available for hire for weddings at The Ritz, offering a variety of suites suitable and licensed for a marriage ceremony. Incorporated into the hotel, these new banquet rooms can be used exclusively by wedding parties.

Added to the original property in the late 1780s, the ground-floor Music Room is the largest room licensed for ceremonies, dominated by enormous floor to ceiling windows with a door leading to the Grand Hall. Situated beneath grand white and green flowered curtains with immaculately pinned pelmets and yellow trim, the room feels spacious and airy. Cream walls with Adamesque pilasters reach up towards an ornate ceiling decked in pastel shades and finished

The Ritz is a sensational building whose far-reaching reputation for breathtaking luxury has found world acclaim

with a delicate white bordered pattern while a low-hanging chandelier adds to the room's ambience. With gold and silver décor that complements elegant table settings, guests dining in the room can be sure of exemplary service.

Passing through the Grand Hall, a luxurious space off which all other available rooms lead, guests will marvel at the two onyx marble pillars which, capped in gold leaf, stretch towards the upper floor. The party make their way through this space towards the chosen function room in the House.

The first of these is the Queen Elizabeth Room, an elegant drawing room and the venue's second licensed space. The vast bay windows which relay fantastic views of nearby Green Park, are dressed with deep velvet curtains which sweep over polished redwood floors. Complemented by original features

such as the restored exotic carpet and white marbled fireplace, the décor is sophisticated and airy. Gold specked ceiling borders blend with subtle decorative features on the room's furniture while a framed mirror sits atop a wide sill and reflects the carefully positioned portrait hung on the wall opposite.

Adjacent to the Queen Elizabeth Room and named after one of the home's previous owners, Lord Wimborne, The Wimborne Room is a small but striking room that can accommodate up to 16 people for dinner. With yellow silk damask walls and matching curtains, a glinting cream ceiling lined with gold leaf shimmers above a low-hanging chandelier which bathes the room in an amber glow. Underfoot, the room's original floorboards have been restored beneath a thick black and cream flower-print carpet where the mahogany

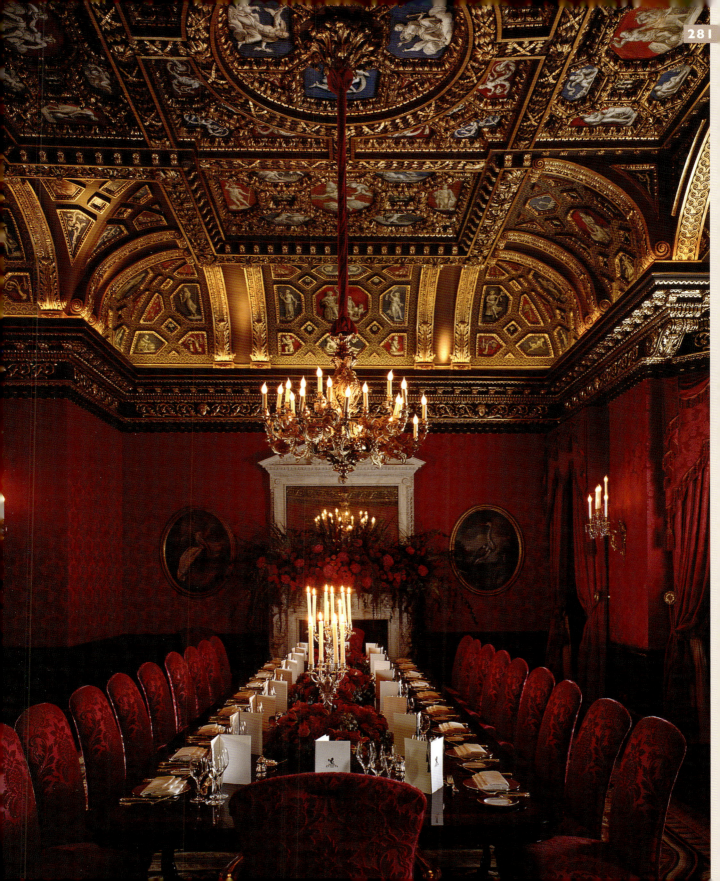

*A lavish dining room is adorned with damask curtains
and an original gold-leaf Kent ceiling*

table, suitable for wedding breakfasts, is placed. Those dining in this room will benefit from finery which includes gold-gilted candlesticks and glass chandelier style wall hangings.

Returning through the Queen Elizabeth Room, couples will find themselves entering the magnificent William Kent Room, a lavish dining room adorned with red damask curtains, soft crimson chairs and an original gold-leaf Kent ceiling, it permits fine views over Green Park. Exquisitely decorated in shades of cerise, this room can host a wedding breakfast for up to 24 guests, seated in plush red chairs around an vast polished mahogany table laid with delicate silverware and flowers.

Surrounded by red damask floral wall-print and matching framboise curtains, the flamboyant décor is in keeping with the Italian Renaissance style in vogue at the time the house

was built. This is offset perfectly by the deep brown of the lower wall design and the perfect accompaniment to the breathtaking Kent ceiling which sits gloriously above the trompe d'oeil upper panels intricately decorated with gold leaf. Widely considered to be one of Kent's greatest works, this ceiling dazzles all who look upon it, with deep-set coffers highlighted in gold surrounded by grisaille paintings depicting the loves of the Gods. Painstakingly restored and re-gilded, it shimmers above diners seated below granting wedding parties a truly royal finish.

Whichever room couples choose to use for their celebrations, they will bask in their luxurious surroundings, admiring views of London's beauty spots as well as the venue's own Italian Garden; the perfect spot for photographs.

FOR A FABULOUS CEREMONY AND RECEPTION

Venue Details

The Ritz London
150 Piccadilly
London
W1J 9BR
t 020 7493 8181
e events@theritzlondon.com
w www.theritzlondon.com

Licence authority:
Westminster Register Office
Westminster Council House
Marylebone Road
London
NW1 5PT
t 020 7641 1161
e registeroffice@westminster.gov.uk
w www.westminster.gov.uk

Licensed for ceremony: The Music Room (60),
The Queen Elizabeth Room (30)

Function rooms available: The Queen Elizabeth Room
(reception 24), The William Kent Rooms (reception 24),
The Music Room (reception 80, evening 120),
The Wimborne Room (reception 16),
Exclusive use of the Ground Floor (evening 220)

Outside space: The Italian Garden

Option of a marquee: ✗

Rooms available for overnight accommodation:
112 guest rooms, 24 suites

Room rates: From £525

Complimentary dressing room for bride available: ✓

SPECIAL NOTES

Licensing hours: Until midnight

Corkage charge: From £36

Catering: In-house

Complimentary Menu Tasting: ✓

Car parking spaces: NCP on Arlington Street,
valet parked via The Ritz

Sound/noise restrictions: No amplified music

Fireworks: ✗

Confetti: ✓ (in specified areas)

Candles: ✓

PA system: ✓

Helicopter landing permission: ✗

Wedding options

The Ritz, renowned for its excellent service, delights in guiding couples through the necessary preparations for their wedding day and can help with all arrangements: from flowers, menus and the cake, to place cards and limousines.

As well as The Ritz's famous Afternoon Tea menu, which includes 17 tea choices, there are a number of menu options for couples to peruse. Ranging from hot and cold canapé menus with 'sweet frivolities', cassolettes and stir-fry stations, to over 20 buffet and dinner menus to choose from, couples can also put together their preferred menu from an extensive list of courses.

Located on the seventh floor of the hotel, The Ritz Salon uses 100% natural plant oils and offers a range of beauty and relaxation treatments. The salon also offers brides and bridesmaids the opportunity to prepare for the day with a Ritz Bridal Hair and Make Up treatment.

The Ritz offers couples a special Honeymoon Package of one night's accommodation, champagne, fruit and flowers on arrival and room service breakfast.

'I believe our day was stunning and will be a special memory for many of our family and friends – this is all down to your impeccable organisational skills!'

'The whole day was perfect in our eyes. From the minute I arrived, when the concierge helped us with our many bags and of course 'the dress', until the room service we had in our room at 2.30am that night, everything was perfect.'

Royal Society of Arts

Fabulous because...

The Grade I listed RSA House offers a series of unexpected rooms behind its Georgian façade, including the enchanting Vaults with fantastic acoustics

Location: Strand

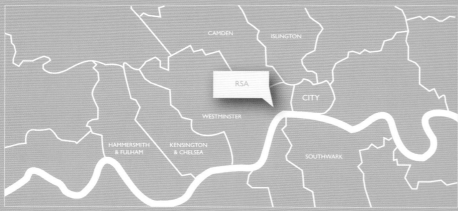

Capacity: Ceremony 200; Wedding breakfast 120; Evening reception 220

Minimum number of guests: 50 on weekends

Guide Price
Per guest (not including venue hire): **£28 – £37**
Venue hire only: **£3114 – £4,994**

When to get married here: All year round

Located in the heart of London, just behind the Strand, the RSA (Royal Society for the encouragement of Arts, Manufacturers and Commerce) occupies a prime location and a unique setting for both ceremonies and receptions. The Grade I listed RSA House was designed for the Society by Robert Adam in the early 1770s. Today the Georgian façade conceals many unexpected delights of both contemporary as well as traditional architecture.

The RSA was founded in 1754 by William Shipley, a painter and social activist. The RSA's initial manifesto, in his words, was 'to embolden enterprise, enlarge science, refine arts, improve our manufactures and extend our commerce' and today the RSA's work is framed by five manifesto challenges that reflect the original mission in twenty-first-century terms. One example is the venue's motto to 'better our environmental policies' which is done by supporting British food producers, purchasing meat and fish from sustainable stocks and preparing dishes on the premises from fresh rather than pre-prepared ingredients. With this in mind, the RSA chefs will create a bespoke menu tailored to any individual requirements.

For couples looking to host a large ceremony, the RSA's Great Room stays true to its name and this spectacular theatre can host up to 200 people. Dominated by a contemporary glass cupola, natural daylight illuminates the epic painting Progress of Human Knowledge and Culture by James Barry which adorns the upper walls, creating a memorable setting for a ceremony.

Below the Great Room lie The Vaults. These originally ran from under the Society's house and the Royal Terrace to the River Thames. Now sympathetically restored, the cathedral-like architecture with high vaulted ceilings and bare brick walls offers an enchanting setting for candlelit ceremonies and atmospheric celebrations. The unusual arrangement provides both an intimate space for a ceremony of 80 guests or, for all the vaults combined, a space for a party of 220.

FOR A FABULOUS CEREMONY AND RECEPTION

The Great Room stays true to its name with this spectacular theatre sure to inspire couples

The vaults have amazing acoustics for a live band or string quartet to play during the ceremony or reception celebration.

Returning to the ground floor, elegant in design, the Benjamin Franklin Room is a grand reception room featuring ornate columns, a Regency crystal chandelier and original Adam fireplaces. It was named after one of the founding fathers of the USA in 1967 to mark the Society's long association with America: Franklin himself was an active member and supported the institution in its early years. Bright and airy with a long window that runs the length of the room, it also affords guests a wonderful view out onto the Strand. The flexibility of the space makes it perfect for both ceremonies and formal wedding breakfasts of up to 100 guests.

The simple, unadorned Tavern Room provides a perfect canvas that can be used to reflect a couple's personal style. Suitable for both ceremonies and intimate celebrations of up to 40 guests, the minimal decorative scheme and solid oak flooring give this room a contemporary feel. The original Adam fireplace provides a beautiful focal point to the room, while natural daylight enhances the light and airy atmosphere.

Once the dining room of the Adelphi Tavern, one of the most fashionable venues in Victorian society, the Adelphi Room is a light and airy room particularly suited to intimate wedding parties. With a beautiful Adam ceiling bathed in pastel tones of blue and pink and featuring inlaid gouache panels depicting Pan celebrating the feast of Bacchus. Large

The cathedral-like architecture with high vaulted ceilings and bare brick walls offers an enchanting setting for candlelit ceremonies

south-facing windows allow daylight to stream in over the wooden floors that are partially carpeted to match the ceiling and highlight beautifully the white period fireplace.

The final room on offer to couples wishing to marry at the RSA is the Romney Room. Once the main drawing room of No2 John Adams Street – a handsome private property – the Romney Room retains its classic Adam dimensions, with large windows, grand white fireplace and curved feature wall. The beautiful Adam ceiling with delicate white detail amid shades of pastel blue, is partially replicated on the carpet. The RSA suggests pairing this room with the Adelphi

Room as a suite of intimate Georgian drawing rooms suited to wedding parties for around 30 people.

The RSA offers dedicated wedding coordinators who will guide couples through the run up to their wedding and be on hand to ensure it all runs perfectly on the day itself. Couples are also offered the Drawing Room as a complimentary retiring room, perfect for the bride's final touches before the ceremony.

Home to a spectacular array of paintings, the RSA is an architectural great that will delight all wedding parties.

FOR A FABULOUS CEREMONY AND RECEPTION

Venue Details

The RSA
8 John Adam Street
London
WC2N 6EZ
t 020 7930 5115
e weddings@rsa.org.uk
w www.thersa.org/weddings

Licence authority:
Westminster Register Office
Westminster Council House
Marylebone Road
London
NW1 5PT
t 020 7641 1161
e registeroffice@westminster.gov.uk
w www.westminster.gov.uk

Licensed for ceremony: Great Room (200), Benjamin Franklin Room (100), Romney Room (30), Adelphi Room (40), Tavern Room (40), The Vaults (80)

Function rooms available: Benjamin Franklin Room (reception 100, evening 150), Romney Room (reception 20, evening 30), Adelphi Room (reception 28, evening 40), Tavern Room (reception 30, evening 50), The Vaults (reception 120, evening 220)

Outside space: ✗

Rooms available for overnight accommodation: ✗

Complimentary dressing room for bride available: ✓

SPECIAL NOTES

Licensing hours: Until 11pm (late licence available on application)

Corkage charge: Wine £15, sparkling wine £20, champagne £26

Catering: In-house

Complimentary menu tasting: ✓

Car parking spaces: NCP at Adelphi and metered parking in surrounding streets

Sound/noise restrictions: No restrictions

Fireworks: ✗

Confetti: ✓

Candles: ✓

PA system: ✓

Helicopter landing permission: ✗

Wedding options

Throughout the build up and on the day itself, the RSA events team will ensure every need is met. A dedicated wedding coordinator can offer advice on everything from flowers to music, lighting to photographers, and will be there on the day to ensure the smooth running of the wedding day.

At a typical wedding at the RSA guests are invited to make their way down the stairs into The Vaults, lit on either side of the steps by candlelight, to where the ceremony is held.

Following the ceremony, guests proceed through the vaulted archways into Vault 1 which can also be lit by candlelight and combined with dramatic coloured floor lights to create a striking drinks reception venue. Guests can enjoy champagne cocktails and a selection of canapés while the couple take advantage of the many photograph locations around this unique historic house.

The wedding breakfast might take place in the grandeur of the Benjamin Franklin Room where the couple's chosen menu is served by friendly and efficient waiting staff. Before the event, couples will have had the opportunity to sample a range of dishes at the menu tasting to ensure they choose the perfect combination.

After the speeches, guests are ushered back down to The Vaults which have been transformed into a stunning party venue. Additional guests can join the party entertained by a DJ or full band until the early hours. A licensed bar is available along with a selection of evening food options.

'I would like to thank you for the effort put into our reception. We had a fantastic day, which is testament to the effort made by the staff on and before the day to ensure it ran smoothly.'

'The food was excellent and drew many unsolicited compliments from our guests. The waiters and waitresses were efficient and performed their duties with cheerful willingness and charm. The venue was splendid, with the Benjamin Franklin Room adding a touch of gravitas that is often missing from civil ceremonies, and with the atmospheric vaults being the perfect spot for the reception and party.'

Skinners' Hall

Fabulous because...

Skinners' Hall has many features of a country house in the heart of the City of London including a charming English courtyard and a roof garden

Location: The City

Capacity: Ceremony 80; Wedding breakfast 170; Evening reception 250

Minimum number of guests: None

Guide Price
Per guest (not including venue hire): From £95
Venue hire only: £3,500

When to get married here: All year round

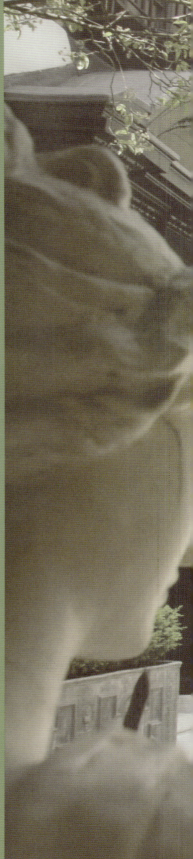

The paintings, tapestries and Coat of Arms create an impressive backdrop to an elegant meal

Skinners' Hall, the 'Country House in the City', lies in the heart of the City of London. The hall is a Grade 1 listed building with architecture and décor reminiscent of a private country house, unexpected, given its central location, and boasts three delightful outside spaces. Exclusive hire of the hall gives couples the opportunity to enjoy maximum comfort and opulence in a grand yet welcoming setting. The Hall can accommodate ceremonies, seated meals and dancing, as well as smaller more intimate celebrations.

Skinners' Hall is the home of The Worshipful Company of Skinners, one of the City of London's Great Twelve Livery Companies. They have owned the site on Dowgate Hill since the thirteenth century, and the building was rebuilt in

1670 after the Great Fire of London. To this day, it retains many original features and so is steeped in history.

When guests enter from Dowgate Hill near the River Thames, they pass beneath the Skinners' Hall crest through the wrought iron gates that lead into a delightful ceremonial courtyard, restored in a cloister style in the late 1770s. This provides an attractive space for guests to gather and gives a taste of the sumptuous tradition of the interior that they are about to enter.

Guests will first enter into the Outer Hall, with its haughty ceiling and high encircling gallery. This is a wonderfully light and impressive space to hold the wedding ceremony, accommodating up to 80 guests, or alternatively the room can be used for a drinks reception before going through to

The roof garden is an enchanting gem hidden from outside view, with its olive trees, fountain and seating

the Banqueting Hall. Three George II carved wood and gilt mirrors, part of a set of nine found in Skinners' Hall, and a grand wooden fireplace resonate the tradition and beauty the hall exudes. The gallery above surrounds a beautiful glass chandelier, originally made for Empress Catherine the Great of Russia. After dinner, the hall can be used as a bar area with additional seating, and in winter, an open fire is the perfect addition to this inviting reception room.

Through wooden arches from the Outer Hall is the breathtaking Banqueting Hall, dating back to 1670 with its dark wooden panelling and artwork. A tall window fills the hall with natural light, and the paintings, tapestries and Coat of Arms create an impressive backdrop to an elegant meal.

This main room of the hall can seat up to 170 guests for a wedding breakfast. Here guests can experience Skinners Hall's rich history, captured by six large Sir Frank Brangwyn murals dated from the beginning of the twentieth century. Couples can also use the charming minstrel's gallery overlooking the hall to position musicians adding to the atmosphere.

For more intimate wedding breakfasts, Skinners' Hall offers the Old Court Room, which can be accessed from the Banqueting Hall or via the Outer Hall. The Old Court Room, with its own small courtyard, also provides an alternative space for a champagne and canapé reception before going through for dinner. This traditional room can host a beautiful mahogany table, which was a gift to the Skinners

Three George II carved wood and gilt mirrors and a grand wooden fireplace resonate the tradition the hall exudes

Company, which can seat up to 30 guests. The room can later be cleared and used for dancing, with its traditional sprung dancefloor. From the Old Court Room there is a robust oak staircase which creates a picturesque setting for the couple and guests to gather for wedding photographs and leads up to the splendid Fountain Roof Garden.

The roof garden, an enchanting gem hidden from outside view, with its olive trees, fountain and seating, provides a refreshing space for guests to relax. In the summer, it is an ideal place to host drinks receptions before attending the formal wedding breakfast and at night, subtle spot lighting creates an atmospheric and calm area to enjoy the night's sky.

In addition to these delightful function rooms, on the first floor there is the Library Drawing Room, which can be used by the bride and groom to find some privacy or as a dressing room.

The hall is run and managed by a private catering company, who have over 30 years experience of wedding catering who will create bespoke, seasonal menus for each couple's occasion and be pleased to advise on all aspects of organising and planning the wedding day. The on-site events coordinator will be on hand throughout the day to ensure the smooth running of the event.

Bringing a country feel to central London, Skinners' Hall offers an intimate and traditional wedding venue.

FOR A FABULOUS CEREMONY AND RECEPTION

Venue Details

Skinners' Hall
8¹/₂ Dowgate Hill
London
EC4R 2SP
t   020 7213 0553
e   sales@skinnershall.co.uk
w www.skinnershall.com

Licence authority:
Islington Town Hall
Upper Street
London
N1 2UD
t   020 7527 6350
e   registrars@islington.gov.uk
w www.islington.gov.uk

Licensed for ceremony: The Outer Hall (80)

Function rooms available: Great Hall (reception 170, evening 250), The Old Court Room (reception 50, evening 150), The Outer Hall (drinks reception 120)

Outside space: Roof garden, courtyard and terrace

Option of a marquee: ✗

Rooms available for overnight accommodation: ✗

Complimentary dressing room for bride available: ✓

SPECIAL NOTES

Licensing hours: Until midnight

Corkage charge: £3–£6 charged per person

Catering: Requisite caterer

Complimentary menu tasting: ✓

Car parking spaces: On street parking (free Sundays and from 1.30pm Saturdays) and NCP nearby

Sound/noise restrictions: No restrictions

Fireworks: ✗

Confetti: ✓

Candles: ✓

PA system: ✓ (in Great Hall)

Helicopter landing permission: ✗

Wedding options

Skinners' Hall's on-site wedding coordinator, with the help of private caterers Party Ingredients, hosted a spring wedding for 60 guests.

For the ceremony, guests were seated in rows with a central aisle and 20 guests watched from the Gallery. The fire was lit and the bride made her entrance through the Banqueting Hall.

After, a drinks and canapé reception was held in the Old Court Room. Champagne and sparkling elderflower were served by waiters circling the room. British canapés, such as chargrilled asparagus tips with hollandaise dipping sauce and minature toad in the hole with English mustard were served. Next to the staircase, a bar was set up, serving alternative drinks.

The Party Ingredients manager advised the best man when to make the announcement to move through into dinner, using a gavel. The bride and groom then received guests as they entered into the Banqueting Hall.

For the wedding breakfast, the couple chose a horseshoe shaped table, seating nine on the top table with remaining guests spread evenly on sprigs. The tables were decorated with table candelabra, ivory linen and napkins tied with ribbon.

For starters, centrepieces on the tables displayed langoustine, king prawns, sliced smoked salmon, watermelon, asparagus, quails eggs and crudités. A carvery buffet in The Outer Hall provided delights such as roasted saddle of lamb basted with rosemary, honey and wholegrain mustard and whole baked Scottish salmon with spinach, tarragon and hollandaise sauce. The dessert was again displayed on tiered central displays and included Croque en Bouche wedding cake with chocolate sauce, garden statuary centrepieces draped with fresh fruits and flowers and a selection of English specialty cheeses.

After dinner, a bar was set up in the Outer Hall with live band and dancing. At 11pm, guests departed to the Threadneedle Hotel for the party to continue.

Soho House

Fabulous because...

Unrelentingly stylish and unapologetically cool, Soho House, set over three floors, merges contemporary spaces with an individual edge, making this venue a must for chic Londoners

Location: Soho

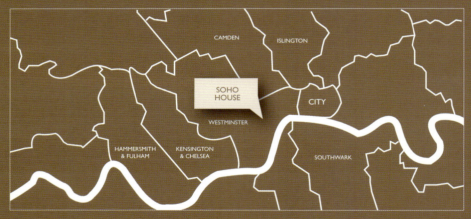

CAMDEN

ISLINGTON

SOHO HOUSE

CITY

WESTMINSTER

HAMMERSMITH & FULHAM

KENSINGTON & CHELSEA

SOUTHWARK

Capacity: Ceremony 60; Wedding breakfast 60; Evening reception 200

Minimum number of guests: None

Guide Price
Per guest (not including venue hire): **£21 – £38.50 + drinks**
Venue hire only: **From £1,000 (minimum spend of £6,000 ceremony and reception, £5,000 reception)**

When to get married here: All year round

Solid oak floors and deep brown leather panelling on the walls make this room confident in its sparseness

Founded as a private member's club, Soho House has a keen following amongst the media, art and film world, located appropriately in the heart of Soho. Set in a beautifully restored eighteenth-century listed building, the venue has an exclusive events section, named Soho House 21. Its intriguing and unconventional split-level layout paired with its edgy, modish décor make this venue ideal for those looking to find an alternative, fresh place to hold their wedding celebrations.

Entering the club through an unassuming, discreet wooden door on Old Compton Street, guests mount wooden slatted steps, aside an exposed brickwork wall up to the reception. The venue is found on four floors, all of which can play a part in the wedding day itself.

Wedding ceremonies are held in the Dining Room 19/21 on the first floor. Surrounded by solid oak floors and deep brown leather panelling on the walls, this room is confident in its sparseness and needs hardly any decoration. Its warm panels lit with candlelight give this ceremony room a rustic feel. The venue's brown leather function chairs can be set up with an aisle between, and a solid oak table is positioned as the central point, usually garlanded with flowers. Adjacent to the member's restaurant (accessed through a different entrance on Greek Street), the bride can make a traditional entrance into the ceremony.

The Dining Room is also where the wedding breakfast takes place at Soho House, and can hold up to 42 guests. With the back wall fully retracted, the Georgian Red Room next

The roof is an enviable outdoor space, with a terrace overlooking the bustling streets of Soho

door creates a perfect extension for a further 18 guests. This room is more traditionally decorated, with red walls and an 'old English' style fireplace. The two rooms together make a delightful space, with their long windows letting in an abundance of natural light and fusion of styles. The long wooden tables can be set up in a variety of configurations depending on individual needs. Some couples choose to sit at the top table in the Red Room, on a large oval table, with their guests around the long, oak tables, placed diagonally across the room.

The atmosphere at a wedding breakfast at Soho House is informal and relaxed, made easy by the venue's unique 'Bring Me Food' style of serving dinner. The courses are served on large wooden boards raised with metal stands and placed in the centre of the tables. Guests are encouraged to serve themselves and share the platters, conducive to sparking conversation amongst those who have not before met.

In the past, couples have used this opportunity to circulate amongst their guests, by swapping seats with a guest through each course of the meal, to ensure they share the day with everyone involved.

Usually before the ceremony and after it has taken place, guests congregate at the top of the house, on the fourth floor in the delightful Roof Deck Bar. When guests arrive at the venue, they are shown up to the top floor before ascending to the ceremony. In the winter, the space is enclosed by a hardy canvas roof, and serves as an additional room for drinks

Mirror panels jar the room's reflections and bring the contents of the room to life

receptions with outdoor heating, while in the summer, the roof is retractable and is an enviable outdoor space on balmy days, with a terrace overlooking the bustling streets of Soho. With its exposed brickwork, foliage and simple decoration, the Roof Deck Bar is an unusual and stylish place to hold a drinks reception for up to 70 people. There is also a covered room on the roof top, white washed with brightly coloured seating.

Situated on the second floor, Bar 19/21 is a retro, stylish space for an evening reception. The distinctive semicircular bar is complemented with the bold statements made through the bar's furnishings: wooden flooring, bold monochrome floral wallpaper, low red lampshades and deep-buttoned brown leather sofas lie along one wall. Mirror panels jar the room's reflections and bring the contents of the room to life. The amalgamation of these strong elements crafts a quirky and

resoundingly hip bar in which to hold a reception. Bands and musicians are welcome to play in this space, while the Roof Deck can be used as a quieter place to relax and can be set up with tables and seating areas. Used in conjunction with the Roof Deck Bar, up to 200 people can be accommodated.

A welcome addition to this venue is found on the third floor. The Cinema, seating 27 people in comfy, high-backed chairs is on the floor between Bar 19/21 and the Roof Deck and comes with the hire of the events floors. It can be used to entertain children during the reception, or to show a favourite home video!

For couples looking for an alternative, modern place to hold their wedding celebrations, Soho House offers a fresh, quirky, unrelentingly cool setting in which guests can feel relaxed and enjoy the party until 3am, Monday to Saturday and until 10.30pm on a Sunday.

Venue Details

Soho House
21 Old Compton Street
London
W1D 5JJ
t 020 7292 0122
e enquiries@sohohouse.com
w www.sohohouse.com

Licence authority:
Westminster Register Office
Westminster Council House
Marylebone Road
London
NW1 5PT
t 020 7641 1161
e registeroffice@westminster.gov.uk
w www.westminster.gov.uk

Licensed for ceremony: Dining Room 19/21 (60)

Function rooms available: Dining Room 19/21 (reception 42), Dining Room and Georgian Red Room (reception 60), Roof Deck (drinks reception 70), Bar 19/21 (evening 100), two-floor hire (evening 200)

Outside space: Roof deck

Option of a marquee: ✗

Rooms available for overnight accommodation: ✗

Complimentary dressing room for bride available: ✓

SPECIAL NOTES

Licensing hours: Monday to Saturday until 3am, Sunday until 10.30pm

Corkage charge: Wine £10, champagne £15

Catering: In-house

Complimentary menu tasting: ✓

Car parking spaces: NCP nearby off Shaftsbury Avenue

Sound/noise restrictions: Music permitted until 3am

Fireworks: ✗

Confetti: ✓

Candles: ✓

PA system: ✓

Helicopter landing permission: ✗

Wedding options

Soho House's unusual layout lends itself to a distinct and stylish day, and the events team take a personal approach to planning each wedding.

A wedding in spring took full advantage of the versatility of this venue. On arrival guests were ushered up to the Roof Deck for pre-ceremony drinks of Chateauneuf and Chablis.

The ceremony was held at 2pm in the Dining Room, in front of 52 guests who also attended the wedding breakfast. The room was simply decorated with candles and candelabras. The bride made her entrance through the private members' entrance to Soho House, and entered the ceremony as a guitarist played.

After the ceremony, the party made their way up to the Roof Deck Bar for a drinks reception with rosé champagne and canapés. Family members remained in the Red Room for wedding photographs.

The wedding breakfast was served at 5pm in the Dining Room, 'Bring Me Food' style. The party enjoyed:

- Tuna carpaccio, pum tomato relish
- Tiger prawns and scallops with chilli and garlic
- Butternut squash, goat's cheese salad
- Sirloin beef, fat chips, bearnaise sauce
- Whole Morroccan baked seabass, spiced couscous
- Baked gnocchi, gorgonzola, spinach
- Lemon drizzle cake
- Pecan tart

Speeches were given between the main course and desert with a champagne toast. At 8pm, evening guests arrived and joined the party in Bar 19/21 where a saxophonist from the band set the mood. The band then played three sets throughout the evening. Guests could also go up to the Roof Deck, where tables had been laid out to provide additional seating areas and background music played.

During the evening reception, guests were served 'tubs' of fish and chips with tartar sauce and bangers and mash. The bride and groom left at 12.15am and the party drew to a close at 1am.

Stoke Park Club

Fabulous because...

Situated on the outskirts of London, this grand manor house, set in 350 acres of land, is a bastion of luxury and has played host to royalty

Location: Stoke Poges, Buckinghamshire

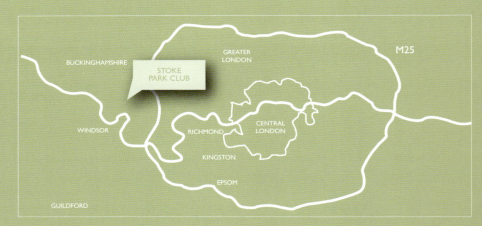

Capacity: Ceremony 120; Wedding breakfast 120; Evening reception 200

Minimum number of guests: 80

Guide Price
Per guest (including venue hire): **£185**
Venue hire only: **Not available**

When to get married here: All year round

Stoke Park Club is a unique manor of extraordinary proportions situated on the outskirts of London. A millennium has left an indelible ambience of elegance upon the 350-acre estate, while a decade of rediscovery has rendered every aspect of the facility a masterpiece of refined indulgence: exquisite works of art and antiques sit comfortably alongside the latest technologies and innovations. The vast estate – which includes a glistening lake, terrace and fountain – has featured in a number of films, including two of the James Bond greats: *Goldfinger* and *Tomorrow Never Dies*. With its rolling acres and 210-year-old Palladian mansion, this venue was named the 'number one country house wedding venue' by *Wedding Venues and Services* in 2006.

For more than 900 years, the Stoke Park Estate has been at the very heart of British heritage, playing host over the centuries to lords and nobleman, kings and queens. The historic parkland which surrounds the current mansion was the product of eighteenth-century designers 'Capability' Brown and Humphrey Repton. Marrying together sprawling lawns and rolling hills, it is offset by the manor itself, originally designed by the world famous English architect James Wyatt. Having worked for George III, Wyatt's work on the Palladian mansion and its surrounding monuments between 1790 and 1813 has caused him to leave behind a suitable legacy, with original features retained and added to in the 200 years since its conception.

The estate was used as a private residence until 1908 when 'Pa' Lane Jackson, founder of the Corinthian Sporting Club, purchased the estate, turning it into Britain's finest club. Jackson engaged the gifted golf architect Harry Shapland Colt to design the estate's championship golf course. The history of the venue is now complemented by a stunning array of modern facilities, which include the inimitable new spa, health and racquet pavilion.

A pristine jewel of white stone set amidst its sweeping acres of historic parkland and exquisite gardens, Stoke Park's Palladian mansion provides a truly breathtaking setting for a

A millennium has left an indelible ambience of elegance upon the estate, while a decade of rediscovery has rendered the facility a masterpiece of refined indulgence

marriage ceremony, civil partnership or wedding reception. Two of Stoke Park's elegantly decorated function rooms are licensed for civil weddings, with breathtaking interiors and spectacular views across the estate. The Club's dedicated, professional team of wedding coordinators and banqueting staff will create a uniquely personal experience, from champagne breakfasts to a sumptuous reception banquets, a live swing band or an awe-inspiring firework display over the fountains and gardens.

With an interior that displays exquisite works of art and antiques, Stoke Park Club does not disappoint from the outset. Couples approaching the mansion circle the elaborate gravel path and arrive in front of an imposing entrance dictated by enormous white columns before ascending the grand steps guarded by two stone lions. These are positioned slumbering atop columns either side of the wide stone steps, and movie buffs will note the familiarity of the location which featured in the dramatic ending to the 2004 film, *Layer Cake*.

Passing into the building, guests will then enter the Great Hall. A lavish place for couples to receive guests, this room is warm and inviting, decorated with warm colours and offset by sunny yellow walls. With chandeliers and ornate marble pillars which reach to meet a finely detailed ceiling border, the

With diamond-like chandeliers and ornate marble pillars, the scene is set for romance

scene is set for romance. Traditional works of art pay homage to the elegance of Stoke Park Club and guests can marvel at one of the largest free-standing staircases in Europe. With its detailed balustrade and imposing position, the bride can make a grand entrance, descending the stairs in front of her guests.

Stoke Park Club has three rooms for couples to choose from, two of these holding civil ceremony licences. The first of these is the Ballroom, situated in the West Wing of the building. This is an elegant room that recalls grand banquets from days gone by; high ceilings with plush mouldings and cornices and an enormous central chandelier. With silk panelled walls in the same delectable shade of pink as the carpets of the Great Hall, the room also boasts an open fire. Seating up to 120 for a ceremony,

natural sunlight pours through large windows which relay glittering views of the fountains and the gardens outside.

The second room licensed for ceremonies is the Repton Room. Named after one of the principle garden architects, it is a small gem with a capacity of 30. Warmly decorated with ochre walls and adorned with large gilded mirrors and original paintings, it is dominated by a tasteful fire surround.

After holding their ceremony at Stoke Park Club, parties can take advantage of the venue's expansive grounds for the wedding photographs with delightful choice of background settings, before beginning the postnuptial celebrations.

Both the Ballroom and the Repton Room can be transformed into banqueting spaces; the Ballroom has a capacity of 60 guests and the Repton Room 27 guests.

FOR A FABULOUS CEREMONY AND RECEPTION

*Guests can marvel at one of the largest
freestanding staircases in Europe*

For larger parties, who have perhaps used the Ballroom for their ceremony, their wedding breakfast can be held in the last room available to couples marrying at the Stoke Park Club, the beautiful Fountain Room.

Overlooking the terrace and gardens with perfect views of the large fountain, the south-facing Fountain Room is decorated in neutral shades of white and cream; complete with deep green marble pillars and thick, sandy coloured curtains. Sunny and spacious, it boasts a delicately engraved ceiling. This room provides the perfect setting for a wedding breakfast and an evening reception for up to 120 people.

With a wedding package that includes room hire of the Fountain Room and Ballroom, couples are also granted access to the Wyatt Room; a circular interconnecting space with deep wooden doors and cream walls decorated with a large mosaic-type print.

Catering at Stoke Park Club is a delight in itself and the acclaimed Executive Chef can create menus that cater for the most discerning of pallets, using the freshest ingredients. Table settings with gold candelabras and flower centrepieces complete an exquisite dining experience.

After the wedding breakfast, guests can then enjoy a magnificent party throughout the club's three rooms, dancing until 1am, whilst also making use of the venue's unparalleled outdoor space. The bride and groom also have use of the bridal suite.

FOR A FABULOUS CEREMONY AND RECEPTION

Venue Details

Stoke Park Club
Park Road
Stoke Poges
Buckinghamshire
SL2 4PG
t 01753 717 171
e info@stokeparkclub.com
w www.stokeparkclub.com

Licence authority:
Chiltern Hills Register Office
Easton Street
High Wycombe
Bucks
HP11 1NH
t 01494 475205
e chilternhillsregistrars@buckscc.gov.uk
w www.buckscc.gov.uk

Licensed for ceremony: The Ballroom
(120), The Repton (30)

Function rooms available: The Ballroom (reception 60,
evening 80), The Fountain Room (reception 120,
evening 120), The Repton (reception 27, evening 30)

Outside space: 350 acres of parkland

Option of a marquee: ✗

Rooms available for overnight accommodation: 21

Room rates: From £225

Complimentary dressing room for bride available: ✗

SPECIAL NOTES

Licensing hours: Until 1am

Corkage charge: Wine £20, champagne £49

Catering: In-house

Complimentary menu tasting: ✓

Car parking spaces: 150+

Sound/noise restrictions: No restrictions

Fireworks: ✓ (fee applicable)

Confetti: ✓ (indoors only)

Candles: ✓

PA system: ✗

Helicopter landing permission: ✓ (fee applicable)

Wedding options

**Stoke Park Club's wedding package gives couples a basis
from which to plan the details of their wedding.**

The package is priced at £180 per adult, with a minimum number
of 80 adults charged (£75 children under 12). The package includes:

- Complimentary menu tasting for bride and groom
- Room hire of the Fountain Room, Wyatt Room and Ballroom
- Two reception drinks per guest on arrival
- Stoke Park Club's master of ceremonies
- Three-course meal with coffee and chocolates
- Half a bottle of house wine per person
- Evening buffet
- Use of silver cake stand and knife
- Stationary to include: place cards, table plan and menu cards
- Complimentary bridal suite
- Bottle of champagne for bride and groom in bridal suite
- Reduced accommodation rate for your guests

(A maximum of five rooms, including the bridal suite,
can be reserved for a one-night stay only. Any additional
rooms must be booked for a two-night minimum stay
basis at £225 per room per night including breakfast.)

A visit to Stoke Park would not be complete without visiting the
acclaimed SPC spa, heralded as 'staggeringly luxurious' in *The
Times*. Its facilities include deep relaxation rooms, Italian marble
steam rooms, an indoor pool complete with in-built hydro-seat
Jacuzzi, and a private atrium with a 5m tropical aquarium.

'It is widely regarded as Excellent'
Conde Nast Traveller – September 2006

'Number One Country House Wedding Venue'
Wedding Venues and Services – August 2006

The Silver Directory

Fabulous Suppliers

The Silver Directory
Wedding Planners

Kathryn Lloyd Wedding Design

South Bank House, Black Prince Road, London SE1 7SJ

t: 020 7828 5535
m: 07721 446167
e: kathryn@kathrynlloyd.co.uk
w: www.kathrynlloyd.co.uk

Smith and Niemierko Ltd

7 Hanson Street, Fitzrovia, London W1W 6TE

t: 020 7580 5010
e: hello@smithniemierko.com
w: www.smithniemierko.com

Lillingston Associates

The Studio, 2A Kempson Road, London, SW6 4PU

t: 07000 710131
e: catherinecs@lillingston.co.uk
w: www.lillingston.co.uk

Wedding By Design

PO Box 700, Weybridge, Surrey KT13 3BR

t: 0870 609 4190
m: 07977 165929
e: info@weddingbydesign.co.uk
w: www.weddingbydesign.co.uk

The Bespoke Wedding Company

166 Clarence Road, Wimbledon, London SW19 8QD

t: 020 8715 3316
e: info@thebespokeweddingco.com
w: www.thebespokeweddingco.com

Kavanagh & Kavanagh Event Management

t: 01242 771288
e: info@kavanagh-kavanagh.com
w: www.kavanagh-kavanagh.com

The Silver Directory
Photographers

Robert Munro

t: 01892 543872
e: weddings@robertmunro.net
w: www.robertmunro.net

Mark Wallis

t: 07841 703111
e: hello@markwallisphoto.com
w: www.markwallisphoto.com

Jules Beresford

t: 07776 183797
e: jules@julesberesford.com
w: www.julesberesford.com

Julia Boggio Photography

t: 020 8543 3349
e: info@juliaboggiophotography.com
w: www.juliaboggiophotography.com

Andrew Errington

t: 07768 635710
e: mail@andrewerrington.com
w: www.andrewerrington.com

Robert Lawler

t: 020 8932 4096
e: info@robertlawler.co.uk
w: www.robertlawler.co.uk

The Silver Directory
Florists

Paula Pryke
The Flower House, Cynthia Street,
London N1 9JF

t: **020 7837 7336**
e: **sales@paula-pryke-flowers.com**
w: **www.paula-pryke-flowers.com**

The Fresh Flower Company
39A North Cross Road,
London SE22 9ET

t: **020 8693 6088**
e: **studio@freshflower.co.uk**
w: **www.freshflower.co.uk**

Wild at Heart
49A Ledbury Road, London
W11 2AA

t: **020 7727 3095**
e: **shop@wildatheart.com**
w: **www.wildatheart.com**

Jane Packer
32–34 New Cavendish Street,
London W1G 8UE

t: **020 7935 2673**
e: **flowershop@janepacker.com**
w: **www.jane-packer.co.uk**

Forever Flowering
Orchard House, Mortlake Road,
Kew Gardens, Surrey TW9 4AS

t: **020 8392 9929**
e: **info@foreverflowering.co.uk**
w: **www.foreverflowering.co.uk**

Monique Alexander Flowers
13 Cascade Avenue, Muswell Hill,
London N10 3PT

t: **020 8444 3037**
e: **info@moniquealexanderflowers.co.uk**
w: **www.moniquealexanderflowers.co.uk**

The Silver Directory
Other Essentials

CATERER

Party Ingredients

Unit 1A Tideway Industrial Estate,
Kirtling Street, London SW8 5BP

t: 020 7627 3800
e: sales@partyingredients.co.uk
w: www.partyingredients.co.uk

CATERER

Rocket Food

Unit 5, Southside Industrial Estate,
Havelock Terrace, London
SW8 4AH

t: 020 7622 2320
e: parties@rocketfood.net
w: www.rocketfood.net

WEDDING CAKES

The Chelsea Cake Shop

66 Lower Sloane Street, London
SW1W 8BP

t: 020 7730 6277
e: info@chelseacakeshop.co.uk
w: www.chelseacakeshop.co.uk

WEDDING STATIONARY

Seventh Heaven Ltd

t: 01480 464217
e: enquiries@seventhheavendesigns.co.uk
w: www.seventhheavendesigns.co.uk

ENTERTAINMENT

Fiona Oliver Smith and Oyster Opera

t: 07770 631431
w: www.oysteropera.com
e: oysteropera@oysteropera.com
w: www.fionaoliversmith.com
e: info@fionaoliversmith.com

ENTERTAINMENT

Saucy Flapdragons

t: 07775 858468
e: info@saucyflapdragons.com
w: www.saucyflapdragons.com

With thanks

Contributing photographers

Jo Newman — Chelsea Register Office p14

Andrew Dent and
Harrow School Collection — Harrow School pp168–173

Dod Miller — LSO St Luke's pp218–223

Dennis Orchard — Stoke Park Club p303

George Powell and 'Red Photographic' — Chelsea Register Office p12
Landmark Arts Centre p62
The Cadogan p118

Contributing editorial & design

Cathy Howes, Beth Law, Lianne Slavin, Holly Bennion, Sally Rawlings and Jaqui Palmer

JULIA BOGGIO©
PHOTOGRAPHY

Julia Boggio is a successful wedding and portrait photographer, based in London and operating nationally and internationally. Julia has been photographing weddings for four years, having previously worked in advertising on some of the UK's leading pharmaceutical brands.

When it comes to wedding photography, Julia's approach is artistic, glamorous and fun. She has a strong belief that using a variety of photographic styles on the wedding day is the key to telling the couple's story effectively. She delivers this in a friendly and respectful manner to enhance her clients' wedding experience.

Julia currently works with a number of high-end venues in the greater London area. You can often find her articles in the bridal press and Julia makes regular appearances on Wedding TV and has also appeared on *Richard & Judy, BBC Breakfast* and *The Oprah Winfrey Show.*

Fabulous Places
to get married in Scotland

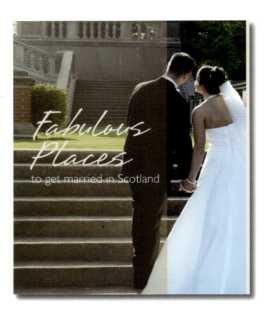

Revealing the most fabulous wedding venues in Scotland, from the grandeur of Edinburgh Castle, to the intimacy of Rosslyn Chapel, made famous by *The Da Vinci Code*, this book provides a real insight into the true essence of a Scottish wedding.

Available March 2008
ISBN 978 1 85458 368 0

Fabulous Places

to get married in England

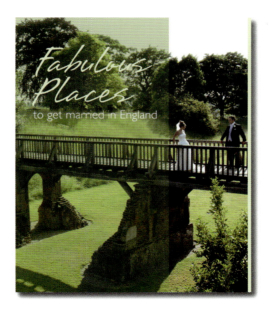

A stylish collection of the most fabulous wedding venues throughout
England, including celebrity favourites, secret gems and a choice of
charming backdrops, from stunning countryside to vibrant cities to
breathtaking coastlines.

Available March 2008
ISBN 978 1 85458 421 2